TREATISE *on the* FUGUE

TREATISE *on the* FUGUE

BY ANDRÉ GEDALGE

Translated and Edited by
Ferdinand Davis

WITH A FOREWORD BY
DARIUS MILHAUD

UNIVERSITY OF OKLAHOMA PRESS
NORMAN

Library of Congress Catalog Card Number: 65-11241
 Manufactured in the U.S.A. First edition.

ACKNOWLEDGMENT

I am deeply indebted to my friends and
colleagues Charles Jones, Donald Lybbert, and Louise Talma,
without whose help, criticism, and encouragement
this book would not have been published.

F. D.

FOREWORD

By Darius Milhaud

I was lucky enough to study with André Gedalge for several years. I have the impression that everything I know, so far as teaching is concerned, I owe to him.

It is absolutely necessary for a composer to have a strong technique: harmony, counterpoint, and fugue. And for the study of the technique of the fugue in all possible details, André Gedalge left us a real monument.

If you are technically strong enough to study and assimilate *Treatise on the Fugue,* you will have achieved not only a great step but an indispensable one.

TRANSLATOR'S NOTE

André Gedalge, born in Paris in 1856, was professor of counterpoint and fugue in the Paris Conservatory from 1905 until his death in 1926. His *Traité de la fugue,* here translated, was first published in 1900. A few years thereafter it was translated into German and Italian. It has been the standard work on the subject in France and Italy for more than half a century.

Many modifications have been made in this translation in accordance with the instructions of Louis Vierne, the composer, who was the organist of the Cathedral of Notre Dame de Paris from 1900 until his death in 1937, and with whom I studied composition from 1931 to 1934. Vierne found it advisable to re-arrange the order of the chapters, which I have done as follows: Chapter X of the original is here Chapter VIII; the former Chapter VIII is here Chapter IX; former Chapter IX is here Chapter X; and former Chapter XIV is here Chapter XIII. The original Chapter XIII is here Appendix B, as the fugues with which it deals require constant writing in three- or four-part invertible counterpoint, a burden which is hardly practical to put on a beginner. Representative scholastic fugues are here in Appendix C.

Furthermore, Vierne added instructions for exercises which have been placed at the end of chapters wherever appropriate, as a guide to the student in organizing his work. The text, too, has been simplified in places to avoid needless repetition, and comments have been interspersed throughout. Almost all of these stem directly from Vierne, though a few derive from my own experience in teaching counterpoint and fugue in Hunter College from 1950 to 1960.

These changes will, I believe, be of great value to the student who seriously works his way through the book. They will also serve to make Gedalge's treatise of greater utility in the classroom. For his great work is not, primarily, a reference book but a textbook on the art of developing a musical idea, which, as Gedalge has well said, is the principal reason for the study of fugue.

FERDINAND DAVIS

New York City
March 13, 1965

CONTENTS

Acknowledgment *page v*
Foreword by Darius Milhaud, *vii*
Translator's Note, *ix*
I. General Definitions, 3
II. The Subject, 5
III. The Answer, 9
IV. The Countersubject, 60
V. The Exposition, 72
VI. The Counterexposition, 114
VII. The Episodes, 119
VIII. The Modulations of the Fugue, 168
IX. The Stretto, 173
X. The Pedal Point, 205
XI. Construction of the Stretto Section, 217
XII. The Musical Composition of a Fugue, 241
XIII. General Summary:
Order and Arrangement of Work in Writing a Fugue, 277
Appendix A: Fugal Subjects, 296
Appendix B: Fugues with Several Subjects, 313
Appendix C: Representative Scholastic Fugues, 336
Index, 424

TREATISE *on the* FUGUE

I

GENERAL DEFINITIONS

1. A fugue is a musical composition based on a theme, in the manner of a periodic imitation. We here deal particularly with the scholastic fugue, so called because it is a modification for teaching purposes of the fugues created by the masters of contrapuntal writing. In order, therefore, to instruct, the scholastic fugue combines systematically elements derived from their fugues, though no single fugue of any of the masters falls within the category of the scholastic fugue. Furthermore, to achieve control and discipline, certain limitations of voice-leading and harmonization are likewise peculiar to the scholastic fugue.

The purpose of the study of the scholastic fugue is the practical application in musical composition of the methods of fugal construction. These devices, and developments of them, can be found in profusion throughout the works of Haydn, Mozart, and Beethoven, and their successors. They constitute the core of compositional technique down to and including the composers of the present day. Thus, from Bach to Alban Berg and Stravinsky, the study and writing of fugues has been an integral part of the education of practically all composers of the first rank—not, of course, expressly to write fugues, but to acquire the technical mastery that only fugal writing can bring.

2. The word "fugue" (from the Latin "fuga," meaning "flight") comes from the imitative character of the composition; that is, the theme of the fugue seems to "flee" from voice to voice, appearing in another part as it leaves that in which it has just been heard.

3. The writing of a fugue, however, requires far more than the imitation of the theme in all the parts of a choir or orchestra. Various rules of modulation and voice leading must be observed; use must be made of all available devices of counterpoint, in order to accompany and develop the theme and present it under various aspects. These devices include double, triple, and quadruple counterpoint; imitation by direct, contrary, and retrograde movement, augmentation, and diminution; and, indeed, the entire range of contrapuntal artifices, provided musical effect is never sacrificed for the sake of contrapuntal ingenuity.

4. The theme of the fugue is called the "subject."

5. The imitation of the subject is called the "answer."

6. A fugue may be written:

a) For unaccompanied voices. This is called a "vocal fugue" and is the style in which the scholastic fugue is written.

b) For various instruments. This is known as an "instrumental fugue."

c) For voices and instruments. This is called an "accompanied fugue."

7. The harmonic limitations of the scholastic fugue are the subject of some disagreement. Some authorities—and these will be followed in this book—limit the harmony permitted to that of strict tonal counterpoint, that is, to the major and minor triads and their first inversions, and the first inversions of the chord of the diminished fifth. No 6/4 chords are permitted, and no unprepared dissonances. Chromatics, however, are allowed, and any number of harmonies may be written within a measure.

However, many authorities permit the free use of the harmonic vocabulary of the eighteenth century. The difference is, fundamentally, one of emphasis: how to obtain a balance between expressiveness and control. This is recognized by Gedalge when he points out: "The student will be inspired by it (the example of Bach) in his schoolwork, while avoiding the liberties of form and writing that Bach could permit himself, but which would be considered matter for reproof in the classroom."

While, therefore, the fundamental harmonies should be of the simplest, great richness and variety can be produced by nonharmonic dissonant notes: neighboring and passing notes, chromatic alterations, and prepared dissonances.

Melodic movements are limited to those of strict tonal counterpoint, that is, the major and minor second, major and minor third, perfect fourth, perfect fifth, minor sixth, and octave.

8. The essential parts of the scholastic fugue are the subject; the answer; the countersubject; the exposition; the counterexposition; the episodes, which consist of passages to various keys in which the subject and answer are heard; the stretto; and the pedal point. Each of these will be discussed in this book.

II

THE SUBJECT

The Subject

9. Not every musical phrase can qualify as a subject of a fugue. Indeed, the requirements of a fugal subject are such that the beginner should not attempt to use subjects of his own, but should confine himself to the many listed in Appendix A at the back of this book.

10. A subject of a fugue is limited by special and narrow considerations of rhythm, of melody, of length, of mode, and of tonality.

Rhythm of the Subject

11. The subject must not have a large variety of rhythms; two or three are enough. Moreover, in the scholastic fugue, all subjects that present an alternation of binary and ternary rhythms must be avoided.

Melody of the Subject

12. The melody of the subject of a vocal fugue, in which style the scholastic fugue is written, should not exceed a minor seventh in extent. This limitation is imposed by the narrow range of the average human voice. As the subject passes from voice to voice it might easily become too high or too low unless, in the first place, it were confined within a narrow compass.

The subject should consist of a clearly defined melodic phrase, complete as to musical sense. No random succession of notes can form a good fugal subject.

13. It is also desirable that the subject be such as to lend itself to numerous combinations of different kinds of imitations. It should, at least, be capable of being arranged in canon with its answer, and this canon should give rise to an invertible harmony, the subject affording a good bass to the answer, and vice versa.

14. The melody of the subject should be harmonizable in four parts, and, when heard in the bass, should be able to sustain good four-part harmony.

Length of the Subject

15. A subject must be "long enough." It is not possible to specify absolutely

the length of a subject. A few notes with one or two rhythms can suffice. However, the following remarks may be helpful:

16. A too-long subject would cause the following inconveniences:

a) As the entries of the subject would be widely separated by its length, the imitative strength of the fugue would be diminished. The impact of the beginning of the subject would be dissipated by the time the subject had ended.

b) As the length of the subject might necessitate the repetition of the same notes or rhythmic patterns, monotony or redundance might result.

c) If, in an attempt to avoid such repetition, the subject comprised a large variety of melodic and rhythmic forms, the unity of the fugue would be destroyed.

17. A too-short subject would, on the contrary, force the entries to occur too close to each other. Modulations would come too near together, making the fugue sound tonally vague. Moreover, the subject might not contain enough material from which a fugue could be created. It must always be remembered that the fugue is made from its subject. All the developments of the fugue are generated, directly or indirectly, by the subject.

Mode of the Subject

18. The subject of a fugue must belong entirely and exclusively to either the major or the minor mode. Any subject presenting an alternation of modes is not suitable for a scholastic fugue.

Key of the Subject

19. The subject must either be entirely in one key, or if it modulates, such modulation must be only to its most nearly related key, that is, the dominant, the key on the fifth degree of the scale of its tonic.

The invariable rule is: A subject can modulate only from its tonic to its dominant, or, reciprocally from the key of its dominant to its tonic.

Consequently, any alterations present in the subject other than those which produce modulation from the tonic to the dominant and vice versa must be understood as chromatic, and, therefore, as not affecting the tonality of the subject.

20. It is apparent, therefore, that the modulations of a subject can occur only in the following ways—That is, the subject may: (a) begin in the tonic and modulate to the dominant; (b) begin in the dominant and modulate to the tonic; or (c) begin and end in the dominant, having modulated to the tonic. It must be clearly understood, however, that the subject, in the main, must belong to its principal key, its tonic.

Head of the Subject

21. The rhythmic or melodic phrase with which a subject begins is called the "head" of the subject.

It should possess trenchant characteristics as to rhythm, melody, and expressiveness.

It may be repeated several times in succession at the beginning of the subject; such repetition gives a particularly energetic or expressive quality to certain subjects (see examples 7, 8, and 9, below).

However, the rhythmic and melodic features of the head of the subject must never be repeated in the middle or the end of the subject.

Examples:

Summary

From the foregoing paragraphs, ¶9–¶21, it should be apparent that the creation of a good fugal subject is beyond the scope of the beginner.

Moreover, it is evident that themes suitable for other kinds of compositions may not be appropriate for a fugue. In sum:

The subject of a fugue must be more than an expressive musical idea. It must embody distinctive features of tonality, modality, rhythm, range, and length. Most importantly, it must be of such a nature as to be capable of generating the development of a fugue. The logical organization of the material generated directly and indirectly by the subject is the basic concern of this treatise. The subject of the fugue is the primal cause of the whole fugal structure.

THE ANSWER

22. After the subject has been stated in its entirety in one voice, it is imitated in another voice. This imitation is called the "answer."

Tonality of the Answer

23. The tonality of the answer cannot be remote from that of the subject as it is promptly followed by another entry of the subject in a different voice.

24. The answer, therefore, must be written in the keys most closely related to the subject, those of the tonic and the dominant.

Modulations of the Answer

25. However, if the order of tonality and modulation were identical to that of the subject, the answer would merely consist of an imitation of the subject at the unison or octave, which would create monotony and would not further the development of the fugue.

26. Therefore, in the answer, the order of tonality and modulation is made to *reverse* the order of the subject. When the subject is in the tonic, the answer is made in the dominant; when the subject is in the dominant, the answer is in the tonic. This basic principle will be developed in the following paragraphs.

It is necessary to make a detailed study of the answer both because of the many possible contingencies and because of the necessity of finding the correct answer. Thus:

I. When the subject is in the key of its tonic, the answer must imitate it in the dominant, that is, the key on the fifth degree of the principal key of the subject. The imitation, therefore, is made at either the fifth above or the fourth below the subject, depending on the arrangement of the parts.

II. Each time the subject modulates to its dominant, the answer must imitate it in the key of the tonic, the first degree of the principal key of the subject. The imitation, therefore, is made at the fourth above or the fifth below, depending on the arrangements of the parts.

27. It can therefore be seen that:

I. When the subject, without modulating, has as its tonic the first degree of the principal key, the answer has as its tonic the dominant of the subject.

II. When the subject, modulating, has as its tonic the fifth degree of the principal key, the answer, making a reciprocal modulation, has as its tonic the tonic of the subject.

From the above principles, the two following rules are derived. These rules apply, without exception, to all subjects of fugues:

Rules for Determining the Answer

28. *First Rule*: Each note, diatonic or altered, belonging in the subject to the key of its first degree (tonic of the subject), must be reproduced in the answer by the note, diatonic or altered, placed on the corresponding degree of the scale of the fifth degree of the subject (dominant of the subject), this fifth degree being taken as the tonic of the answer.

In this case, the answer imitates the subject degree by degree, alteration by alteration, at the fifth above or the fourth below.

29. *Second Rule:* Each note, diatonic or altered, belonging in the subject to the key of its fifth degree (this fifth degree being considered temporarily, by modulation, as tonic of the subject), must be reproduced in the answer by the note, diatonic or altered, placed on the corresponding degree of the scale of the first degree of the subject, this being taken as tonic of the answer when the subject begins on or modulates to the dominant.

In this case, the answer imitates the subject degree by degree, alteration by alteration, at the fourth above or the fifth below.

Fundamental Harmonies of the Answer

30. The above two rules give rise to the following harmonic principle:

The fundamental harmonies that are defined in the key of the dominant by any fragment of the melody of the answer must be homologous to the fundamental harmonies which the corresponding fragment of the subject has defined in the tonic, and vice versa.

31. The purpose of the above rules is to maintain the fugue in the general tonality of the tonic of the subject.

Suppose, instead of following these rules, the answer, though modulating, were made in exact imitation of the subject. This is what would result: Whenever the subject modulated to the dominant, the answer would modulate to the dominant of the dominant, that is, to the key on the second degree of the principal key of the subject. Since the second degree is remote, harmonically, from the tonic, it would be difficult, once the answer were made, to return promptly to the principal key in which the subject must be restated.

Such remoteness would also destroy the reciprocity of tonic and dominant. Moreover, the tonality of the fugue would be weakened by the immediate wandering away from the key of the subject.

Real Fugue

32. When the subject does not modulate, the fugue is called a "real" fugue, and the answer, a "real" answer. Obviously, the rules just given cannot apply to a "real" fugue, but only to a "tonal" fugue, that is, one in which the subject begins on or modulates to the dominant.

When the subject so modulates, or, beginning on the dominant, modulates to the tonic, the fugue is, as we have just seen, called a "tonal" fugue, and the answer a "tonal" answer. And, obviously, it is to such subjects that the rules given in ¶24–¶31 above apply.

(N.B. The term "real" fugue derives from the nature of the answer, which is an identical, i.e., "real" imitation of the subject at the fifth above or the fourth below.—F.D.)

Modulation by Characteristic Alterations

33. It will be recalled that the simplest way of modulating from any key to its dominant is by the use of "characteristic alterations," that is:

a) In major, by the alteration, ♯, or ♮ annulling ♭, of the fourth degree of the principal key, which then becomes the seventh degree of the key of the dominant.

b) In minor:

1. By the alteration, ♯, or ♮ annulling ♭, of the fourth and sixth degrees of the principal key, which become, respectively, the seventh and second degrees of the key of the dominant, and
2. By the alteration ♭, or ♮ annulling ♯, of the seventh degree of the principal key, which becomes the third key of the dominant.

Therefore, every subject which, according to its mode, presents such alterations or implies them in its harmony is considered as modulating to the dominant.

Careful analysis of the harmony of the subject is, therefore, essential, as the alterations may be merely chromatic, and thus not affect the tonality of the subject. Correct analysis will avoid a false answer, which, as will be seen, is a fundamental defect in a fugue.

Special Modulations of the Fugue

34. Other conventions exist, special to the fugue, all of which have as their purpose the maintenance of the answer close to the tonality of the subject.

These conventions deal with the beginning, or head of the subject, and with its ending.

The four following rules formulate these conventions. The rules assign exactly to each note the degree of the scale that it should occupy, either in the tonic or in the dominant. These rules are the corollary of the principle stated in ¶30: The fundamental harmonies of the key of the dominant in a fragment of the melody of the answer must be homologous to the fundamental harmonies of the tonic in the corresponding fragment of the melody of the subject, and vice versa.

Harmonic Function of the First Degree

35. *First Rule:* The first degree of the scale of the tonic, the principal key of the subject, is always considered as the fundamental note of the triad chord placed on the tonic when:

a) It is heard as first or last note of the subject:

Example:

b) The head of the subject progresses to the first degree, having begun on the dominant or the mediant (or in exceptional cases foreign to the scholastic fugue, on any other degree) either directly or in sounding other scale tones:

Example:

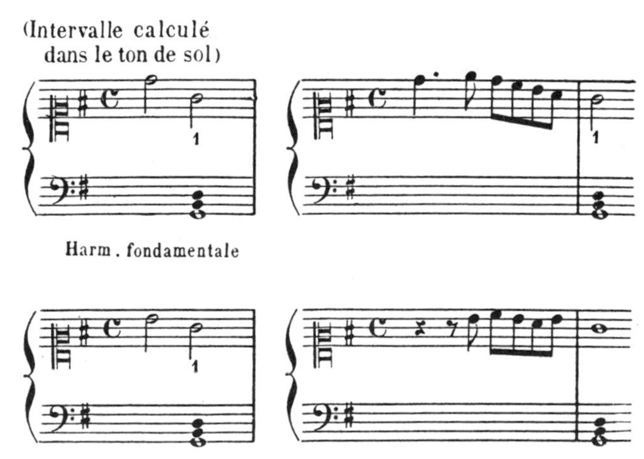

Harmonic Function of the Third Degree

36. *Second Rule:* The mediant, third degree of the scale of the principal key of the subject is always considered, harmonically and tonally, as the third of the triad placed on the tonic when:

a) It is heard as first or last note of the subject.

Example:

b) The head of the subject progresses to the third degree, having begun on the dominant or any other degree, either directly or in sounding other scale tones.

Example:

Harmonic Function of the Fifth Degree

37. *Third Rule*: The fifth degree of the principal key of the subject is always considered as fundamental note of the triad on the first degree of the dominant:

a) When it is heard as first or last note of the subject.

Example:

In consequence, all subjects beginning or ending on the fifth degree are considered as modulating from or to the dominant.

b) When the head of the subject progresses to the fifth degree, having begun on the tonic or the mediant or any degree other than the fifth, either directly or by sounding various scale tones.

Example:

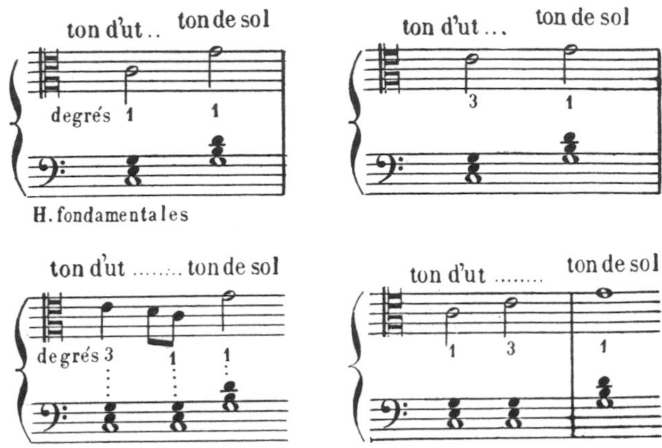

In consequence, all subjects progressing at the start from the tonic or mediant to the fifth degree are considered as modulating to the key of the dominant.

Harmonic Function of the Seventh Degree

38. *Fourth Rule:* The seventh degree of the scale of the principal key of the subject, *unaltered* in the minor mode (since in minor the altered seventh degree would either change the mode to major, or retain its character of leading note, which could not end a subject), such unaltered seventh degree is always considered as the third of the triad on the first degree of the dominant:

a) When the head of the subject progresses from the tonic or dominant to the fifth degree by way of the seventh degree.

Example:

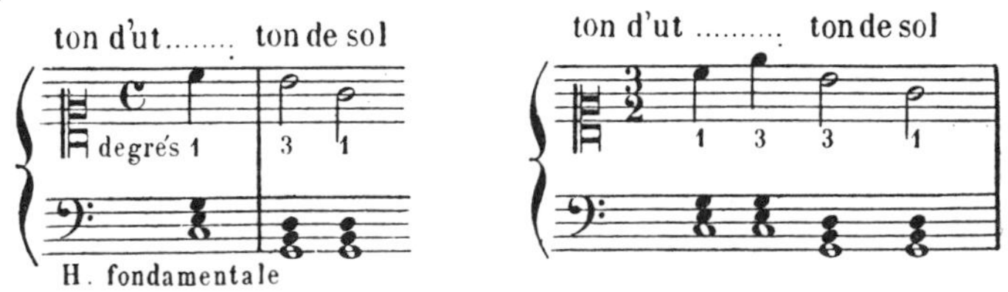

b) When the subject ends on the seventh degree of the principal key.

Example:

In consequence, all subjects ending on the seventh degree of the principal key, unaltered in minor, are considered as modulating to the key of the dominant, and ending on the third of the triad placed on the first degree of the key of the dominant.

Non-modulating Subject: Real Answer

39. A subject does not modulate when it begins and ends on the tonic or mediant without sounding the fifth degree.

In this case, the answer reproduces the subject degree by degree in the key of the dominant, that is, at the fifth above or the fourth below.

Example:

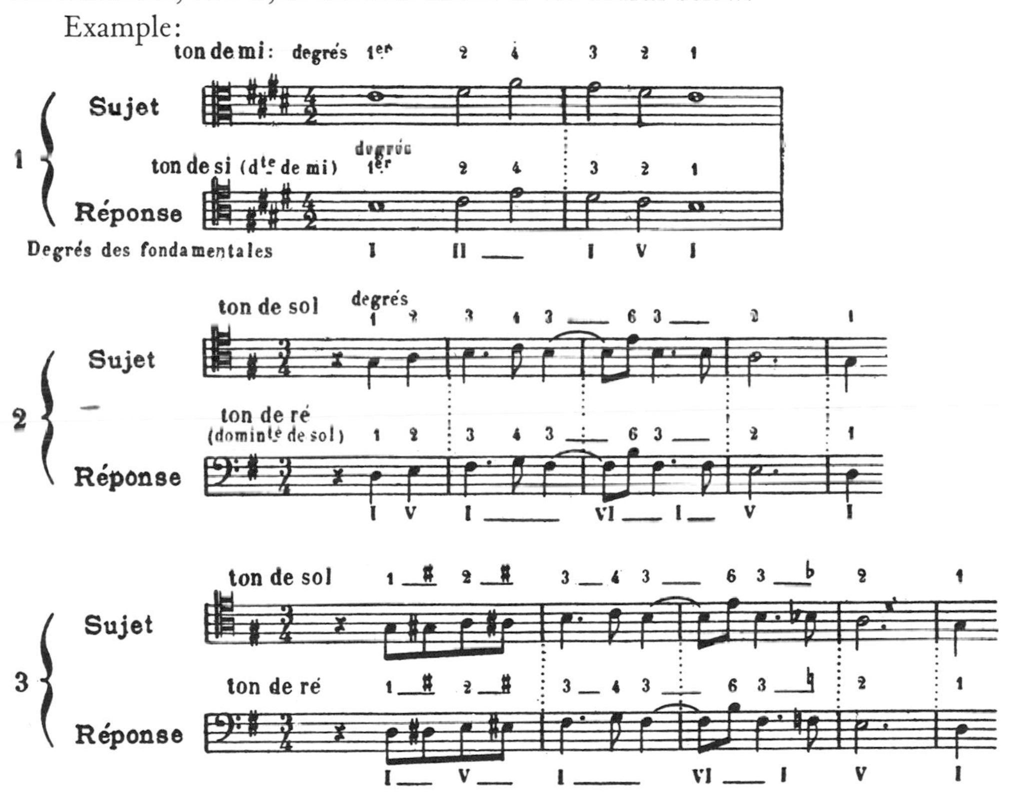

40. A subject does not modulate when, either beginning or ending on the tonic or mediant, it does not progress *directly* to the dominant, or to the seventh degree followed by the dominant, but uses the dominant either as a passing note, an appoggiatura, or in a sequence.

Example:

Intervalles calculés dans le ton de la ♮ mineur (ton du 1er degré du Sujet).

If we omit the melodic passing notes of this subject, its musical sense is very evidently as follows:

Thus, in the first measure, the fifth degree is heard only as a passing note; in the second measure and on the first beat of the fourth measure, it is part of a sequence; finally, on the last beat of the fourth measure, it is again a passing note.

A real answer must, therefore, be given.

Example:

41. The following subjects treat the fifth degree in similar ways, and should also be given a real answer:

Subject Beginning on the Fifth Degree: Tonal Answer

42. Every subject that begins with the dominant is considered as starting in the key of the dominant.

The dominant, in this case, is considered as tonic of the key on the fifth degree of the subject (¶37).

Answer to it must be made by the first degree of the principal key.

Example:

Return to the Principal Key

43. But, as has been said in ¶20, the subject must belong, in the main, to the tonality of its first degree. It must, therefore, re-enter this tonality, and in so doing sound the principal scale tones.

In consequence, once the dominant is heard as first note of the subject and taken as tonic of the key of the fifth degree, all the notes that follow are counted as degrees in the tonic scale, provided they do not have characteristic alterations of the key of the dominant, or that such alterations are not implied in the harmony.

The answer to these degrees (if unaltered) is made by the corresponding degrees of the key of the dominant.

It is of the utmost importance to keep in mind that the subject is considered as returning to its tonic key *immediately* after the dominant is heard. Only the presence of characteristic alterations or evident harmonic implications can maintain it in the key of the dominant.

Example:

44. If, on the contrary, characteristic dominant alterations, written or implied, are present, the answer must be made by the corresponding degrees of the tonic.

Example:

It is evident that the ♮ placed before the C in the first note of the second measure is a chromatic accidental, and does not affect the tonality of D major in which the subject begins. This tonality is affirmed by the ♯ placed on two occasions in front of the C; by the harmonic sense of the first two measures; and by the subject's melodic sense, which may be reduced to this outline:

In view of these factors, we conclude that characteristic alterations are present; that modulation to the dominant is implied in the harmony, and the subject therefore requires the following tonal answer:

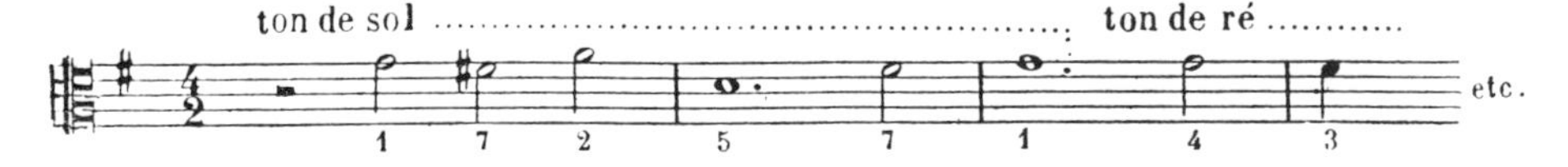

Exception: Harmonic Function of the Altered Fourth at the Beginning of the Subject

45. When a subject begins on the fifth degree followed by the raised (altered) fourth degree, and immediately returns to the fifth degree, this raised

fourth degree is always considered as leading note of the dominant.

The answer is always made by the tonic, leading note, and tonic of the principal key.

Example:

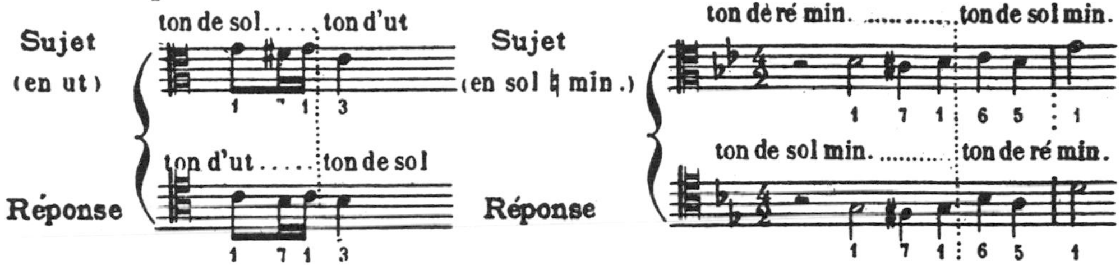

46. Apart from the above instance, in which the raised fourth degree becomes a sort of lower neighboring tone of the dominant, it retains its character as the altered fourth degree of the principal key.

Examples:

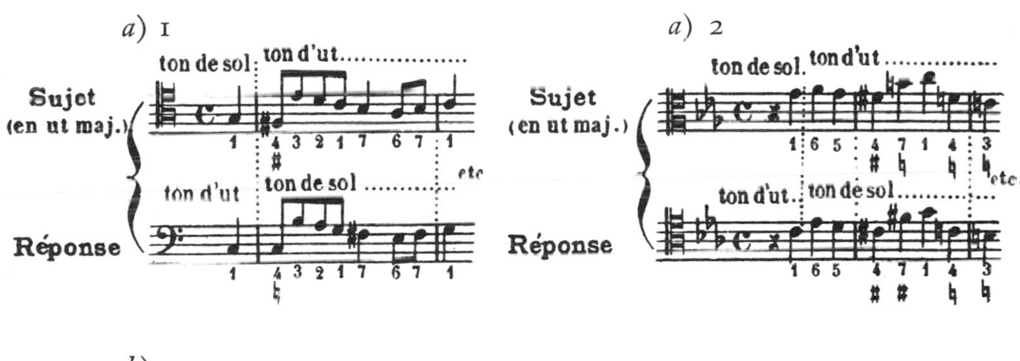

But note that, in example (*a* 1) above, the answer does not follow the rule even though the raised fourth degree is considered as the altered fourth degree of the principal key. This is because if the answer to this alteration were under these circumstances made by the corresponding alteration in the dominant, an imitation by contrary movement would be produced, as in (*b*).

As imitation by contrary movement is never permitted in the answer, we are obliged to make the answer by oblique movement and ignore the alteration.

47. The imitation by contrary movement that we have just seen in ¶46 occurs in the answer each time the subject, beginning on the dominant, progresses to the mediant or tonic by descending chromatic movement.

To avoid this forbidden imitation, the answer must repeat unaltered the fourth degree until the fourth degree of the principal key is actually imitated by it.

Example:

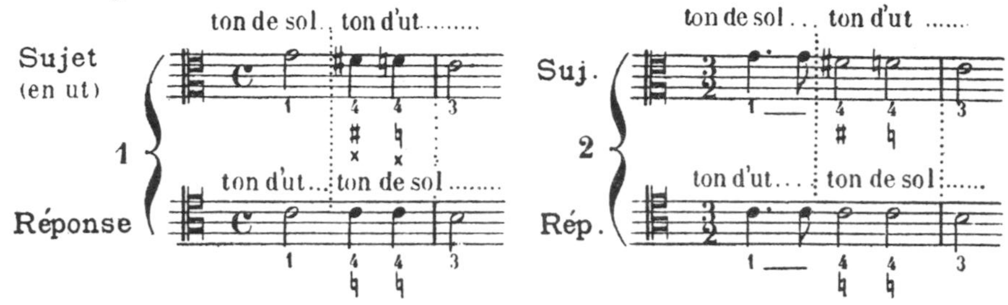

48. It is apparent from the above examples that the subject is completely deformed when so imitated in the answer. Therefore, a real answer is usually given to subjects which descend chromatically from the dominant to the mediant or tonic.

One guiding principle controls these and other exceptional cases: In case of doubt, choose that answer which least deforms the subject.

No doubt arises when the subject, before sounding the altered fourth degree, progresses to another degree by non-chromatic movement. The answer then follows the general rule.

Example:

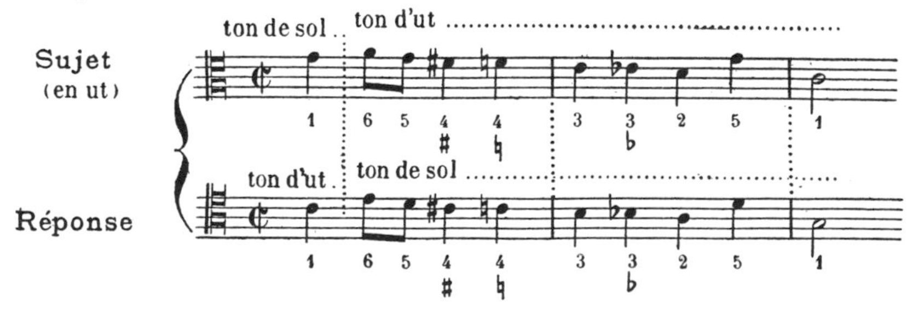

The whole question of chromatic subjects and their answers is discussed further in ¶92–¶98.

49. The two tables below recapitulate all the different ways in which a subject can progress from the dominant to the first degree, either descending or ascending, together with the appropriate answers.

a) Head of the subject progressing from the dominant to the tonic by descending movement:

b) Head of the subject progressing from the dominant to the tonic by ascending movement:

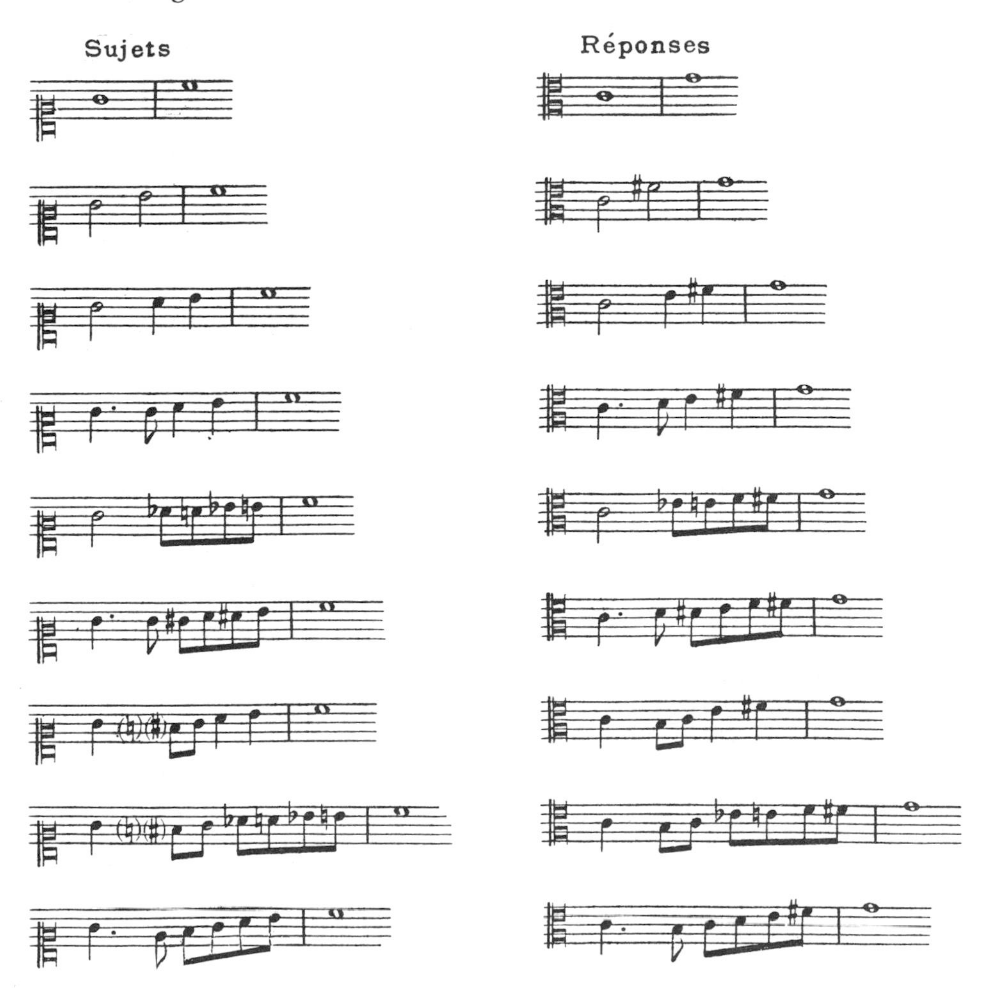

50. When the subject begins on the dominant and sounds various notes before progressing to the tonic or mediant, the following tables apply. They indicate the diatonic or chromatic alterations brought about at each interval:

51. Practical application of the above tables to heads of subjects progressing from the dominant to the tonic, ascending or descending, can be shown as

follows:

ton de ré
ton de sol
Sujet
1
ton de sol
ton de ré
etc.
Réponse
ton de si
ton de mi
Sujet
2
ton de mi
ton de si
Réponse
ton de mi
ton de la
Sujet
3
etc
ton de la
ton de mi
Réponse
ton de mi
ton de la
Sujet
4
etc.
ton de la
ton de mi
Réponse
ton de mi
ton de la
Sujet
5
etc.
ton de la
ton de mi
Réponse

ton de ré ton de sol
Sujet
6
1 4 3 2 3 1 6 5 5 5 4 3 4 3
etc.
ton de sol ton de ré
Réponse
1 4 3 2 3 1 6 5 5 5 4 3 4 3
ton de la ton de ré
Sujet
7
1 5 6 6 7 1
etc.
ton de ré ton de la
Réponse
1 5 6 6 7 1
ton de sol ton d'ut
Sujet
8
1 5 6 4 2 5
etc.
ton d'ut ton de sol
Réponse
1 5 6 4 2 5
ton de la ton de ré
Sujet
9
1 4 2 3 4 3 2 3 5 1
etc.
ton de ré ton de la
Reponse
1 4 2 3 4 3 2 3 5 1
ton de sol ton d'ut
Sujet
10
1 3 1 6 5 4 5 4 3
ton d'ut ton de sol
Réponse
1 3 1 6 5 4 5 4 3

ton de ré ton de sol
Sujet
11
ton de sol ton de ré
etc.
Réponse
ton de la ton de ré
Sujet
12
ton de ré ton de la
Réponse
ton de sol ton d'ut
Sujet
13
ton d'ut ton de sol
Réponse
ton de sol ton d'ut
Sujet
14
ton d'ut ton de sol
Réponse
ton de ré ton de sol
Sujet
15
ton de sol ton de ré
Réponse

THEORETICAL TONAL SIGNIFICANCE OF THE FIFTH DEGREE

52. We have just seen that a subject that begins on the fifth degree of the principal key really begins on the first degree of the key of the dominant, and returns thence to the principal key.

Likewise, when it is heard in the head of the subject, the fifth degree always assumes the character of the first degree of the key of the dominant. It is, therefore, evident that any subject that begins on the tonic or mediant and progresses immediately to the dominant or the seventh degree of the principal key modulates to the first or third degree of the key of the dominant.

Therefore, in its fundamental harmony, such a subject formulates a cadence to the key of the dominant.

53. The first melodic movement of a subject that begins on the tonic or mediant and progresses to the dominant must always take one of the following forms:

Either the subject progresses from the tonic or mediant to the dominant

a) Directly:

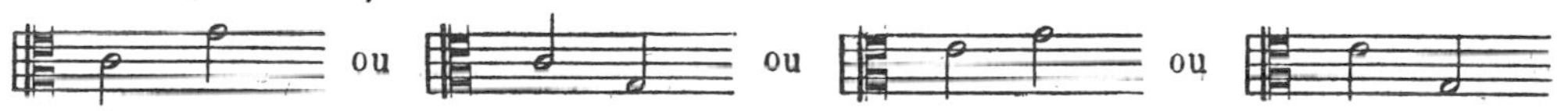

b) Or by sounding the mediant immediately before the dominant

1. either as the only note between the tonic and the dominant:

2. or after other degrees (excepting the fifth) of the principal key:

c) Or by the mediant immediately followed by the tonic, or with interposition of degrees other than the fifth of the principal key, the tonic, however, in all instances immediately preceding the dominant:

d) Or beginning on the tonic or mediant, and sounding before the dominant is heard any other degrees of the scale, provided the note heard immediately before the dominant is neither the tonic nor the mediant:

54. In cases (*a*), (*b*), and (*c*) above, the notes preceding the dominant all belong to the tonic key.

In case (*d*), however, all the notes between the tonic and/or mediant and the dominant are taken as degrees in the scale of the dominant. In other words, when the note immediately preceding the dominant is neither the tonic nor the mediant, all the notes between the tonic and/or mediant and the dominant are considered as being in the key of the dominant.

Analysis of the First Three Cases in ¶53

55. Theoretically, the following reasons justify the tonal attributions to the various degrees:

Modulation implies a cadence. Such a cadence is composed either of a succession of chords of the fourth and fifth degrees, or one of them, or of chords of the second and fifth degrees, either in fundamental or inverted state, progressing to the tonic chord of the new key.

In this process of modulating from the first degree of the scale to the dominant, at a certain moment the first degree ceases to belong to the principal key, but becomes the fourth degree of the key of the dominant.

If such modulation is made by the immediate succession of the two degrees, confusion between the two keys is produced on one note which belongs half to each key; this accounts for the well-known indeterminate effect of the plagal cadence.

Such an effect would be produced in the first three cases in ¶53, where the note immediately preceding the dominant is either the tonic or the mediant. The tonic chord cannot, however, simultaneously have the attribution of the chord of the first degree of the principal key and the fourth degree of the dominant.

Therefore, under such circumstances, the chord always maintains its quality of first degree of the principal key, the mediant being considered as third of the same chord. And, therefore, the notes preceding it are considered as *not* having modulated.

The Fourth Case in ¶53

56. Here, however, the note immediately preceding the dominant is neither the tonic nor the mediant, and the confusion described above does not arise. In fact, once the tonic or the mediant has been heard, the dominant attracts into its key all the notes that separate it from the initial note of the subject. Analysis will show that all the harmonies of such intervening degrees necessarily become part of a cadence to the dominant.

Example:

That the notes attributed to the key of G are actually in that key may be shown by omitting the first note in the examples in ¶56 and ¶58 (below). Harmonization of the rest of the notes as of the cadence to G major will be evident.

57. In the example in ¶56, it is the mediant, the second note of the subject, which is the equivocal note, as it might belong either to the key of C or G, as third of the chord on the first degree of the principal key, or as third of the chord on the fourth degree of the dominant. However, as the tonal attraction is stronger toward the new key than toward that already heard, and as the note in question cannot be equally divided between the keys of C and G, it is necessary to attribute to it the function of the sixth degree of the dominant scale, and to consider it as the third of the chord on the fourth degree of that key.

58. If the subject in its progress from the tonic to the dominant does not sound the mediant but passes through other degrees, the equivocal situation arises on the tonic, as in the first three cases in ¶53. Here, however, the tonic cannot lose its function as the first degree of the principal key, but the degrees that follow it can only, harmonically and tonally, belong to the key of the dominant.

Example:

Head of the Subject Progressing to the Fifth Degree, or to the Seventh Degree Followed by the Fifth: Tonal Answer

59. Applying the preceding analyses, we may state that: A subject modulates to the dominant when, having begun on the tonic or mediant, it progresses directly to the dominant or seventh degree (unaltered in minor), followed by the fifth degree.

In such cases, the fifth degree of the principal key is considered as the first degree of the key of the dominant, and the answer is made by the first degree of the tonic. Likewise, answer is made to the tonic by the first degree of the dominant, and to the mediant by the third degree (mediant) of the dominant. (See ¶¶35, 36, and 37.)

Examples:

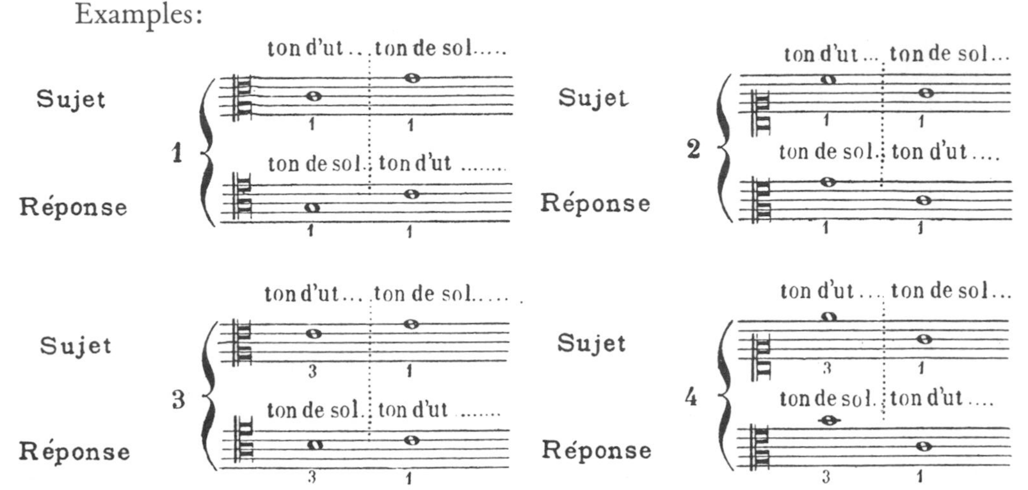

Note that in example 4, above, the answer must be made by an interval of a seventh to an interval of a sixth in the subject; subjects with such an opening are avoided in the scholastic fugue because of this unvocal interval in the answer.

60. When the subject, beginning on the tonic or the mediant, progresses to the seventh degree (unaltered in minor) followed by the fifth, the seventh degree is always considered, harmonically and tonally, as the third of the triad placed on the first degree of the key of the dominant (¶38).

The answer is made by the third degree of the principal key followed by the tonic.

Examples:

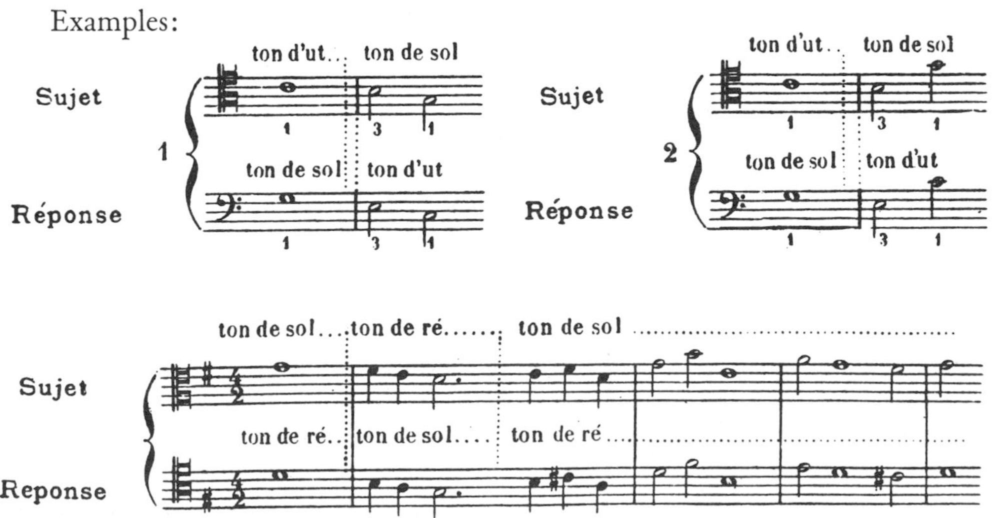

61. In cases in the minor mode similar to the above, if the seventh degree is altered, it always preserves its character of leading note. Answer is made by the

altered (raised) seventh degree of the key of the dominant.

Example:

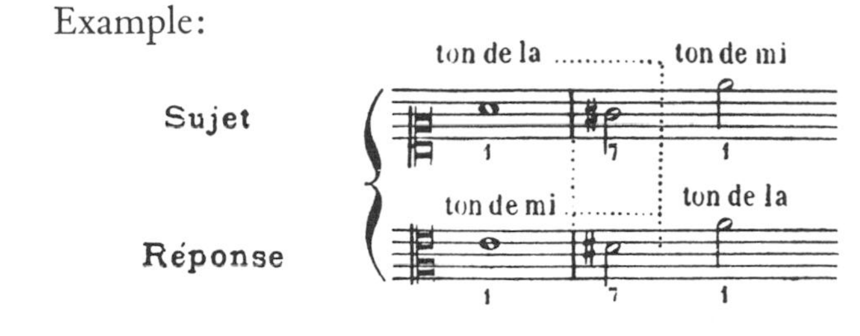

Tonal Function of Various Other Degrees in the Head of the Subject

62. As we have seen, a subject modulates to the dominant when, having begun on the tonic or mediant, it progresses to the dominant or seventh degree (unaltered in minor) followed by the dominant, and in so doing sounds other degrees.

All these degrees must be counted as intervals in the scale of the principal key of the subject, provided that the note immediately preceding the dominant or the seventh degree is the mediant or tonic.

Answer is made by the corresponding degrees of the key of the dominant.

Examples:

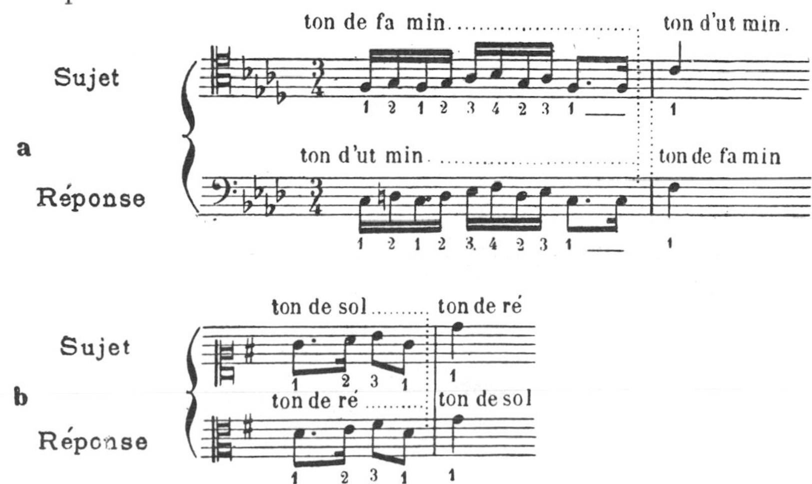

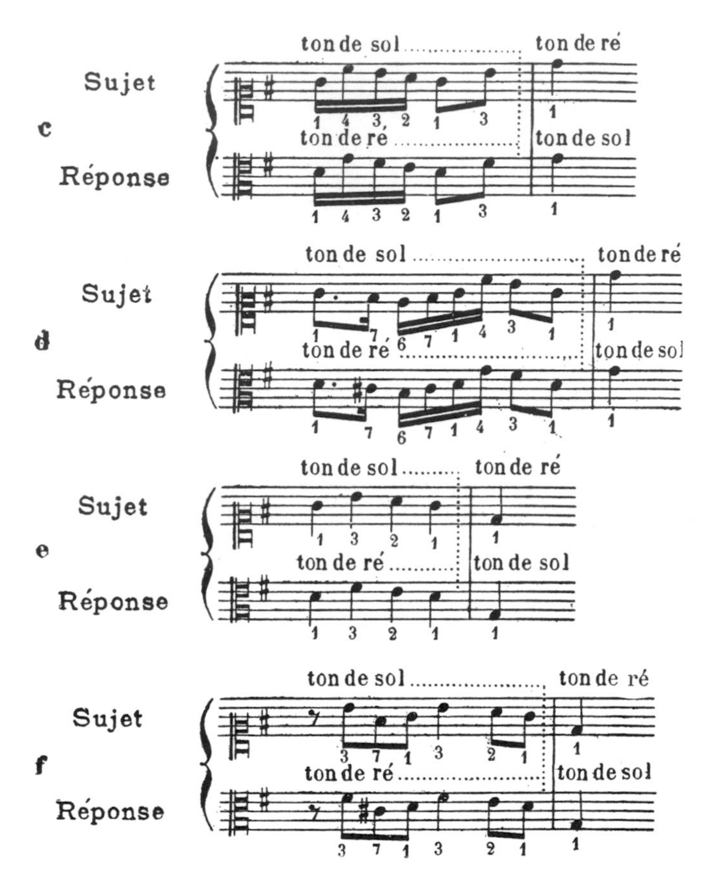

63. In every other case, after the tonic or mediant is heard as the first note of the subject, all the notes that compose the first melodic movement progressing to the dominant or non-altered seventh degree followed by the dominant must be calculated in the scale of the dominant.

Answer is made by the corresponding degree in the scale of the tonic.

The unaltered fourth degree is no exception to this rule. It is always considered, in this context, as the seventh degree of the key of the dominant, and answer is made by the seventh degree of the tonic key.

Example:

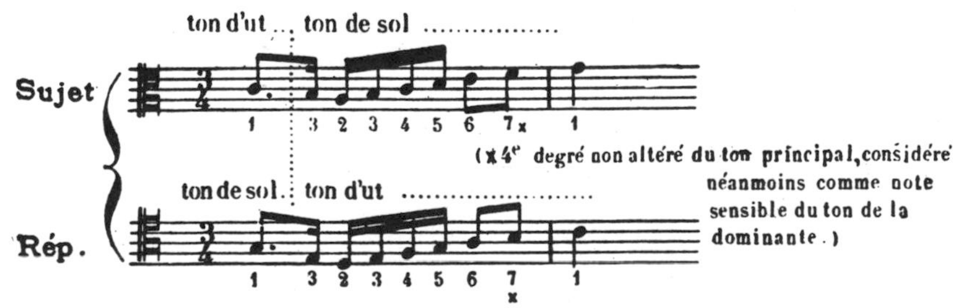

In the above example, the fourth degree of the tonic (F in the key of C) is considered as the leading note of the dominant key even though it is not altered by the ♯ characteristic of the latter key. Answer is made by the leading note of the tonic. It can be seen that the scale of C in the answer is the only possible response to the similar scalewise passage in the subject. Any other arrangement would badly distort the subject, and the musical sense of the subject would be lacking in the answer.

64. Likewise, the seventh degree of the tonic scale, whether or not altered in minor, when found in the first melodic movement and even though used as a neighboring or passing note, is always considered as the third degree of the dominant scale.

Example:

In the minor mode, the requisite alterations of the minor scale must be regarded.

Example:

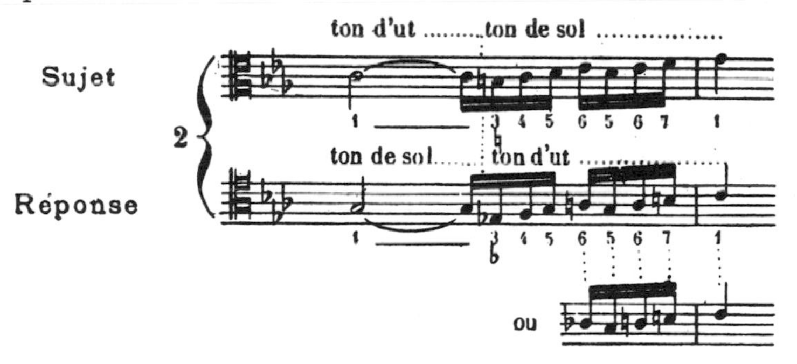

65. This rule (¶64) explains an answer by Johann Sabastian Bach, *Well-Tempered Clavier,* Fugue XVIII, which some theoreticians have claimed is false. Answering this subject:

Bach rightly considers it as modulating from the second note, F double-sharp, to the key of the dominant, since the note heard immediately before the dominant, C-sharp in the second measure, is neither the tonic nor the mediant. The double-sharp of the F in the first measure is evidently only a chromatic accidental. All the notes between the second G of the first measure and the D of the second measure must, therefore, be considered as belonging harmonically to the cadence of D-sharp minor. Bach treats his subject as if it had this form:

which would have as answer:

and, therefore, by analogy, he makes his answer:

and not, as certain theoreticians have suggested:

which would not make sense either musically or harmonically.

Another simple test of the correctness of Bach's answer is to substitute an F-sharp for the F double-sharp, which would give B-natural in the answer. Moreover, by transposing the subject into the major mode, it will be seen by analogy that Bach's is the correct answer.

66. The following answers can be explained by the same reasoning:

67. Subjects beginning on the tonic and progressing to the fifth degree, with their answers:

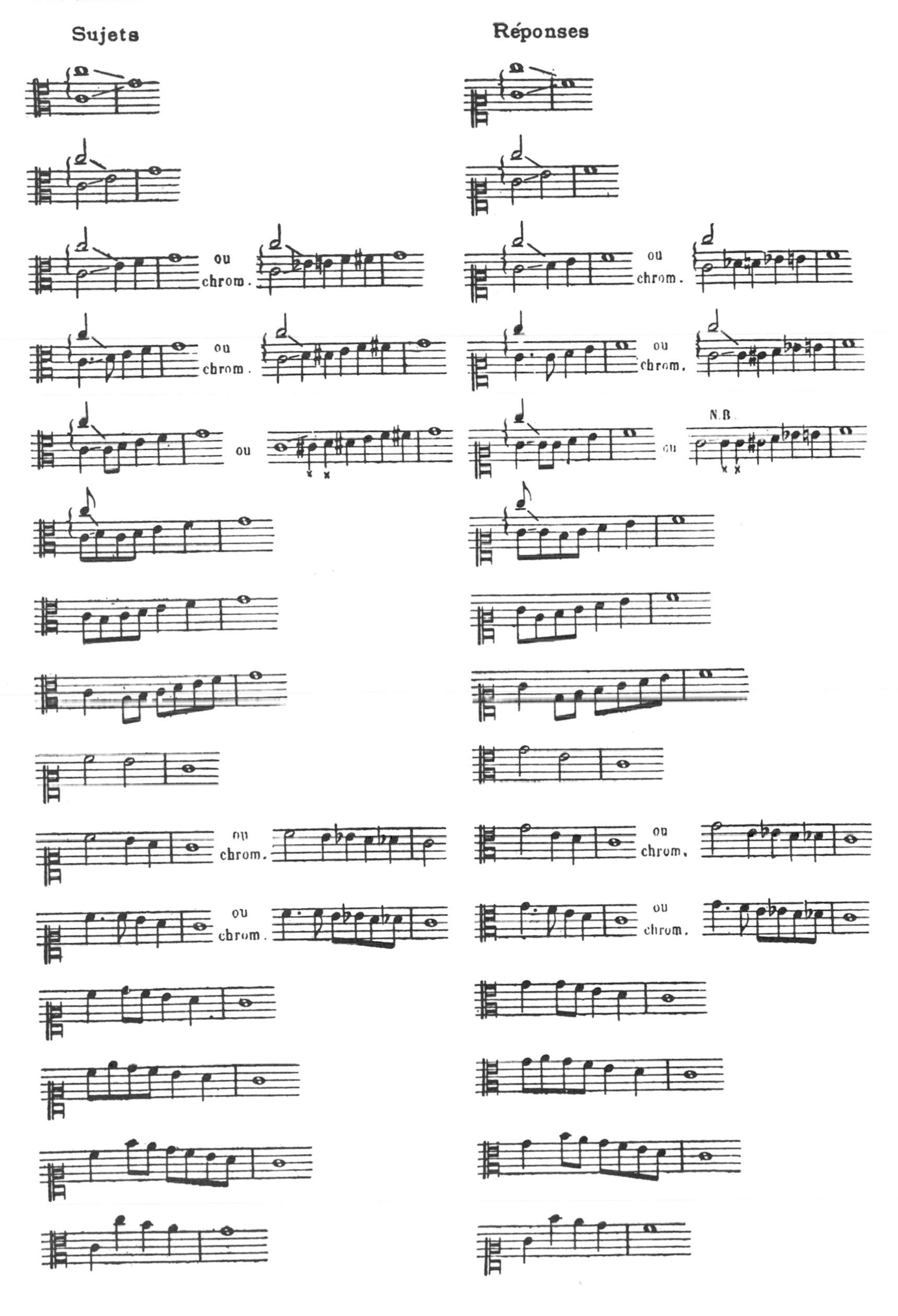
Sujets
Réponses
ou
chrom.
ou
chrom.
ou
chrom.
ou
chrom.
ou
ou
N.B.
ou
chrom.
ou
chrom.
ou
chrom.
ou
chrom.

N.B. See ¶92 for further remarks concerning chromatic subjects.

68. When the subject begins on the tonic or mediant and sounds various notes before arriving at the dominant, or the seventh degree followed by the dominant, the following tables may be applied:

Fourth Degree of the Principal Key Considered as the Seventh Degree of the Key of the Dominant

69. It has been said (¶63) that, when the subject progressing to the dominant sounds the fourth degree of the principal key, this fourth degree, even though unaltered, must be treated harmonically as the leading note of the key of the dominant. Actually, this fourth degree is considered as subtonic of the natural scale of the dominant; this scale—produced by the overtones of a sonorous chord—has its seventh degree, or subtonic, unaltered.

The fifth degree of the principal key, under these conditions, having ceased to be the dominant but having become the tonic of the key of the dominant (¶37), it is impossible to consider the fourth degree either as fundamental of the triad on the fourth degree, or the third of the triad on the second degree of the principal key, as neither of these chords can decide a modulation to the key of the dominant.

On the other hand, it is logical to consider it as subtonic of the dominant key, as it then becomes the third of the dominant of the dominant, a chord which does take part in the perfect cadence to the dominant.

70. Moreover, it should be noticed that, in accordance with this analysis, the harmonies of the fragment of the answer are homologous to those in the corresponding fragment of the subject (¶30). Likewise, it follows the principle stated in ¶29: Each note belonging in the subject to the key of the dominant must, in the answer, be reproduced by the note placed on the corresponding degree of the principal key.

Tonal and Harmonic Analysis of the Subject

71. It should be apparent by this time that the tonality and harmony of a subject of a fugue cannot be analyzed in the same way that analysis of an ordinary melodic phrase is made. The function of tonic of the key of the dominant attributed to the fifth degree of the principal key when heard in the head of a fugal subject gives a special tonal attribution to the notes that immediately precede the dominant when these are other than the tonic or mediant of the principal key, as has been seen in ¶56.

72. For example, if the following subject were to be analyzed from the point of view of tonality considered as an ordinary melodic phrase, harmonies of the key of E-flat would be attributed to its first and second measures:

But, analyzed from the special point of view of the fugue, the B-flat of the principal key (its fifth degree) on the second beat of the second measure, on which the first melodic movement ends, must be considered as tonic of the dominant key. It therefore follows that, by this modulation to the dominant, a cadence in the dominant key must be made, and such cannot be made by the harmonies attributed to the notes G and C in the third and fourth beats of the first measure of the example. Therefore, these notes must have the following harmonies in the key of B-flat attributed to them:

These harmonies must bring about in the answer the homologous harmonies in the key of E-flat:

In the example (*b*), the G on the third beat of the first measure might, alternatively, have been analyzed as the third of the chord on the fourth degree of the key of B-flat, instead of being taken as the fifth of the chord on the second degree of that key. This would have served quite as well as the above analysis, as the cadence would have been just as strongly defined by the fourth degree followed by the fifth. Homologous changes in harmony would then have been made in the answer.

73. Obviously, in the above instance a real answer is conceivable, but the harmonies envisaged in (*b*) and (*c*) are the only ones both logical and compatible with the tonal answer, and that is what concerns us here. However, it should be clearly understood that this way of envisaging the harmony of the subject is purely theoretical, and has as its sole object the close conformity of the tonality of the subject and answer. As has been said, the subject analyzed by itself as an ordinary musical phrase could be harmonized quite differently.

Return to the Principal Key

74. When the dominant has been heard, either as the first note of the subject, or after the tonic or mediant followed or not by other degrees, the subject must return at once to the principal key (¶43).

All the notes that follow the dominant under such circumstances must be calculated as degrees of the scale of the tonic of the subject, unless altered by a characteristic alteration of the key of the dominant, or unless such alteration is clearly implied in the harmony.

In other words, by a convention special to the fugue, the subject can modulate once only to the dominant. It can only do so again by means of characteristic alterations of the dominant key.

Examples:

tons de mi . si ... mi ... si ... mi
Sujet
tons de si . mi . si ... mi ... si
Réponse
MENDELSSOHN
ton de sol ... ton d'ut
Sujet
ton d'ut ... ton de sol
Réponse
HAENDEL
ton de mi . ton de la
Sujet
ton de la . ton de mi
Réponse
KIRNBERGER
ton d'ut ton de sol ... ton d'ut
Sujet
d
ton de sol ... ton d'ut ... ton de sol
Réponse
A. GEDALGE
ton de la . ton de mi . ton de la ... ton de mi ... ton de la
Sujet
e
ton de mi . ton de la . ton de mi ... ton de la ... ton de mi
Réponse
A. GEDALGE
ton d'ut . ton de fa . ton d'ut ... ton de fa
Sujet
f
ton de fa ton d'ut ton de fa ... ton d'ut
Réponse

Real Answer to a Tonal Subject

75. In certain unusual cases in which the subject progresses to the dominant, a real answer instead of a tonal answer is permitted, as when

a) A tonal answer would be antimusical, as in the case of some chromatic subjects (¶48).

b) The tonal answer deforms the subject.

Example:

Evidently a real answer is proper for this subject, thus:

Such cases occur rarely. They usually arise when the melody of the subject takes at its beginning the form of a sequence, and are, therefore, easy to distinguish.

76. For a subject such as the following, the real answer is likewise preferable to the tonal, as the latter deforms the melody of the subject. In case of doubt, the governing principle has been stated in ¶48: Choose the answer which least deforms the subject.

Example:

It is apparent in the above case, where the tonal answer is made, that the unaltered fourth degree of the principal key must be considered as the subtonic of the natural scale of the dominant, and must, in the answer, be answered by the leading note of the principal key. This so changes the character of the melody that it is better to make a real answer. This is generally advisable each time a subject ends on the dominant preceded by the unaltered fourth degree of the principal key.

Further Analysis: Modulation to the Dominant by Characteristic Alteration (Tonal Answer)

77. A subject modulates to the dominant each time one of its notes is affected by a characteristic alteration of that key, or such alteration is implied in its harmony. (¶43, ¶74).

In such cases (¶28, ¶29), each fragment of the subject belonging to the key of the dominant is reproduced in the answer, degree by degree, alteration by alteration, in the principal key of the subject.

Example:

This subject is in F major; it ends on the dominant and, moreover, has the characteristic alteration of the dominant on the note before the last, the ♮ placed before the B, fourth degree of F, becoming, because of that alteration, the seventh degree of C, dominant of F.

The answer, therefore, must end on the tonic of the principal key, F, preceded by its seventh degree in this manner:

78. But it is evident that in the subject the modulation takes place before the characteristic alteration is heard.

It is not always easy to determine the exact moment when modulation to the dominant takes place. Frequently two or more tonal interpretations of the subject may be more or less defensible. Nevertheless, it is certain that of all possible interpretations, one is preferable to all others.

The purpose of the following analysis is to find the best tonal interpretation of the above subject.

Subject Analyzed

79. In the subject in ¶77, let us, for the sake of discussion, admit that the subject can be divided into two distinct melodic phrases:

The first phrase begins on the tonic and does not progress to the dominant; we must, therefore, answer it by the same intervals in the scale of the dominant:

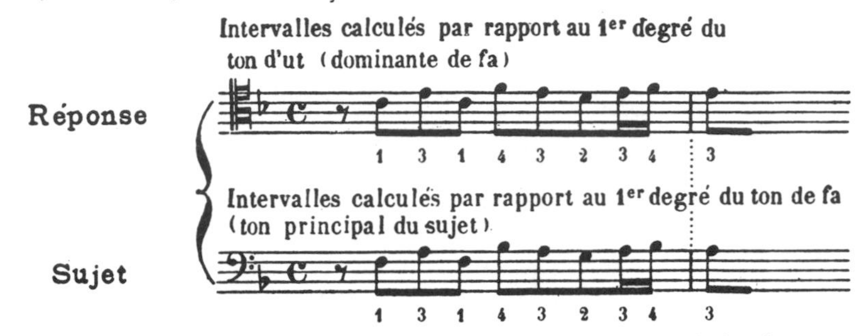

80. In the second phrase, the fundamental bass notes of the harmony are:

It is evident that the G, fundamental of the second note of this phrase, can only be part of one major chord belonging to the key of C; this necessarily implies that modulation to the dominant (key of C) must begin on the first note of the second phrase.

As this phrase belongs entirely to the key of the dominant, the answer is made by reproducing, degree by degree, all the corresponding degrees of the tonic of the subject, thus:

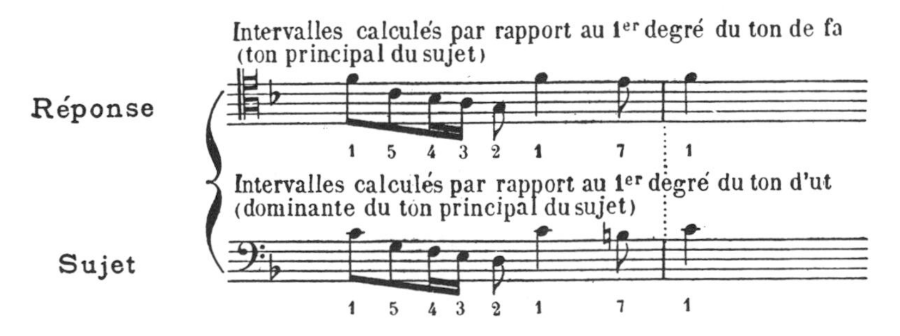

Combining both phrases of the subject, we have this answer:

N.B. Another method of determining the tonality of the second phrase is to lower the second C in the second measure an octave, together with the B-natural and C that follow it. The descending scale from G to C so produced is evidently the scale of C major, as, indeed, are all the notes from the first to the last C, inclusive. Moreover, there is no stronger way of asserting tonality than by sounding the complete scale, or a substantial consecutive fragment of the scale of a key.

81. The following false answers given in a competition are cited here to illustrate how easily one can go astray in an analysis, as well as to show the processes by which the mistakes were made. Let us see in each case what harmonies are inferred in the subject, and the tonal impossibility of justifying the harmonies.

Example 1:

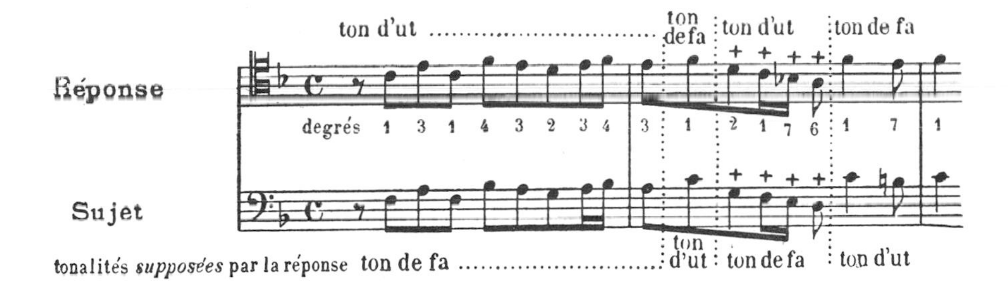

In this false answer we are obliged to suppose that the fragment of the subject indicated by the + signs belongs to the key of F; the answer thereto, in what should be the key of C, shows B, its seventh degree, flatted, that is, affected by the characteristic alteration of the key of F, which is absurd. Such an answer could only have been justified if the subject were:

which it most certainly is not.

82. The two following answers can be analyzed in a like manner. It will be seen that they are inexplicable from the viewpoints of both harmony and tonality. The student should examine them carefully.

Example 2:

Example 3:

83. The following subject,

is in G minor, begins on the tonic, and modulates to the key of the dominant, since it ends on the fifth degree preceded by the characteristic alteration of the key of the dominant.

It can be divided into three phrases:

The first and second phrases are obviously in the key of G minor.

The first phrase (head of subject) progresses to the mediant from the tonic, passing through the second degree. Following the rule, these intervals must be calculated in the key of G minor, the principal key, and the answer must be in the dominant, D minor:

The second phrase can have only these fundamentals:

The answer to the first two phrases joined together is, therefore:

84. Doubt, therefore, seems limited to the first D of the third phrase:

since, obviously, all five notes at the end of the subject belong to the key of D minor, the dominant.

The first note of the third phrase can be only the fundamental, the third, or the fifth of a chord.

a) It is certainly not the fundamental of the tonic chord of D minor, as the note preceding it is E-flat, the third of the chord on the fourth degree of G minor, which chord, in strict part-writing, it could not follow. Nor is it the fundamental of the major triad on the fifth degree of the key of G minor, as the tonality of D minor cannot be introduced by a D major chord.

b) Likewise, it cannot be the third of the B-flat major triad placed on the sixth degree of D minor.

c) The sole remaining alternative, therefore, is to consider it the fifth of the G minor triad which becomes, because of the C-sharp immediately following, attracted into the key of D minor, of which it is part of the triad on the fourth degree. This D, therefore, has as fundamental harmony G in the key of D minor, and must be considered as the first degree of the key of D minor.

The third phrase has, therefore, these fundamental harmonies:

Fondamentales

And the analogous fundamental harmonies of this fragment of the answer must be:

The entire answer, therefore, is:

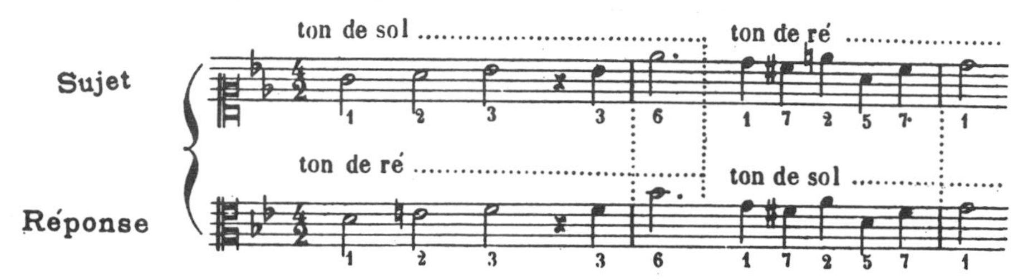

SUBJECT ENDING ON THE DOMINANT OR THE SEVENTH DEGREE
(TONAL ANSWER)

85. As has been seen, a subject modulates to the key of the dominant when it ends

a) On the dominant (¶37). In this case, the dominant is considered as the first degree of the key of the dominant, and the answer ends on the first degree of the principal key.

b) On the seventh degree (unaltered in minor) of the principal key (¶38). The seventh degree is considered as the third degree of the key of the dominant, and the answer ends on the third degree of the principal key. Examples:

86. To find an answer to these subjects, we apply the same analytic procedure as before. Subject 1, ¶85:

This subject may be divided into three phrases:

The first phrase, according to the rule, requires the following answer:

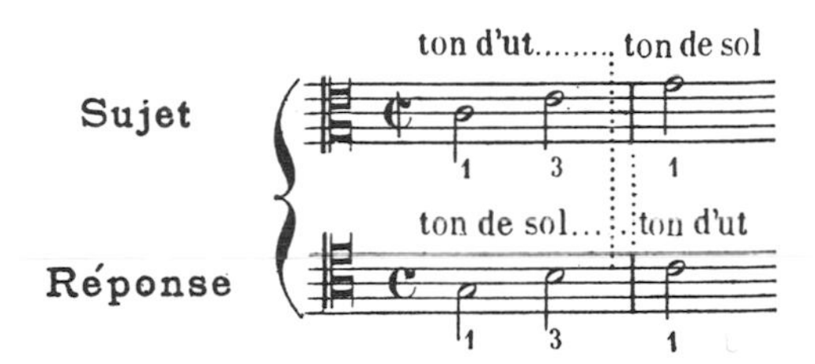

The subject, having modulated to the dominant, must return to the principal key.

In the second phrase there are no characteristic alterations of the key of the dominant, nor is any such alteration implied in the harmony. The passage, therefore, belongs to the principal key of the subject, and the answer is as follows:

In the third phrase, the final note G must be considered as the first degree of the key of the dominant of C. This implies that the modulation is made on the C, the first note of the phrase, which should therefore be considered the fourth degree of the key of G, and should have the following answer:

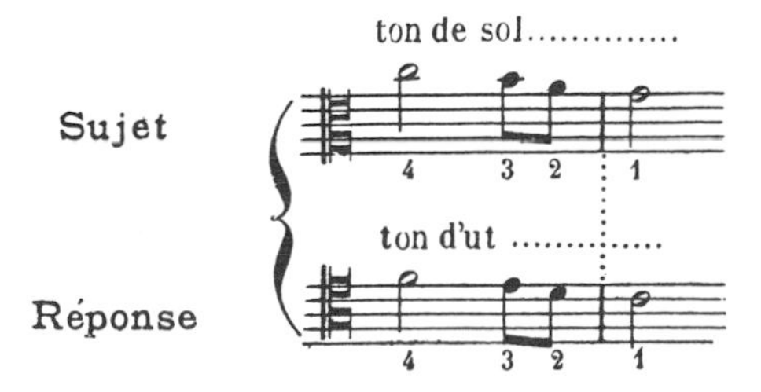

Note, again, that the phrase forms part of a descending scale (¶ 80) which strongly asserts the G major key.

The complete answer is:

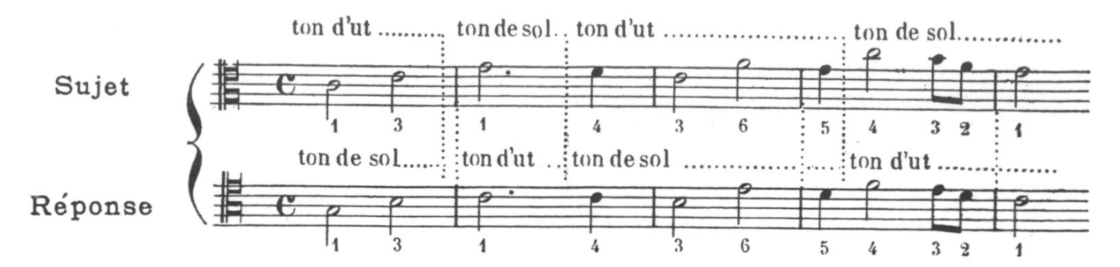

87. In analyzing subject 2 in ¶85,

it will be found that the last phrase in its entirety,

belongs to the key of E-flat, dominant of the principal key. According to the rule, the final note, G, must be considered as the third of the dominant; consequently both the A-flat and B-flat that precede it imply D-natural in their respective harmonies, D-natural being characteristic of the key of E-flat. Moreover, this passage is a fragment of a scale (¶80).

No other difficulties being present, the answer to this subject is:

88. Application of the above analyses and procedures has given answers to the following subjects. They should be carefully studied:

c
Sujet
ton d'ut .... ton de fa .... ton d'ut..........
tr
Réponse
ton de fa .. ton d'ut .... ton de fa..........
tr
d
(A.THOMAS)
Sujet
ton de sol... ton de ré.. ton de sol.. ton de ré
Réponse
ton de ré..... ton de sol ton de ré.. ton de sol
e
(A.GEDALGE)
Sujet
ton de si .. ton de fa.. ton de si .... ton de fa ....
Réponse
ton de fa . ton de si. ton de fa .... ton de si ....
f
(A GEDALGE)
Sujet
ton de ré ton de la ton de ré .... ton de la........................
Réponse
ton de la ton de ré ton de la .... ton de ré ....
g
(A.GEDALGE)
Sujet
ton de si . ton de mi .... ton de si
Réponse
ton de mi ton de si .... ton de mi
h
(A.GEDALGE)
ton de mi ton de si ton de mi .... ton de si ....
ton de si ton de mi ton de si .... ton de mi ....

Mutation

In each of these examples it is apparent that the answer undergoes a change in comparison with the subject each time it modulates *to* the dominant or returns *from* the dominant to the principal key. This modification is called "mutation."

Mutation consists of the omission or addition of the interval of a second between two notes of the answer, one of which is considered as belonging to the tonic, the other to the dominant key of the subject.

It is of the utmost importance that mutation be made correctly.

89. Mutation, in certain cases, causes imitation by oblique movement in the answer. But in no case (¶46) can mutation be permitted to induce imitation by contrary movement.

Further Analysis of Mutation

90. Mutation causes the *omission* of the interval of a second (major or minor, according to mode) in the answer, whenever:

1. The subject progresses from its beginning from the *tonic* to the *dominant,* or a degree in the dominant key, by *ascending* movement. Example:

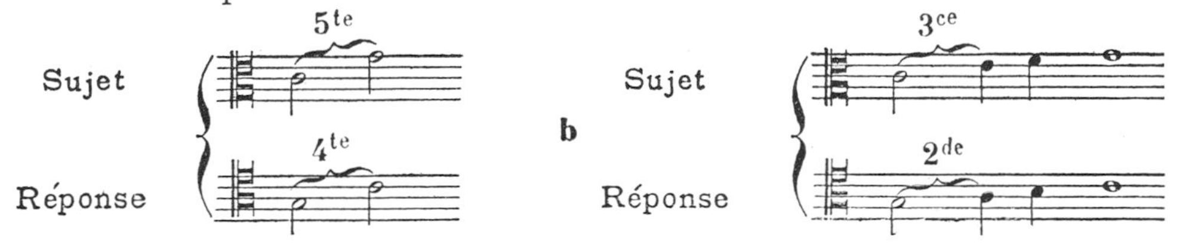

2. The subject progresses from its beginning from the *dominant* to the *tonic,* or a degree in the tonic key, by *descending* movement. Example:

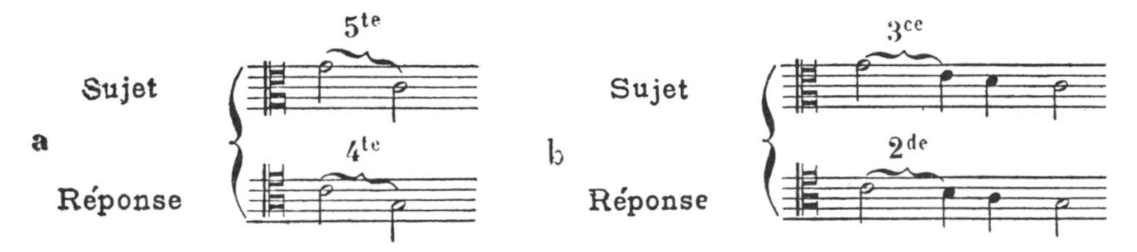

91. Inversely, mutation causes the *addition* of the interval of a second (major or minor, according to mode), whenever:

1. The subject progresses from its beginning from the *tonic* to the *dominant,* or a degree in the dominant key, by *descending* movement. Example:

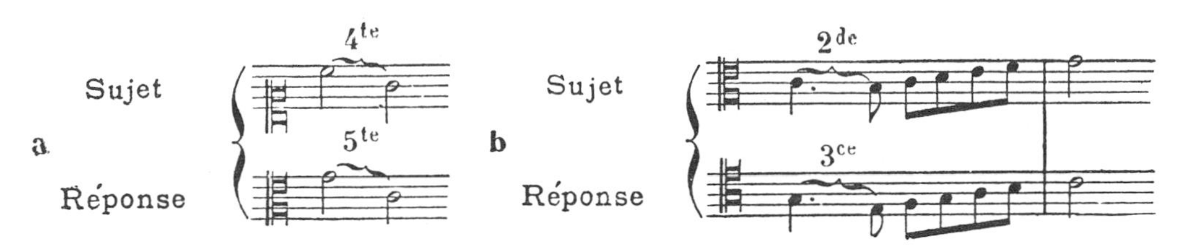

2. The subject progresses from its beginning from the *dominant* to the *tonic,* or a degree in the key of the tonic, by *ascending* movement. Example:

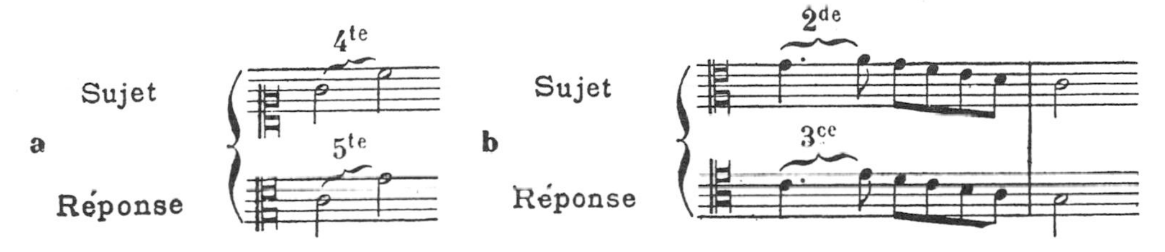

Like changes are produced in the answer each time the subject modulates from the tonic to the dominant, and vice versa.

Further Observations on Chromatic Subjects

92. As has been seen (¶47 and ¶48), chromatic subjects require special attention because of the possibilities they offer of causing an answer in imitation by *contrary* movement, which is always forbidden.

For instance, imitation by contrary movement would be produced in the answer if, in this chromatic subject which progresses from its beginning from the dominant directly to the tonic, by descending movement,

the chromatic alteration of the fourth degree of the tonic were reproduced in the answer.

Likewise, in the case of a chromatic subject which progresses directly from the tonic to the dominant by ascending movement,

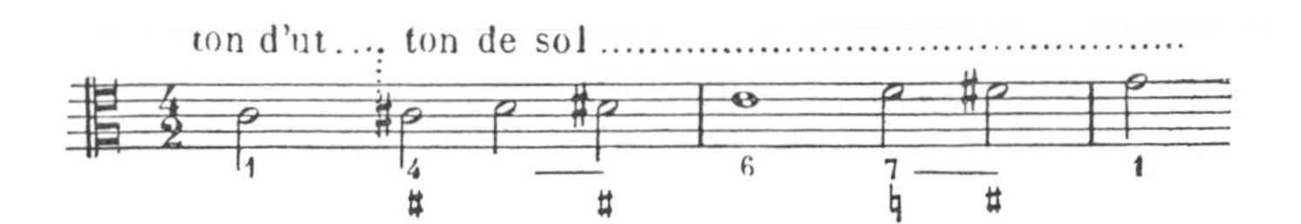

an answer by contrary movement would be given if we reproduced the chromatic alteration of the fourth degree of the dominant key, which would give G followed by F-sharp.

93. To understand how a correct answer may be arrived at for each of the foregoing subjects, they must be examined with their chromatic intervals omitted:

The following would be the answer if the subject were changed from chromatic to diatonic:

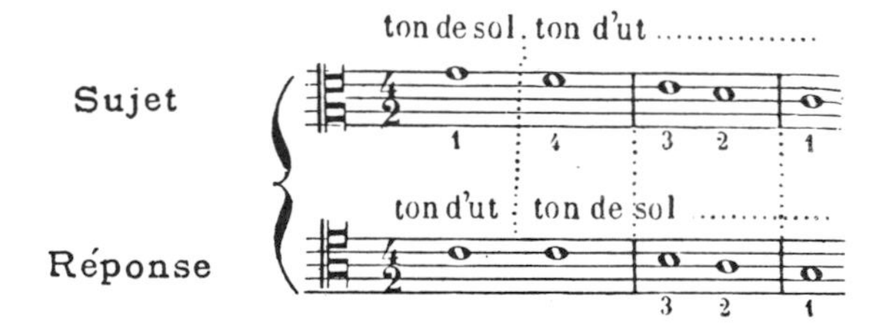

It is possible, in the subject, to insert a chromatic interval between the first and second notes. This is not possible in the answer, as the second note is the same as the first. Therefore, it is necessary to repeat this note in the answer until the subject has progressed to the natural fourth degree of the dominant key,

from which the answer may imitate the chromatic movement of the subject.

In these cases, an altered interval must be answered by a natural interval which produces imitation by oblique movement. Such movement is permitted.

94. Using analogous procedures in the case of a subject progressing directly from tonic to dominant by ascending chromatic movement (subject 2 in ¶92), the following answer is obtained:

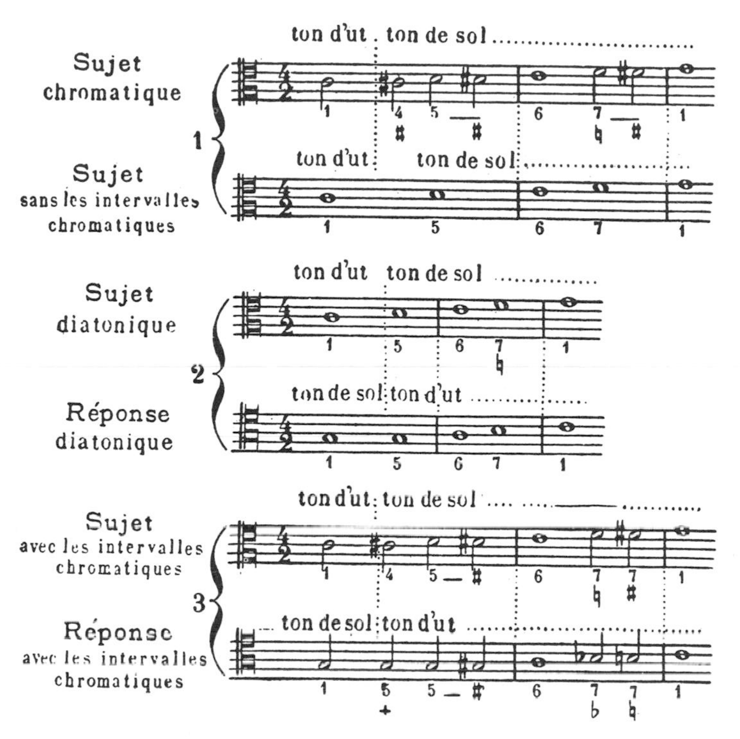

In this example, the fifth degree of the principal key must be repeated, since it is impossible to interpose a chromatic semitone between the first G of the answer (taken as tonic of the dominant key) and the G that immediately follows it, which is considered as the fifth degree of the tonic key, C.

When the subject takes the following forms, however, it is evident that such distortion of the melody of the subject will not occur in the answer. To these subjects, therefore, answers should follow the general rules:

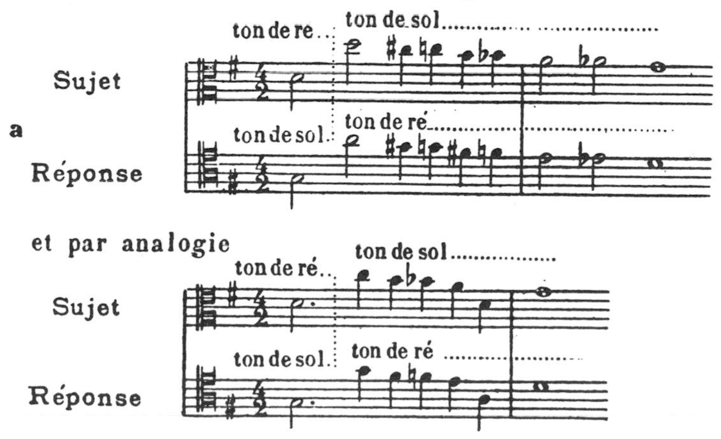

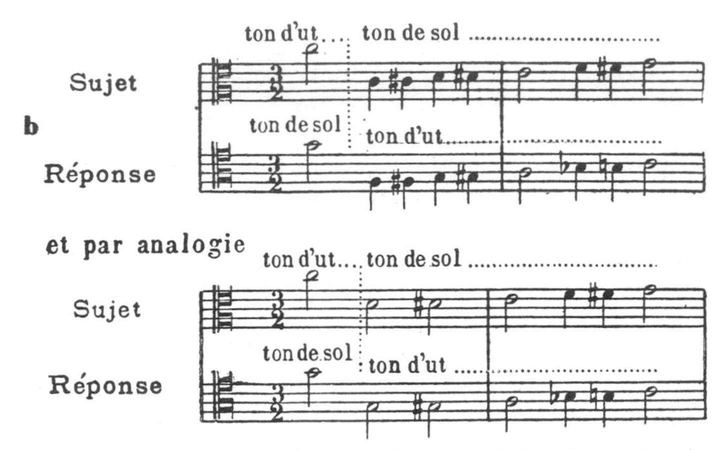

95. In certain cases the subject, having modulated to the dominant key, returns to the tonic or mediant by chromatic movement. Here the procedure must be the same as in ¶93, and answer is made by oblique movement.

Example:

Oblique movement likewise occurs in the answer when the subject, having progressed from dominant to tonic, returns to the dominant by chromatic movement, and then proceeds again to the tonic or mediant by chromatic movement.

Example:

N.B. Subjects of this nature are rare. Because the subject is distorted in the above answer, a real answer would be acceptable to all and preferable to most theoreticians.

96. The situation is entirely different when the chromatic movement of the subject:

1. Ceases, or returns to the tonic or mediant before reaching the dominant.

Example:

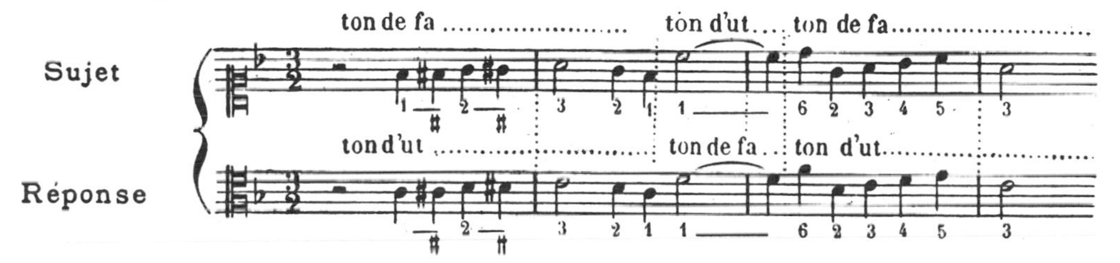

2. Sounds, immediately after the tonic, any degree other than the altered first degree of the tonic, or the second degree of the tonic lowered by a chromatic semitone.

Example:

Answers to subjects of this nature should be made according to the general rules.

97. In any event, when a subject progresses directly and chromatically from dominant to tonic by descending movement, or from tonic to dominant by ascending movement, a real answer is preferable whenever the tonal reply too greatly distorts the subject.

Example:

98. These chromatic subjects have been analyzed at length since they not only furnish special difficulties but also serve as illustrations of the method of analyzing a subject from the particular viewpoint of the answer.

Observations on Various Exceptional Subjects

99. Theoretically, it could be concluded from what has been said in this chapter that

1. A subject should begin only on the tonic, mediant, or dominant.
2. A subject should end only on the tonic, mediant, dominant, or the seventh degree (unaltered in minor).

Of course this is not always the case. Fugue XXI in the second book of Bach's *Well-Tempered Clavier* begins on the second degree. And, in free composition, a subject may begin on any degree, and the composer may answer to or imitate it as he wishes. Nevertheless, it is possible, by applying the preceding rules, to give a logical answer and a rational interpretation to such subjects.

Subject Beginning on the Seventh Degree in Major

100. In the major mode, a subject beginning on the seventh degree is always considered as beginning on the third degree of the dominant. The answer is, therefore, made by the third degree of the tonic.

Example:

Since the fifth degree of the principal key is always considered the first degree of the dominant key, the seventh degree of the principal key can only be considered the third of the triad of the fifth degree, and the answer must be made by the third of the chord of the first degree.

Subject Beginning on the Altered Seventh Degree in Minor

101. In the minor mode, when a subject begins on the altered (raised) seventh degree, it is always considered as the leading note of the principal key. Answer is made by the leading note of the dominant key.

Example:

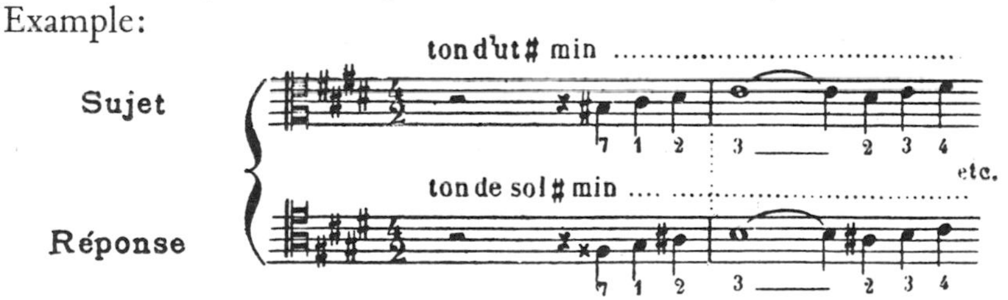

This altered seventh degree cannot be considered the third of the triad on the fifth degree of C-sharp minor, as that is a minor chord.

In the scholastic fugue it is impossible to begin a subject with the unaltered seventh degree of the principal key in the minor mode. The answer would have to be either by the unaltered seventh of the dominant key, which would result in unidentifiable modality and tonality, or (¶100) by the third degree on the tonic, which would produce similar results. Even if a real answer were made, vagueness of key and modality would ensue.

Subject Beginning on the Altered Fourth Degree

102. The altered (raised) fourth degree of the principal key at the beginning of a subject is always considered the leading note of the dominant key. Answer is made by the seventh degree (altered in minor) of the principal key.

Example:

Subjects Beginning on the Second, Fourth, or Sixth Degrees

103. If the subject begins on the second, unaltered fourth, or sixth degrees of the principal key, it is considered as beginning in the tonic, and answer is made according to the rules governing subjects so beginning (¶35 and following).

Example:

It is almost impossible to begin a subject on the fourth or sixth degrees without evoking tonalities of which these notes are the respective tonics. Such subjects should, therefore, be avoided, as it is *anti-fugal* for any uncertainty as to the mode or key of the subject to exist. Actually, the key and mode of the subject tend to be uncertain if it begins on any other degree than the tonic, mediant, or dominant.

Summary

104. I. A subject of a fugue does not modulate when, beginning on the tonic or mediant, it does not progress to the fifth degree, or if it does, only sounds the fifth degree secondarily, as a passing note, appoggiatura, or in a harmonic sequence.

II. A subject modulates to the dominant key when, beginning on the tonic or mediant, it progresses to the fifth degree either directly or in sounding various notes of the keys of the tonic or dominant.

III. A subject modulates to the dominant key when it begins on the dominant, or ends on the dominant or seventh degree (unaltered in minor).

In such cases, the dominant of the subject is considered as the tonic of the key on the fifth degree, and the seventh degree of the subject (unaltered in minor) is considered the third degree of the dominant key.

IV. When the subject begins on the tonic or mediant and progresses to the dominant, or to the seventh degree immediately followed by the dominant, and in so doing sounds various other notes, these notes are calculated in the tonic key of the subject, provided that the note immediately preceding the dominant is the tonic or mediant.

In every other case, these notes are calculated in the key of the dominant, even the unaltered fourth degree, which is considered the seventh of the key of the dominant.

V. A subject modulates to the dominant each time it presents a characteristic alteration of that key, or such alteration is clearly implied in the harmony.

VI. The dominant having once been heard as the tonic of the key on the fifth degree—either as first note of the subject, or in the head of the subject following the tonic or mediant—all the notes that follow it are considered intervals in the scale of the tonic. The subject can only remain in the dominant key by a characteristic alteration of that key, expressed or implied. Otherwise, the subject immediately returns to its principal key.

VII. Every interval belonging in the subject to the tonic scale must be reproduced in the answer by the corresponding interval in the dominant scale, with whatever alterations affect it.

Every interval belonging in the subject to the dominant scale must be reproduced in the answer by the corresponding interval in the tonic scale, with whatever alterations affect it.

Exercises

Write at least fifty answers to subjects chosen from those listed in Appendix A at the back of this book. Choose first those subjects having long note values, simple rhythms, and few notes.

IV

THE COUNTERSUBJECT

Definition

105. The countersubject is a counterpoint, invertible at the octave or fifteenth with the subject, which, entering shortly after the subject, accompanies it at each of its subsequent entries.

Requisite Qualities of a Countersubject

106. I. The countersubject should have nothing in common with the subject except its tonality. It should not resemble the subject in either melody or rhythm. Nevertheless, the countersubject should be in the same general style as the subject: it should *contrast* but not *contradict.* The countersubject should lend variety without destroying the unity of the fugue.

II. Subject and countersubject must be capable of giving good harmonic basses to each other. This is essential, since both pass successively through all the voices, and each in its turn appears in the bass part.

III. The countersubject must always enter after the subject, preferably immediately after the head of the subject. At the latest, it should enter after the first mutation of the subject, if any.

The purpose of the countersubject's making its entry after the subject is to maintain the supremacy of the subject as the most important element of the fugue, as well as to avoid the confusion which might be caused by simultaneous entries.

While it is possible to give a subject as many countersubjects as there are parts of the fugue in excess of that in which the subject is proposed, we here confine ourselves to fugues with single countersubjects.

Example:

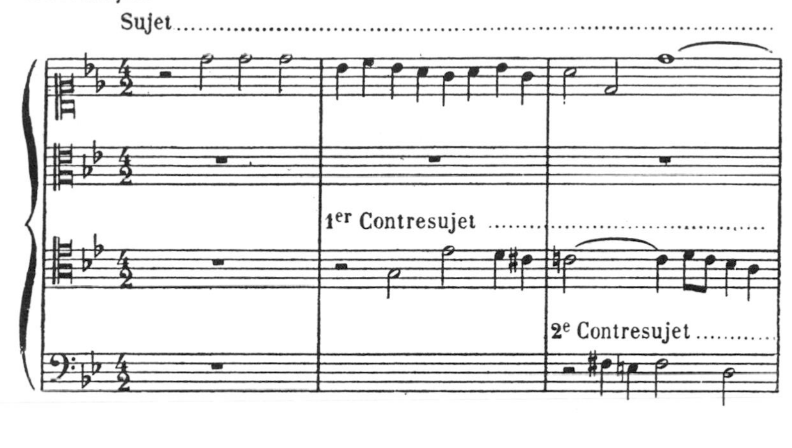

IV. The principal beats in a measure must be sounded by either the subject or the countersubject. The countersubject should not simultaneously with the subject sound notes of the same value. When there are rests in the subject, the countersubject should fill them in, and, reciprocally, rests or notes of long values should be used in the countersubject while the subject moves rapidly.

Example:

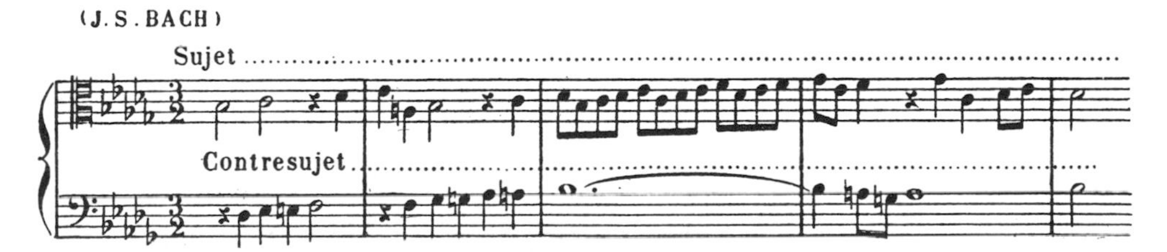

V. The harmonies induced by the countersubject should be as rich and varied as possible. Prepared dissonances should be used whenever feasible.

Frequent changes of harmony within the measure should be avoided, and all notes whose harmonization is unnecessary should be treated as passing or neighboring notes, that is, as nonharmonic.

Example:

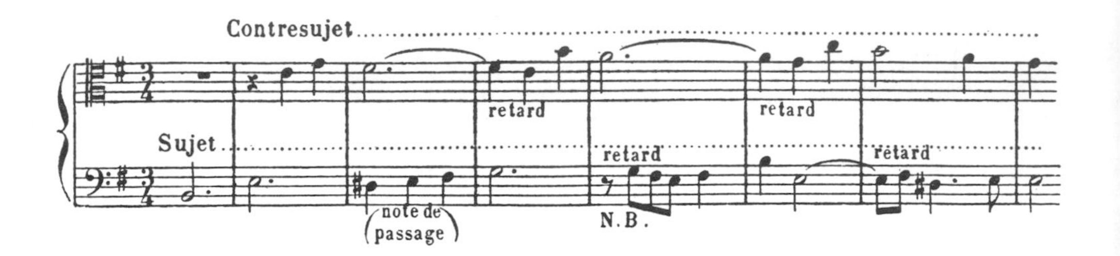

N.B. In the above, each time the last note in a measure is followed by a rest and is repeated at the beginning of the next measure, it should be considered as a suspension, provided the note following it descends a degree. It should be treated harmonically as if a syncopated note had been sustained. Measures 4 and 5 above should be considered harmonically as if the melody had been written as follows:

VI. With chromatic subjects, a diatonic countersubject is generally advisable.

A chromatic countersubject is frequently employed when the subject lacks a strongly marked character.

Mutation in the Countersubject

107. The countersubject likewise accompanies the answer. If the answer does not modulate, the countersubject is simply transposed into the key of the answer.

However, if the answer modulates in response to the mutations of the subject, the countersubject when heard with the answer must make corresponding mutations.

108. When the beginning of a subject necessitates a mutation in its answer, the countersubject must not begin until after the place where mutation occurs (¶106, III).

Example:

109. The difficulties to be encountered if the countersubject is begun before the mutation are illustrated in the following example. The countersubject, of course, must undergo the same mutations as the answer (¶107). In the example, the figures above the notes indicate the degrees of the scale.

Example:

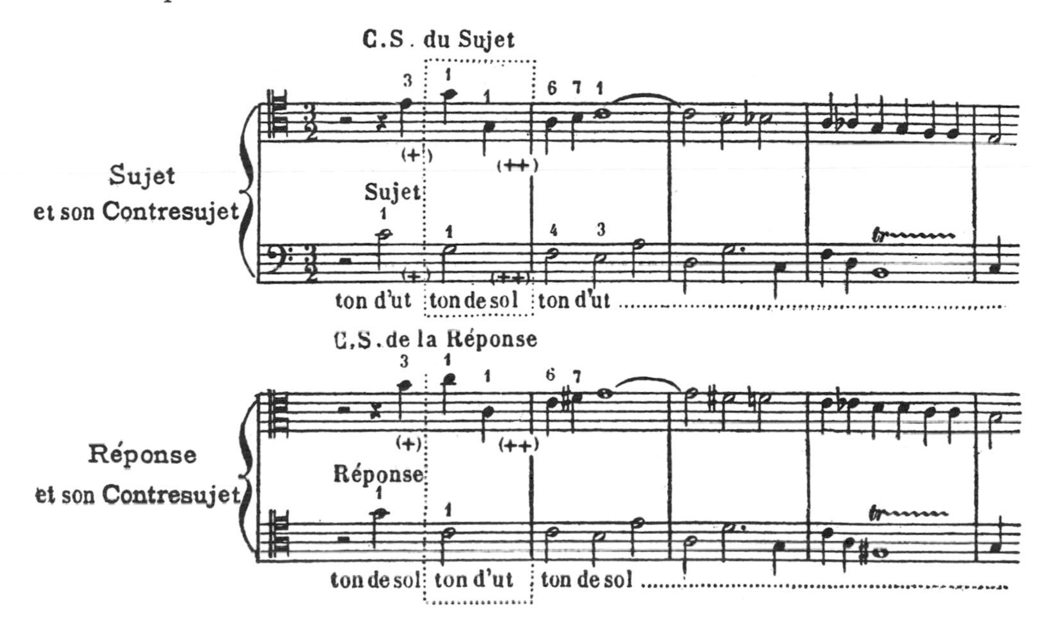

In the head of the above countersubject, there are two mutations which correspond to the change of intervals marked + in the answer as compared with the subject, as follows: the countersubject of the answer begins with the interval of a second instead of the third at the beginning of the countersubject of the subject. Also, the sign ++ indicates where, on the contrary, an interval of a second in the countersubject of the subject requires an interval of a third in the countersubject of the answer.

Note that the subject and answer in this case present mutations that are the inverse of those of the countersubject, that is, an addition of a degree between two intervals of the answer as compared with the subject corresponds to an equal omission in the countersubject, and vice versa.

110. This shows the distortions inevitable when beginning a countersubject before the first mutation of the subject, and the necessity, therefore, of beginning the countersubject *after* such mutation.

111. Moreover, the countersubject undergoes as many changes as there are mutations in the subject. The effect of these mutations in the answer render it essential never to work out the countersubject primarily in relation to the answer, but always with the subject.

Use of Suspensions

112. The omission or addition of an interval produced by a mutation in the answer frequently renders difficult the use of suspensions in the countersubject, as such suspensions, harmonically correct in the countersubject of the subject, cannot be resolved properly in the countersubject of the answer.

This difficulty may sometimes be overcome by repeating a note in the countersubject of the subject, if the mutation causes the omission of an interval in the answer.

Example:

Here we see that the mutation which, in the answer, causes the omission of an interval adds one in the same place in the countersubject of the answer.

If, in the countersubject of the subject, resolution of the suspension had been made without repeating a note,

the countersubject of the answer would have been:

which would have produced a prohibited unresolved dissonance of the second. Furthermore, the B-flat and the E-flat would have made a forbidden 6/4 chord, as the B-flat could be analyzed only as a real note, instead of a passing note.

The countersubject of the answer might also have been written like this:

However, in addition to being awkward harmonically, this would have too greatly distorted the melodic line of the countersubject. It would be better, therefore, instead of writing a banal and tasteless consonant harmony, to use the device just described, and repeat a note in the countersubject of the subject.

Note that in this case, as in all similar instances, the resolution of the dissonance in the countersubject of the answer is not made on the same beat as in the countersubject of the subject. This is not considered important; what is important is that the dissonance resolves.

Further Classification of Fugues

113. Formerly "simple fugue" was the name given to a fugue in which the countersubject was replaced by various noninvertible counterpoints. This sort of fugue is now practiced only, if ever, in "free composition."

The terms "double," "triple," and "quadruple" fugue, likewise formerly in vogue, have now been abandoned for the less pedantic and more accurate description of fugues with one, two, or three countersubjects.

As before stated, this book concerns itself primarily with the four-part fugue with one countersubject.

114. Of course, if two or three countersubjects are used, they must be combined according to the rules of two- or three-part invertible counterpoint.

115. Although it is possible to write a fugue without any countersubject, it is impossible to write a good fugue with a bad countersubject. Therefore, its construction is of the greatest importance.

Construction of the Countersubject

116. A subject having been chosen, we must first determine its fundamental harmonies. Once these have been established, we take as an outline of the countersubject those notes of its fundamental chords which are invertible with the subject, which give the best bass to the subject, and to which the subject can serve as a good harmonic bass. It will be found that some invertible notes give a much better effect than others, so careful choice must be made.

With these notes the outline of the countersubject is shaped. To it must be added those which will best suit the form and character of the melody of the subject.

Example:

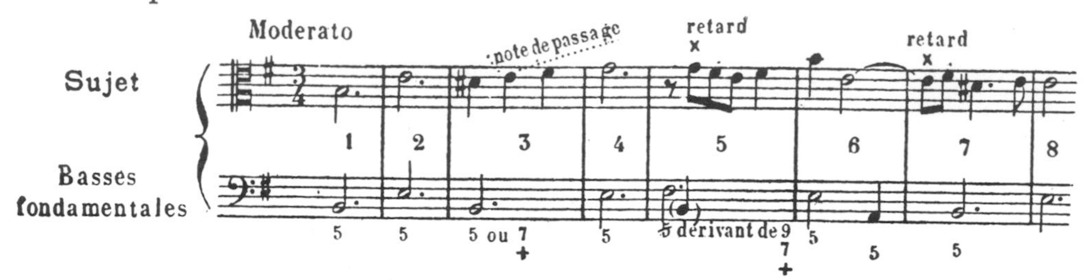

117. This subject is composed of eight measures. As has been said in ¶108, the countersubject should begin immediately after the first mutation in the head of the subject. We therefore postpone the entry of the countersubject until the second measure of the subject.

I. *Second Measure:*

Of the three notes that make up the fundamental triad of the harmony of this measure,

two, E and G, are invertible with the E of the subject; both are equally good as basses, and, inversely, the subject can serve as a good bass to them. We may, therefore, use either.

II. *Third Measure:*

To avoid too many harmonies, we will consider E on the second beat a passing note. Since the fundamental, B, is not an invertible interval, we have the choice of only D-sharp and F-sharp. However, as D-sharp is the leading note, it cannot, harmonically, be doubled. This obliges us to choose F-sharp as the first beat of the countersubject in this measure. For the third beat, we have the choice of F-sharp or D-sharp.

III. *Fourth Measure:*

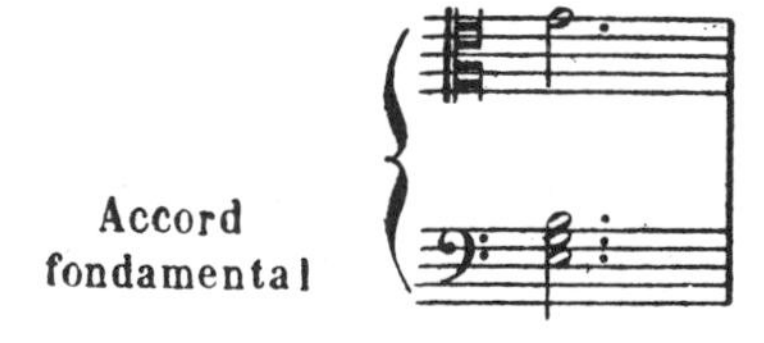

Each of these three notes is invertible with the G of the subject; they are all serviceable as basses, although the fundamental or the third is preferable.

118. Putting these four measures together, we have the following outline of the countersubject:

Continuing in a similar manner with the remaining four measures, the skeleton of the countersubject is this:

Now, examining measures 3 and 4, we see that if we retain the F throughout measure 3, it can be tied to a quarter-note F in measure 4, thus preparing a dissonance of a second, which will resolve by descending a degree to E, forming a third with the G of the subject. This is an invertible dissonance, producing the seventh descending to the sixth when inverted. Such prepared dissonances, as has been noted in ¶106, V, serve greatly to enrich the harmony:

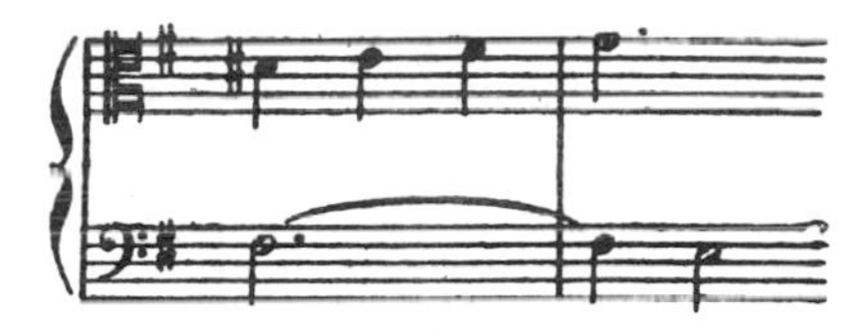

Likewise, in the sixth measure, we can on the first beat suspend the A of the preceding measure:

Here, then, is the complete harmonic outline of the countersubject:

119. Harmonically, this countersubject is adequate, but in its present form it offers no material for contrapuntal development. The sixth measure alone has "character."

It is, therefore, necessary to compose a melody on these harmonies which is appropriate as an accompaniment to the subject. As far as possible it must not resemble the subject either in rhythm or in melody.

120. As we begin the countersubject in the second measure, we must avoid starting on the first beat, in order to make its entry more apparent. Then, since both E and G are available as invertible intervals, we will use both in succession, so that all the beats in the measure will be marked. (N.B. ¶106: The countersubject should mark the beats not marked by the subject; and conversely, it is usually unnecessary for the countersubject to move while the subject does, certainly not in equal melodic units with the subject.)

In the fourth measure we will likewise mark the third beat with either G or B, and in the seventh measure we will mark the third beat by using A as a passing note.

We have now two versions from which to choose the definitive countersubject. Both are equally good harmonically; the first is better melodically; but the second, because of the contrary movement it brings to the second, third, fourth, and fifth measures, may prove more interesting contrapuntally.

This raises the question: is there only one best countersubject for every subject?

It is difficult to answer this categorically, as so much depends on the nature of the subject. However, it may be said that there is most likely only one best set of fundamental harmonies invertible with the subject; the differences that may exist will probably be confined to the melodic and rhythmic design of the countersubject.

Chromatic Countersubjects

121. Certain subjects can only be harmonized chromatically because of the danger, if treated otherwise, of harmonizing a subject in the major mode as if it belonged to minor, and vice versa. This, of course, would destroy the modality

and tonality of the fugue.

122. Take, for example, this subject:

C. SAINT-SAËNS

It is evident that the second measure cannot have the tonic, F, as fundamental, because owing to the flatted A such a chord would be in the minor mode. Therefore a harmony such as the following is necessary:

123. Likewise, the following subject, which modulates in the third measure to the subdominant minor, must not be considered (nor must any other subject) as beginning in minor and ending in major. A chromatic countersubject is therefore essential:

MASSENET

124. As can be seen from the above countersubject, it is always useful to consider the possibility of a chromatic sequence while exploring the harmonic possibilities of the subject. Such sequence produces the richest possible harmonies in the countersubject, and in many cases is preferable to any other.

125. The following examples are designed to show at a glance the different phases in the development of the countersubject from the simple, fundamental harmonies to the completed rhythmic countersubject, as well as the countersubject of the answer with its appropriate mutations.

1
Sujet
retard
Basses fondamentales
Notes des accords fondamentaux renversables à l'8e avec le sujet
Ebauche du Contresujet
Contresujet définitif
Contresujet
+ mutation
mutation
Réponse
2
retard
Basses fondamentales
Notes des accords fondamentaux renversables à l'8e avec le sujet
Ebauche du Contresujet
Contresujet définitif
Contresujet
mutation
mutation
Réponse

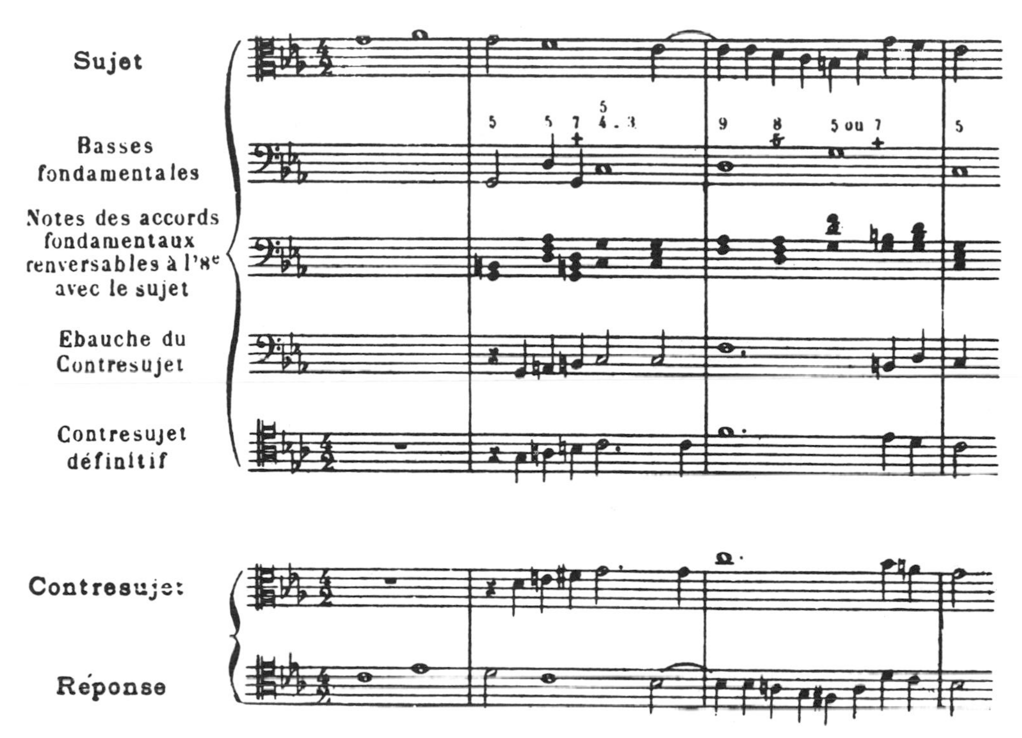

Such are the successive operations necessary to construct a countersubject. With experience and practice the notes essential to the countersubject will become evident at first sight, and the work of analysis will become largely instinctive.

Exercises

From the subjects to which you have already written satisfactory answers, choose thirty-six that interest you most. To them write both countersubjects and countersubjects to their answers.

V

THE EXPOSITION

Definitions

126. To begin a fugue, the subject is stated in one of the parts, followed by the answer in another part; a third voice restates the subject, to which the answer responds in the fourth part.

These four successive entries constitute the exposition.

127. Although we here concern ourselves primarily with four-part fugues, the general rule is: The exposition never has less than four entries; the subject always alternates with the answer.

Entry of the Countersubject

128. Although the countersubject occasionally may be exposed at the first entry of the subject, it is better, in order that the principal themes of the fugue be clearly apprehended, that they enter successively. Therefore, the general rule is: The subject is first stated alone; the countersubject is first heard with the first entry of the answer.

129. (N.B. This paragraph and ¶130 are included for the student's information. They will not be followed in this course.)

If there are several countersubjects, the first can be sounded at the second entry, and the others at the third and fourth entries, in order to clarify the fugue.

130. If the subject is composed of notes of long duration, or if it has a weakly defined melody, the countersubject may be stated at the first entry, to increase the interest of the beginning of the fugue.

The Subject Must be Heard in a Corresponding Voice

131. A subject first stated in one voice must later appear in a voice of corresponding range. In the exposition, a subject in the bass must later be exposed in the alto, and vice versa; likewise, a subject in the tenor must be heard at its next entry in the soprano, and vice versa. But, in the exposition, a subject first heard in the soprano or tenor must not be heard in the bass or alto.

132. When the countersubject first enters as an accompaniment to the

answer, it must be heard in the part that has just stated the subject.

133. The answer should enter as soon as the part stating the subject has finished.

Frequently, this rule cannot be observed, owing either to conflicting rhythms with the end of the subject or to some modulation of the answer.

Example:

It is evident that if we make the answer enter immediately after the last note of the subject, we will distort the rhythm of the theme, since the beats struck by the answer would not be in the same parts of the measure as those of the subject.

Example:

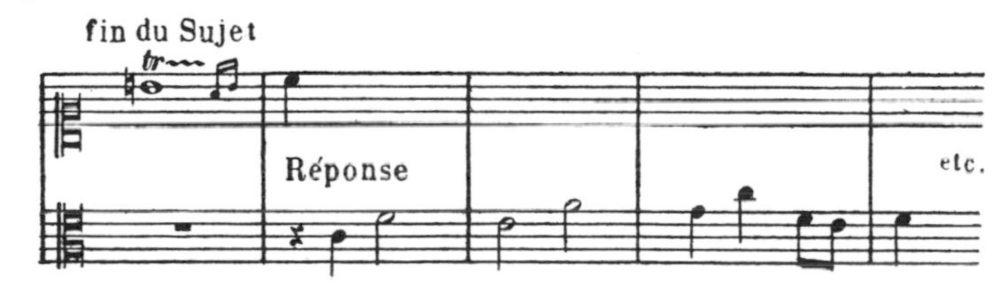

The answer must, therefore, be arranged so that it begins on the same beat as the subject.

Coda of the Subject

134. The remainder of the last measure of the subject is, therefore, filled by a coda. This is a melodic fragment which serves to lead into the answer, and which is continued by the entry of the countersubject, from which it should be separated by a short rest, so that the countersubject's entry may be clearly heard.

Example:

The coda should be written in the style of the countersubject, so that the latter will appear its natural consequence, just as the coda also acts as a natural continuation of the subject.

135. The coda, as well as every melodic and rhythmic figure heard in any

voice during the exposition, becomes an integral part of the fugue and serves in its later development.

A coda must likewise be added if the note that ends the subject and that which begins the answer, although forming a consonant interval, do not belong to the same key, or, if the subject ends on the beat at which the answer should enter. See ¶156.

In certain cases a coda is added even though the answer can enter on the last note of the subject. See the example in ¶172, eighth measure, where a coda is added to improve the melodic line, and to avoid a unison.

On the other hand, musical considerations may lead to the omission of a coda which, at first glance, seemed necessary. No rule can cover all cases, as the nature of the subject is the determining factor. See the expositions illustrated in ¶155–¶176.

Second Coda

136. It frequently happens that, even though the answer can enter on the last note of the subject, the second entry of the subject cannot be made on the last note of the answer, where a coda, therefore, becomes necessary.

This coda can be more developed, composed of two or three measures. Use can be made of it if the subject and countersubject do not provide enough material for future development, but with this restriction: It must be used at once in the parts in which neither the subject nor countersubject nor the answer and its countersubject are being heard.

Because of the new melodic and rhythmic elements supplied by it, this coda is sometimes written even though alternate entries of subject and answer can be made without interruption.

Avoidance of Unison

137. The last note of the subject and the first of the answer must not be in unison. The octave is permissable. Therefore, the first entry of the subject may be placed in a voice of corresponding range to that in which it is given.

Example (subject given in the alto):

In the alto, unison is produced with the first note of the answer. The subject is therefore placed in the bass:

and thereby the first note of the answer is at the octave instead of unison.

Avoidance of unison, as we have seen in ¶134 and ¶136, may also be made by writing a coda for the subject.

Free Parts

138. When the part which first states the subject has finished, another part makes the answer. The first part continues in simple counterpoint which it interrupts by a short rest, before sounding the countersubject. This simple counterpoint is called a "free part." It is distinguished from the coda in that it occurs *after* the entry of the answer.

Continuing the exposition, once the answer is finished, a third voice states the subject, while the voice that made the answer continues with the countersubject as the first part did, and it in turn accompanies the third entry by a free part in simple counterpoint. Then the fourth voice makes the answer, accompanied by the countersubject in the voice that has just stated the second entry of the subject, while the other two parts continue in simple counterpoint in the same style as the subject and countersubject.

139. These free parts must have definite melodic lines, and must not consist merely of harmonic filling.

140. (N.B. As in ¶129 and ¶130, this paragraph and ¶141 are solely for the record.)

If the fugue is in two parts, each voice states the subject and answer; the part which first proposed the subject makes the answer at the fourth entry, and the voice which made the answer at the second entry states the third entry of the subject.

141. In a three-part exposition, the voice which stated the subject for the first time makes the answer at the fourth entry; the other two entries sound (1) the answer at the second entry, and (2) the subject at the third entry.

In more than three parts, each voice in the exposition sounds once only either the subject or answer.

The following tables, ¶142–¶154, give arrangements of entries of subject and answer in two, three, or four parts.

Examples of Arrangements of Subject and Countersubject in Two, Three, and Four Parts

142. Two parts:

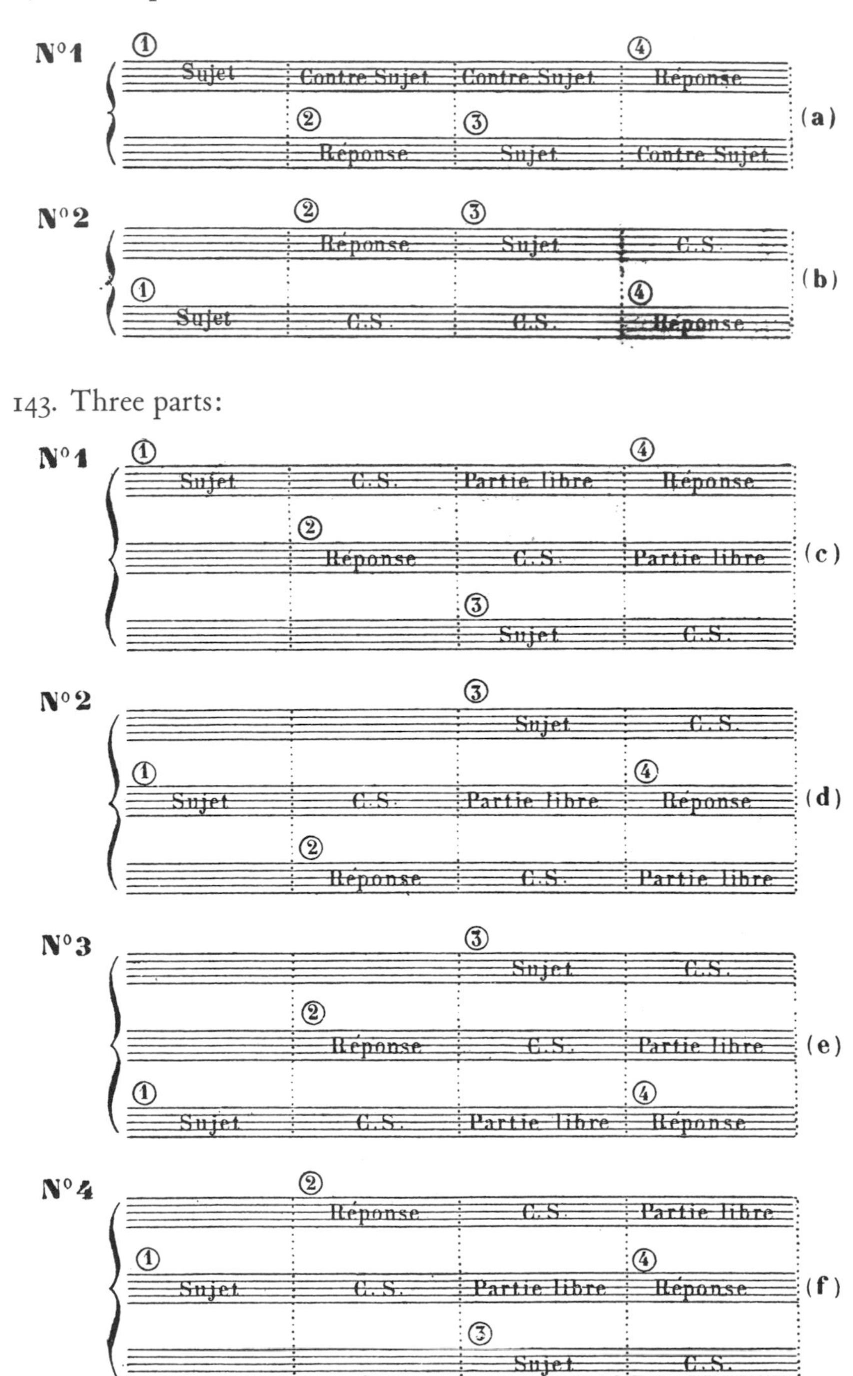

143. Three parts:

144. Four parts:

No 1 (g)

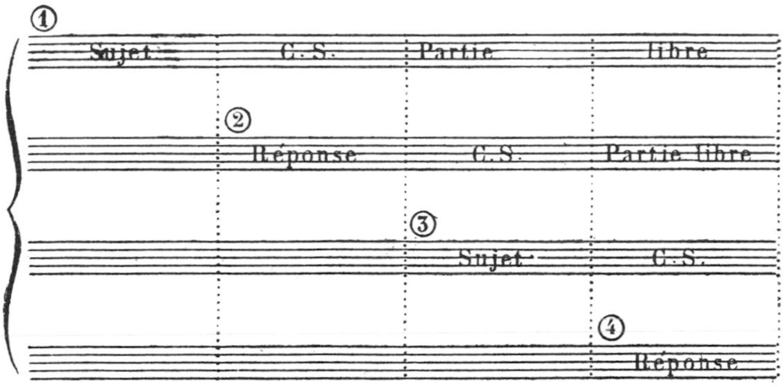 ① Sujet	C.S.	Partie	libre
	② Réponse	C.S.	Partie libre
		③ Sujet	C.S.
			④ Réponse

No 2 (h)

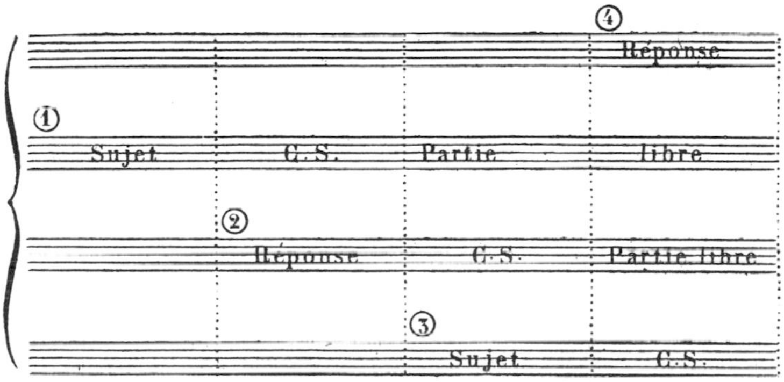

			④ Réponse
① Sujet	C.S.	Partie	libre
	② Réponse	C.S.	Partie libre
		③ Sujet	C.S.

No 3 (i)

		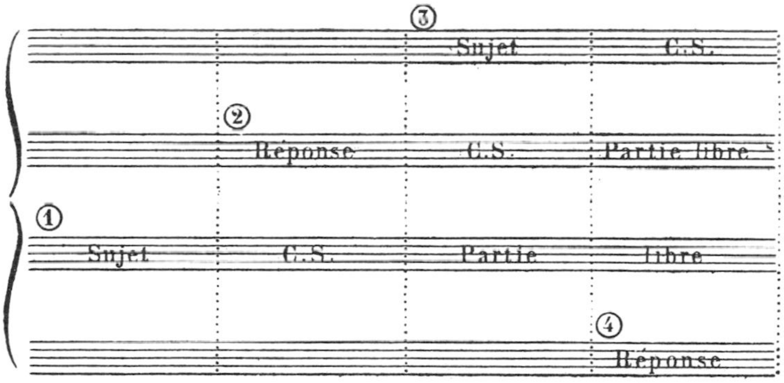 ③ Sujet	C.S.
	② Réponse	C.S.	Partie libre
① Sujet	C.S.	Partie	libre
			④ Réponse

No 4 (k)

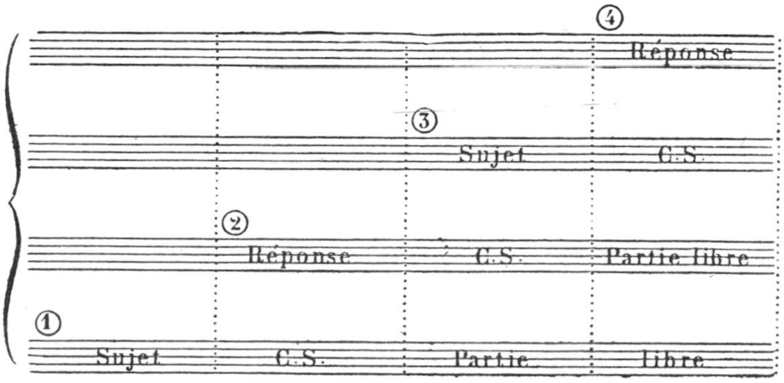

			④ Réponse
		③ Sujet	C.S.
	② Réponse	C.S.	Partie libre
① Sujet	C.S.	Partie	libre

145. Three parts:

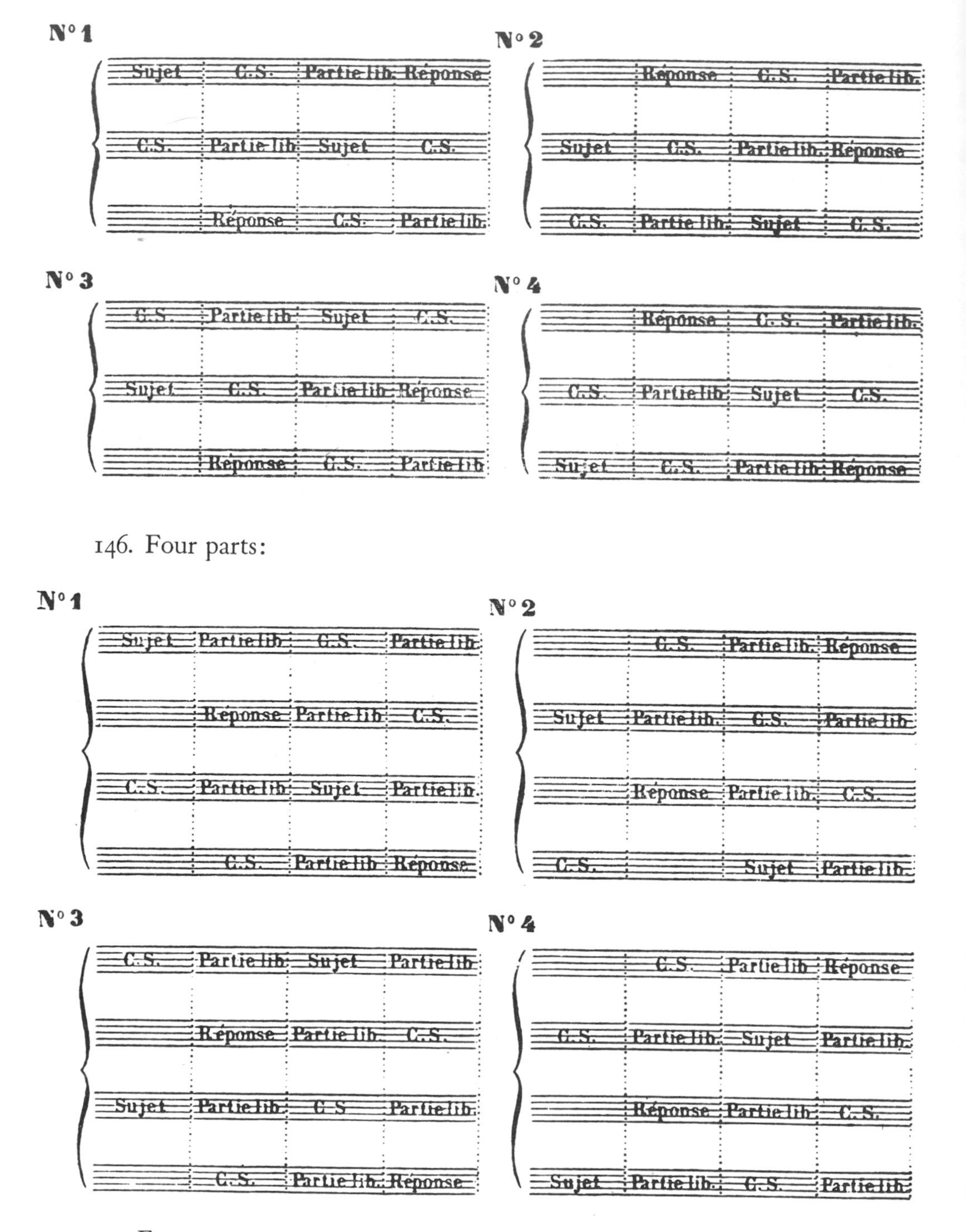

146. Four parts:

147. Four parts:

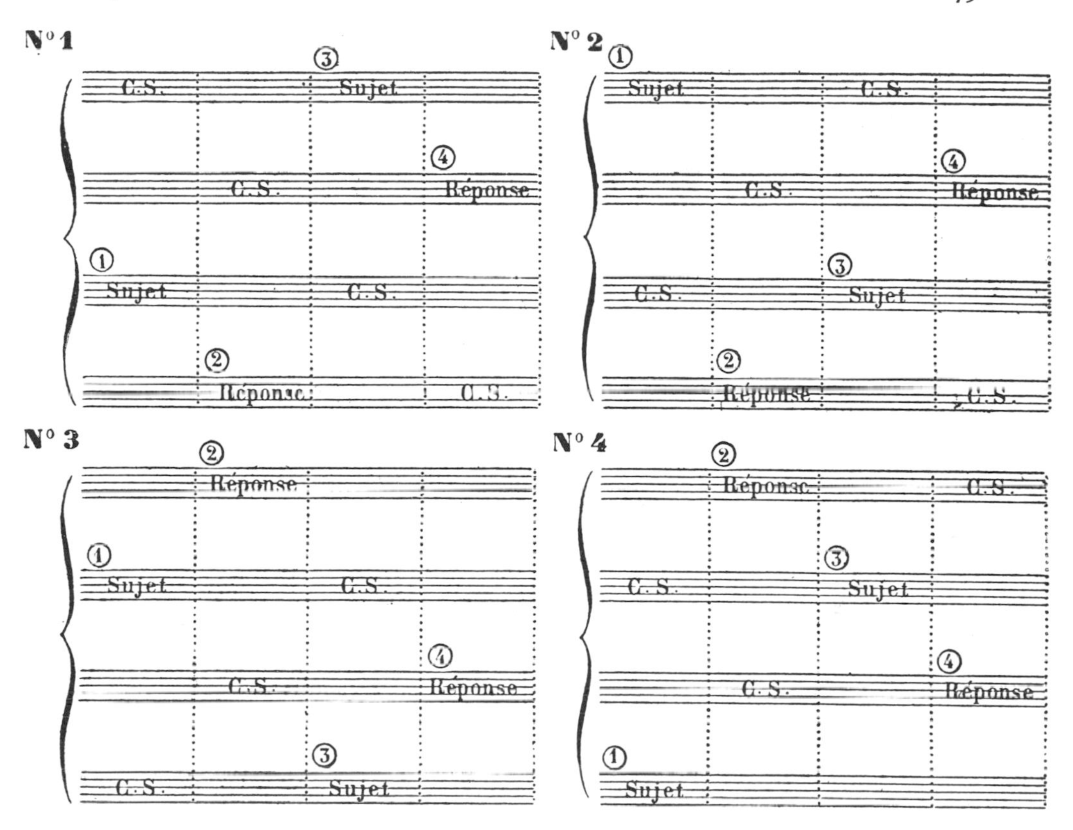

148. Avoid arranging subject and answer so that they appear in voices of similar range, i.e., soprano-tenor, or alto-bass, as in these examples:

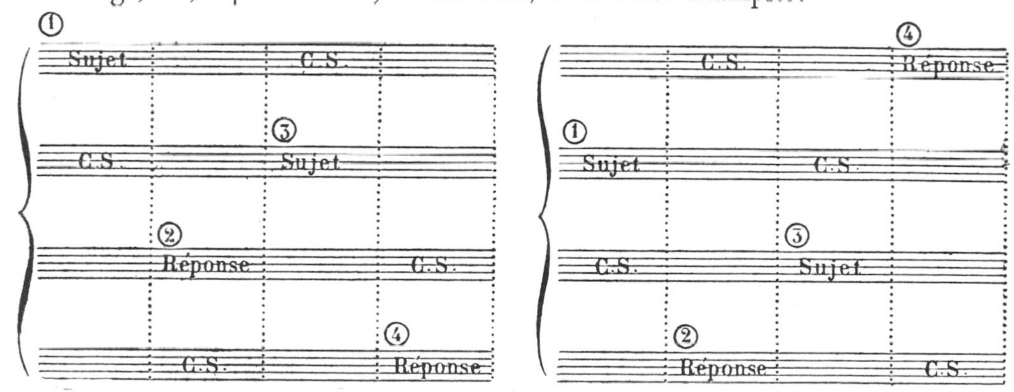

149. The countersubject should always appear in a voice of corresponding range to the subject.

Expositions with Two Countersubjects: These, as Well as Those With Three Countersubjects as Shown Below, Are for Reference, and Not to Be Used

150. Three parts:

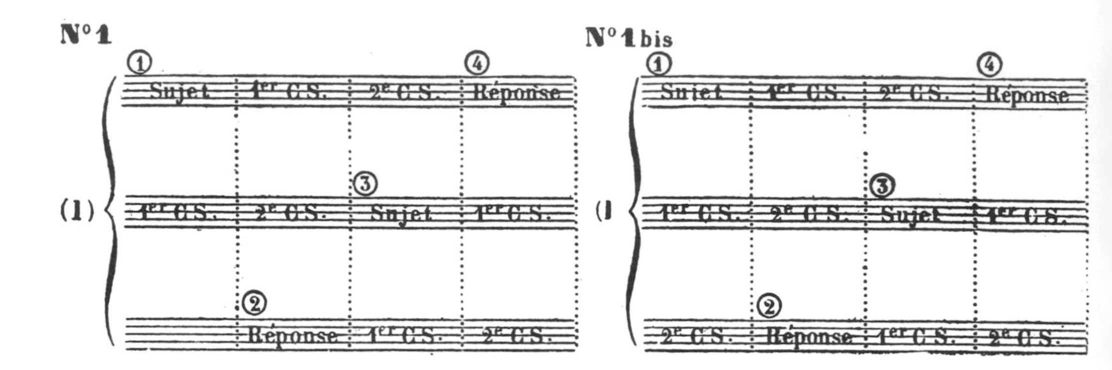
N° 1
Sujet 1er C.S. 2e C.S. Réponse
(l)
1er C.S. 2e C.S. Sujet 1er C.S.
Réponse 1er C.S. 2e C.S.
N° 1 bis
Sujet 1er C.S. 2e C.S. Réponse
(l
1er C.S. 2e C.S. Sujet 1er C.S.
2e C.S. Réponse 1er C.S. 2e C.S.

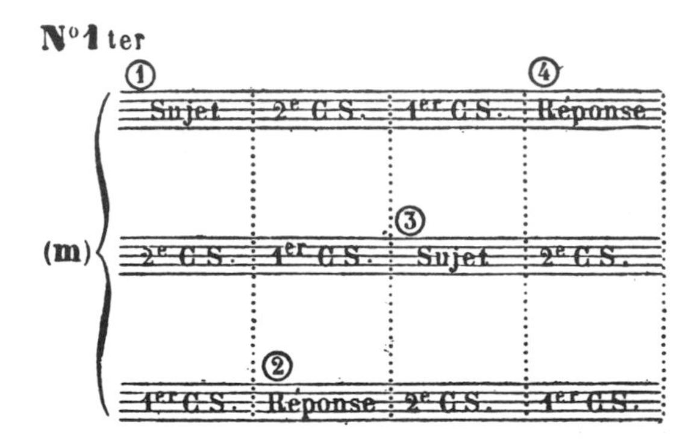
N° 1 ter
Sujet 2e C.S. 1er C.S. Réponse
(m)
2e C.S. 1er C.S. Sujet 2e C.S.
1er C.S. Réponse 2e C.S. 1er C.S.

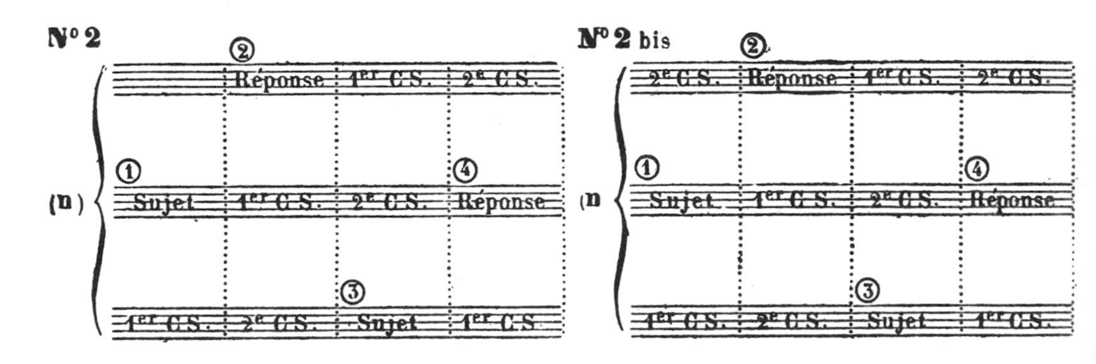
N° 2
Réponse 1er C.S. 2e C.S.
(n)
Sujet 1er C.S. 2e C.S. Réponse
1er C.S. 2e C.S. Sujet 1er C.S.
N° 2 bis
2e C.S. Réponse 1er C.S. 2e C.S.
(n
Sujet 1er C.S. 2e C.S. Réponse
1er C.S. 2e C.S. Sujet 1er C.S.

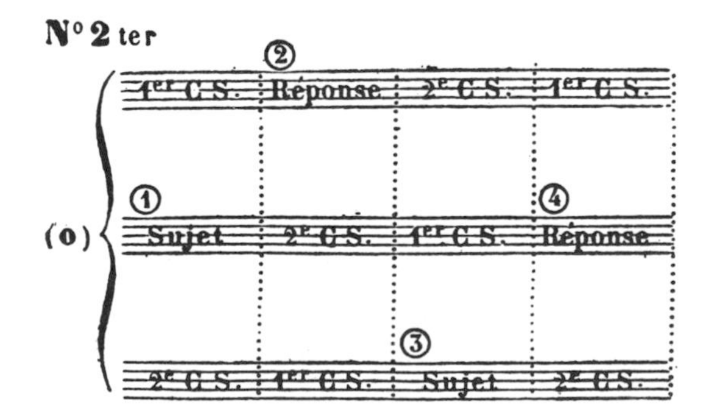
N° 2 ter
1er C.S. Réponse 2e C.S. 1er C.S.
(o)
Sujet 2e C.S. 1er C.S. Réponse
2e C.S. 1er C.S. Sujet 2e C.S.

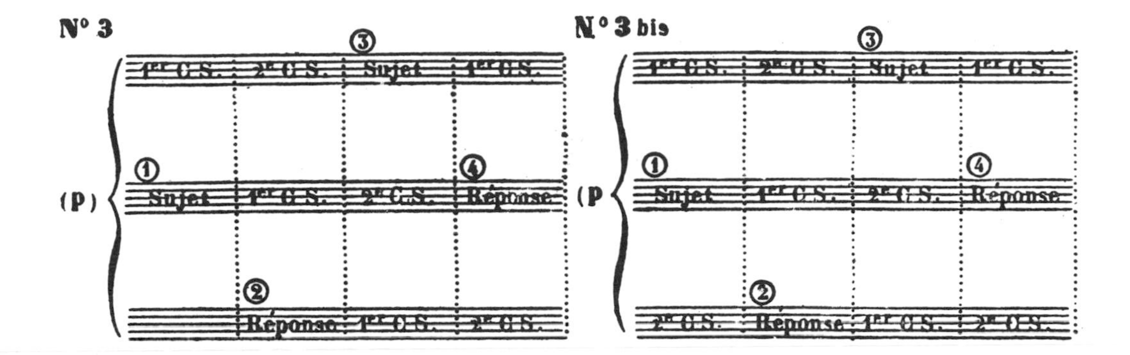
N° 3
1er C.S. 2e C.S. Sujet 1er C.S.
(p)
Sujet 1er C.S. 2e C.S. Réponse
Réponse 1er C.S. 2e C.S.
N° 3 bis
1er C.S. 2e C.S. Sujet 1er C.S.
(p
Sujet 1er C.S. 2e C.S. Réponse
2e C.S. Réponse 1er C.S. 2e C.S.

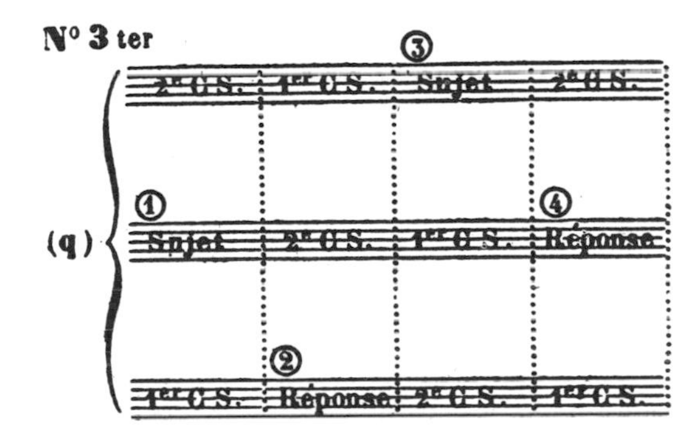
N° 3 ter
2e C.S. 1er C.S. Sujet 2e C.S.
(q)
Sujet 2e C.S. 1er C.S. Réponse
1er C.S. Réponse 2e C.S. 1er C.S.

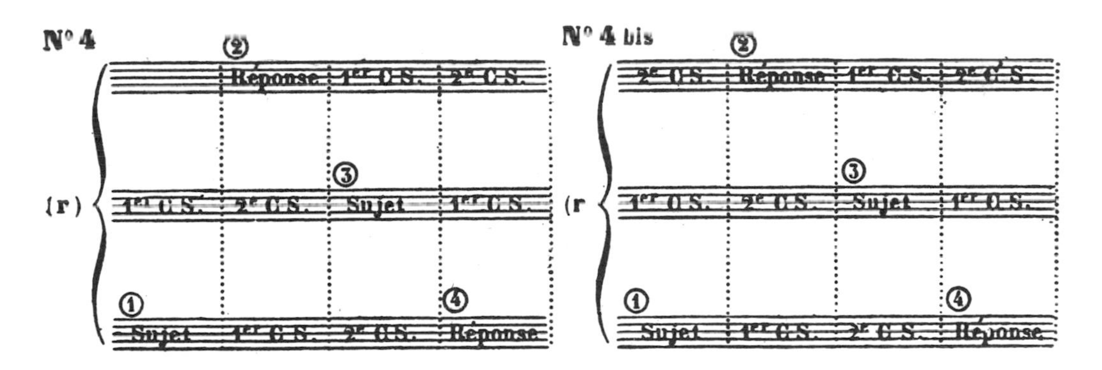
N° 4
Réponse 1er C.S. 2e C.S.
(r)
1er C.S. 2e C.S. Sujet 1er C.S.
Sujet 1er C.S. 2e C.S. Réponse
N° 4 bis
2e C.S. Réponse 1er C.S. 2e C.S.
(r
1er C.S. 2e C.S. Sujet 1er C.S.
Sujet 1er C.S. 2e C.S. Réponse

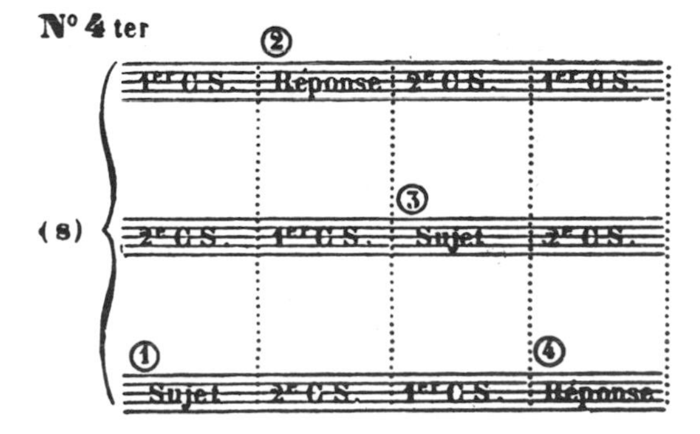
N° 4 ter
1er C.S. Réponse 2e C.S. 1er C.S.
(s)
2e C.S. 1er C.S. Sujet 2e C.S.
Sujet 2e C.S. 1er C.S. Réponse

151. Four parts:

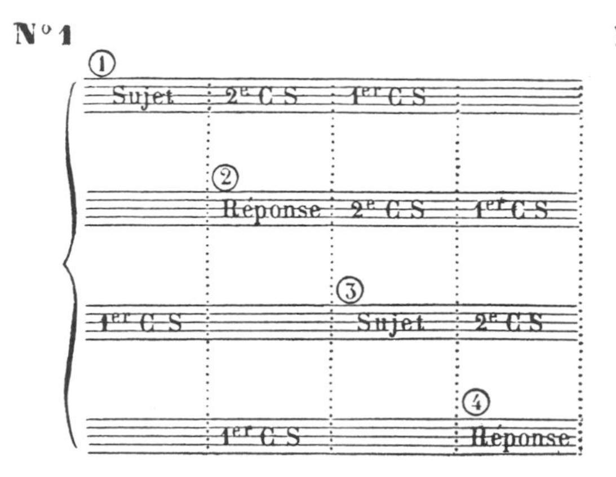

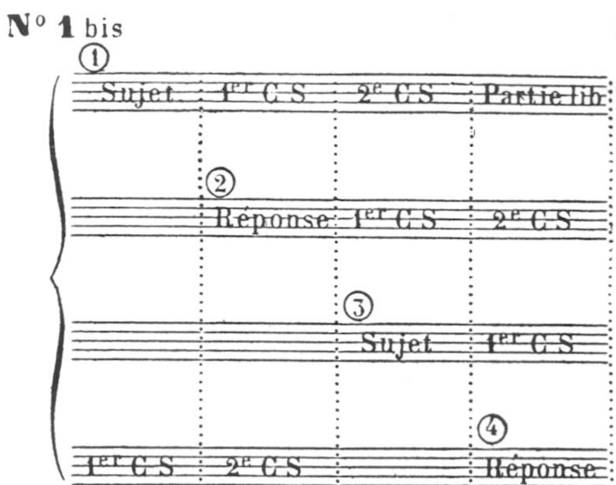

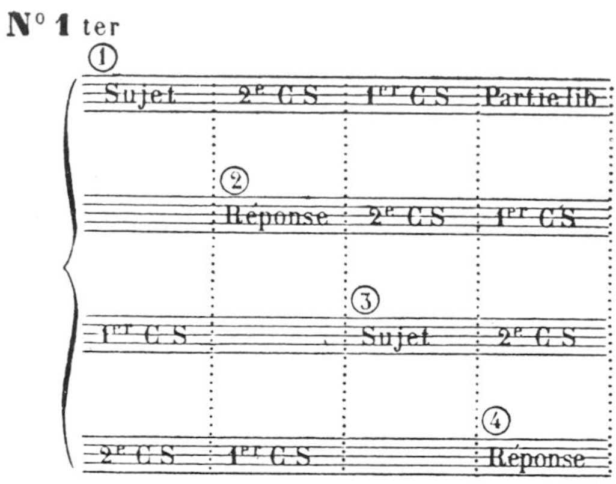

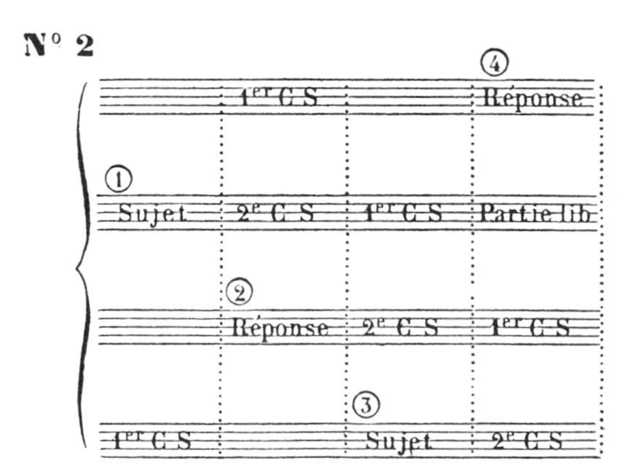

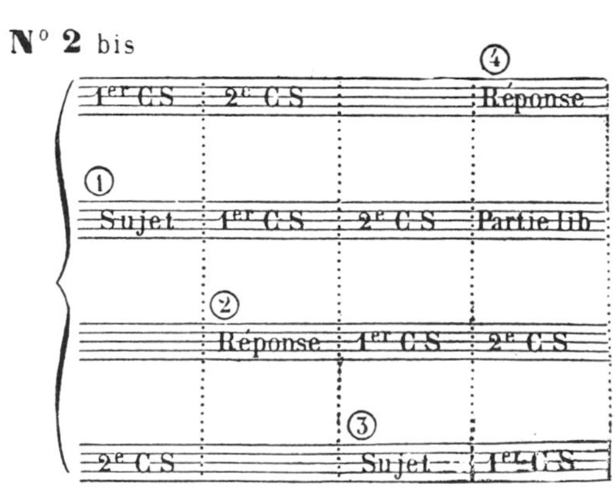

N° 2 ter

2e C.S	1er C.S		④ Réponse
① Sujet	2e C.S	1er C.S	Partie lib.
	② Réponse	2e C.S	1er C.S
1er C.S		③ Sujet	2e C.S

N° 3

1er C.S		③ Sujet	2e C.S
	② Réponse	2e C.S	1er C.S
① Sujet	2e C.S	1er C.S	Partie lib.
	1er C.S		④ Réponse

N° 3 bis

2e C.S		③ Sujet	1er C.S
	② Réponse	1er C.S	2e C.S
① Sujet	1er C.S	2e C.S	Partie lib.
1er C.S	2e C.S		④ Réponse

N° 3 ter

1er C.S		③ Sujet	2e C.S
	② Réponse	2e C.S	1er C.S
① Sujet	2e C.S	1er C.S	Partie lib.
2e C.S	1er C.S		④ Réponse

N° 4

	1er C.S		④ Réponse
1er C.S		③ Sujet	2e C.S
	② Réponse	2e C.S	1er C.S
① Sujet	2e C.S	1er C.S	Partie lib.

N° 4 bis

1er C.S	2e C.S		④ Réponse
		③ Sujet	1er C.S
	② Réponse	1er C.S	2e C.S
① Sujet	1er C.S	2e C.S	Partie lib.

N° 4 ter

2e C S	1er C S		④ Réponse
1er C S		③ Sujet	2e C S
	② Réponse	2e C S	1er C S
① Sujet	2e C S	1er C S	Partie lib

152. Four parts:

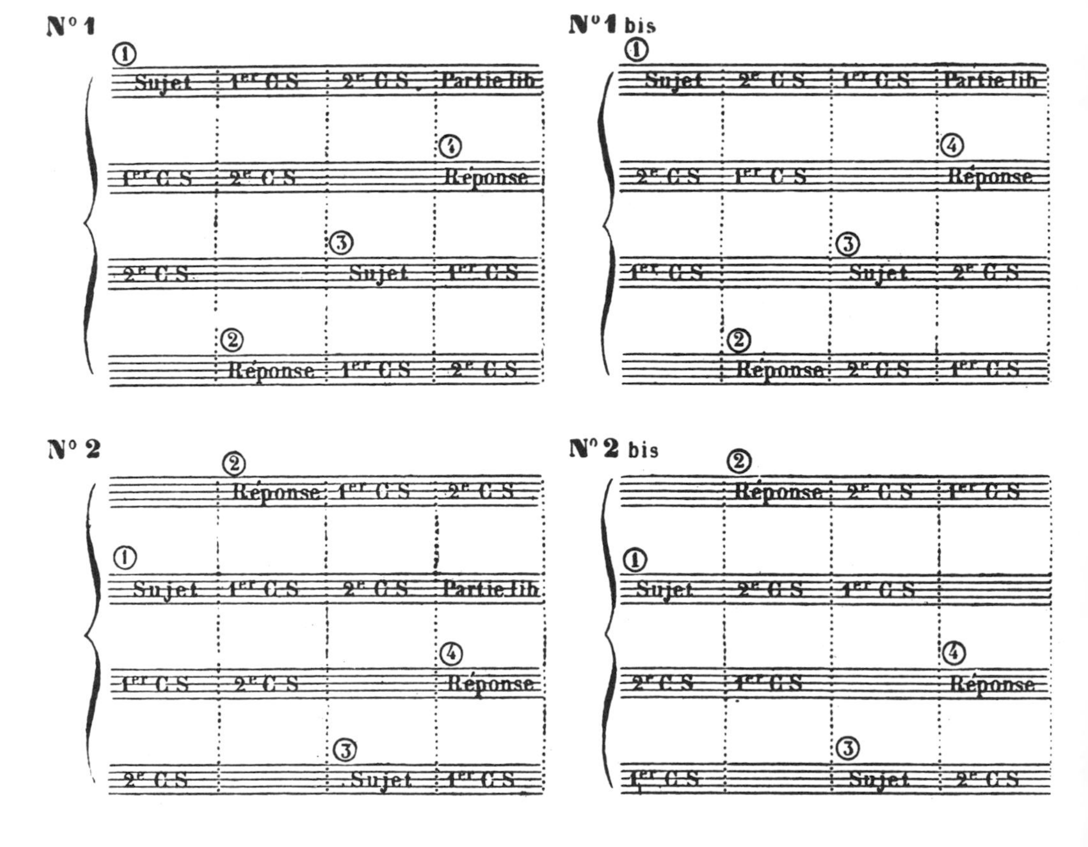

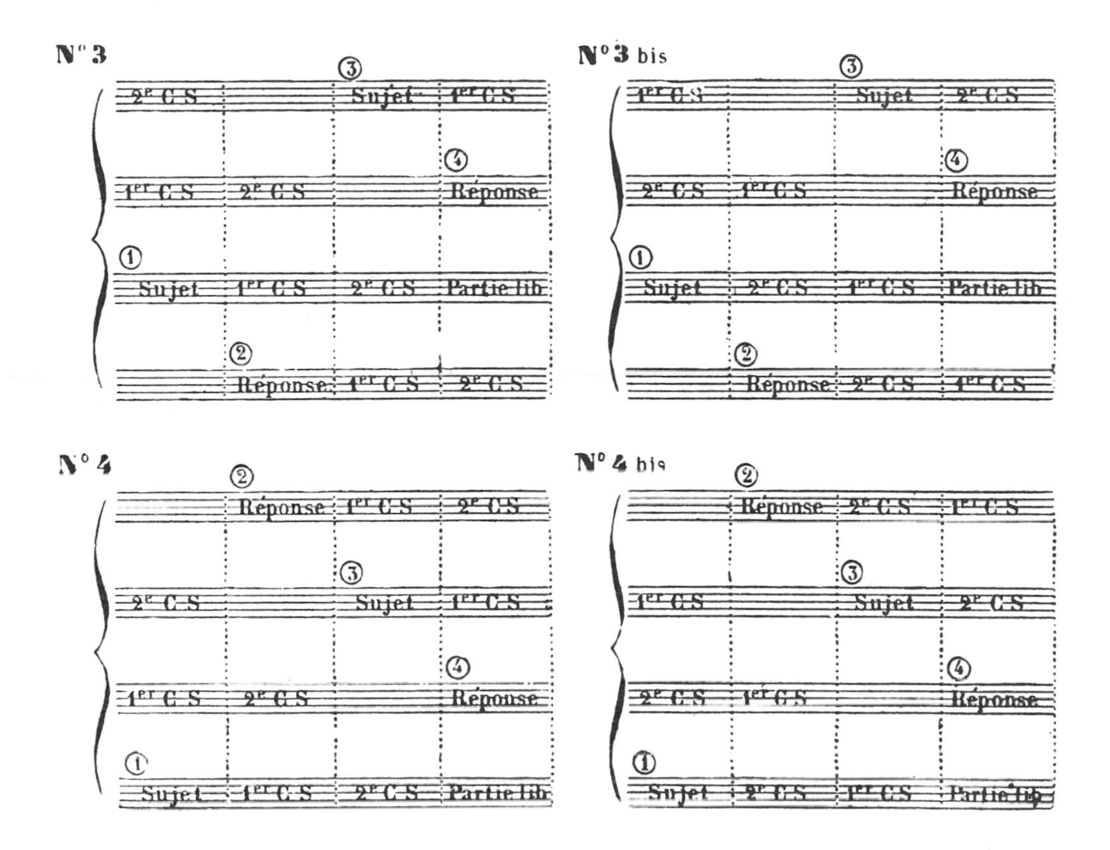

Expositions with Three Countersubjects

153. Four parts:

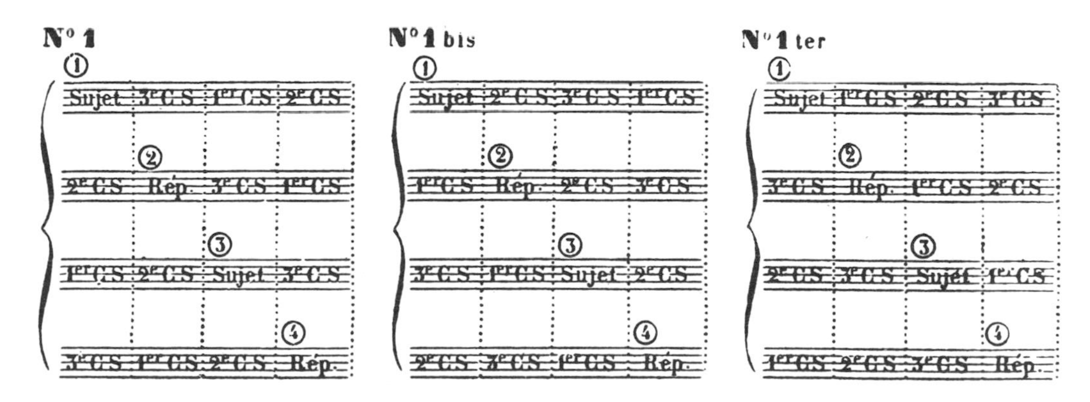

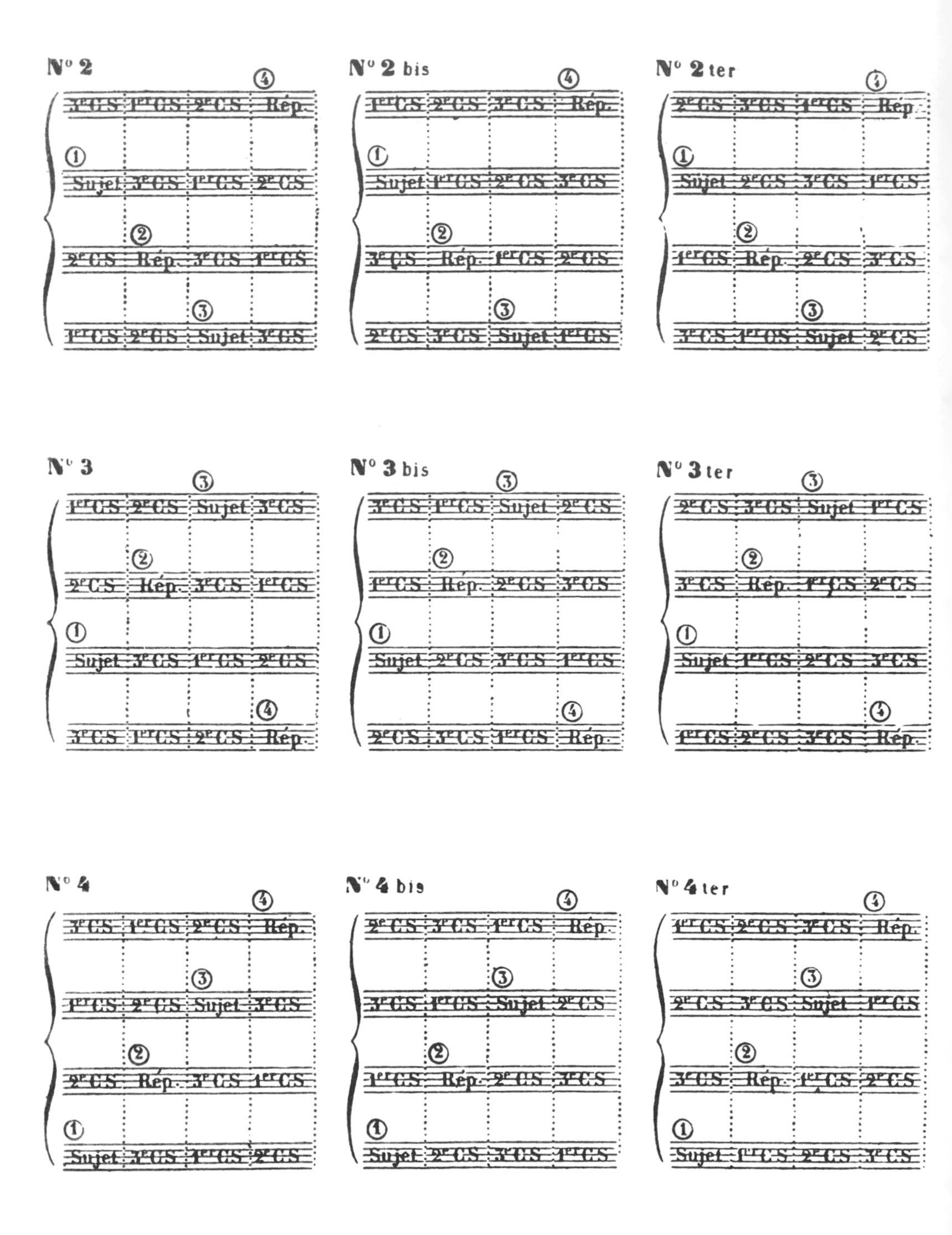

154. Four parts:

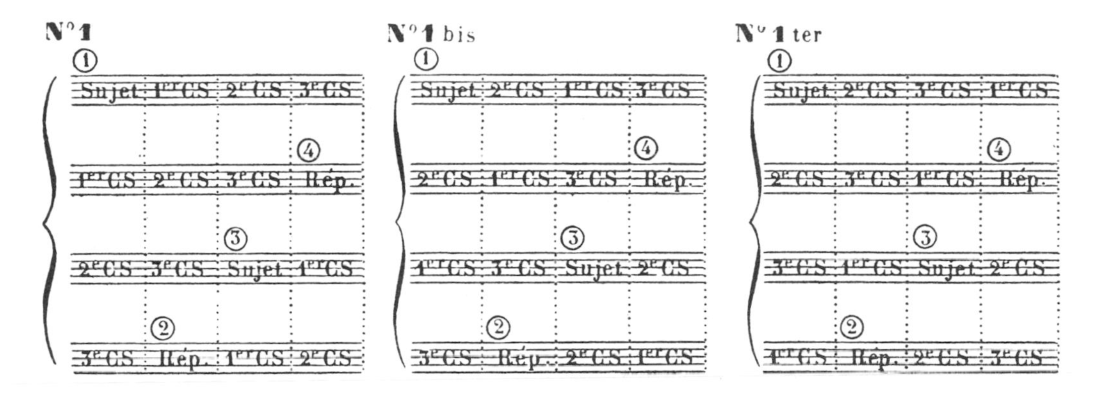

155. Exposition of a two-part fugue in instrumental style. Subject by André Gedalge:

(N.B. This example, as well as others given below which are not written in the style of the scholastic fugue, and those in three parts with multiple countersubjects, are here copied from Gedalge's original book for the record, but not as models for the student. As has been said, his fugues should be in vocal style, in four parts, with one countersubject.

In the above example, the coda between the second and third entries is rather long. The purpose of this is to place in relief the return of the subject in the principal key; at the same time it prevents the immediate repetition in the same voice of the principal motif of the fugue.)

156. Exposition of a vocal fugue in three parts with one countersubject. Subject by André Gedalge:

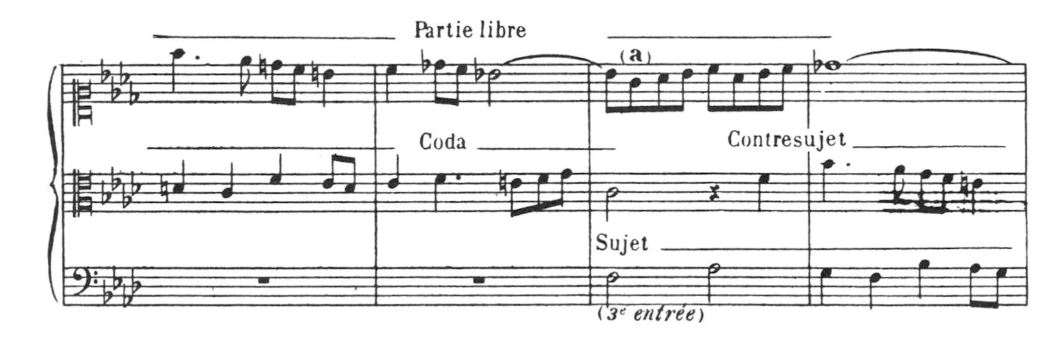

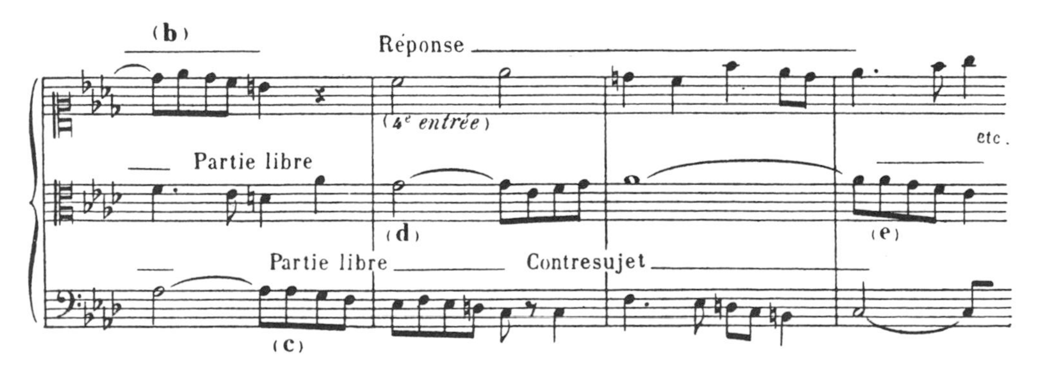

The free part (*a*) is composed of imitations of the coda. At (*b*), (*c*), and (*e*) the imitations are in contrary movement. At (*d*) the imitation is in direct movement.

157. Exposition in four parts of a calm and expressive subject by E. Paladilhe:

At (*a*), (*b*), and (*c*) the apparent 6/4 chord produced by the melodic movement of the subdominant and tonic should not be regarded as "real," since it results from the use of the first degree as an ornament of the subdominant. Analyzed by the rules of strict tonal counterpoint, the harmony is that of the subdominant.

At (*d*), as the soprano ends, the alto continues the highest melodic line without altering its musical sense.

This brings up an important point: For the sake of the melodic continuity of the fugue, when one part ceases, another must take up the melodic line in a manner that does not do violence to the preceding. All parts should combine in contributing to the general melodic line of the fugue.

158. Exposition of a calm and expressive subject in vocal style. Subject by Ambroise Thomas:

At (*a*), (*b*), and (*c*) the two free parts imitate each other. By emphasis on this figure in the exposition, we are warranted in using it prominently in the further developments of the fugue.

In certain music schools this incidence by a major second (*d*) is forbidden. As no reason has ever been given for this prohibition, I think it should be permitted in strict style. (N.B. In strict counterpoint, entry on a second is forbidden, no doubt because it presents problems in intonation. Therefore, I disagree with this observation of Gedalge's.—F.D.)

159. Subject by André Gedalge (instrumental style):

Sujet

Note that the free part (*a*) is devised so that its melody leads naturally to that of the countersubject. At (*b*) the free parts are made of fragments of the countersubject, and imitate each other. (N.B. This is good, provided subject and countersubject furnish ample material. Otherwise the creation of new melodies is essential in the free parts.—F.D.)

160. Exposition in which the use of a coda of the subject is avoided (instrumental style). Subject by Reber:

Moderato.
Sujet
Partie libre
Contresujet
Sujet
Partie libre amenant le contresujet
Contresujet
(a) Réponse
Partie libre
Contresujet
Réponse

161. In the above exposition, after the first entry of the subject, a coda to introduce the answer could have been made in this way:

Here are two reasons for omitting the coda and, instead, modulating immediately to the dominant:

a) The subject ends on a measure devoid of either melodic or rhythmic interest; therefore, any coda would appear foreign to the nature of the subject.

b) No matter how the coda were designed, because of the harmonies defined by the answer, it would have to repeat the same chords (B, A, and E) which the countersubject imposes; it would, therefore, be redundant and monotonous.

162. Exposition of an instrumental fugue. Subject by André Gedalge:

In this exposition, the rhythm and melody of the subject are such that the answer can begin on the fourth beat, even though the subject begins on the second beat (¶133).

At (a) the free part begins the rhythm of the countersubject, to which it is joined without interruption. At (*b*), in the measures that follow, the free parts sound imitations of fragments of the countersubject. But note the warning in ¶159, under (*b*).

163. Exposition of a lively subject. Subject by André Gedalge:

Contresujet
Partie libre
Coda
Contresujet
Sujet
Partie libre
Partie libre
Contresujet
Réponse

164. Exposition of a solemn subject in vocal style:

The free part at (*a*) is imitated by the tenor at (*c*). At (*b*) the alto makes an unprepared seventh. This sort of neighboring note, though musical, is not always permitted in examinations. (N.B. Avoid this.—F.D.)

165. Exposition of a subject in instrumental style:

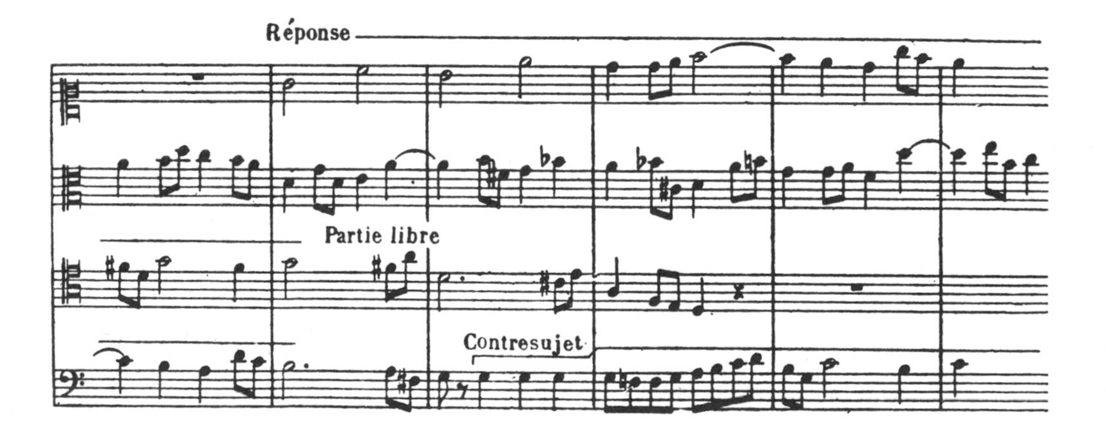

At (*b*) the two free parts combine to repeat the melodic form of the free part at (*a*). Beginning at the third entry, the two free parts make continuous imitations of melodic and rhythmic patterns which recall the rhythm of the first free part at (*a*). They thereby create an attractive melodic quality throughout the entire exposition, and avoid dryness and inexpressiveness—faults into which it is easy to fall with this sort of subject.

166. Exposition of a calm and expressive subject containing melodic passages of many notes. Subject by André Gedalge:

167. Exposition of a vocal fugue, calm in character. Subject by André Gedalge:

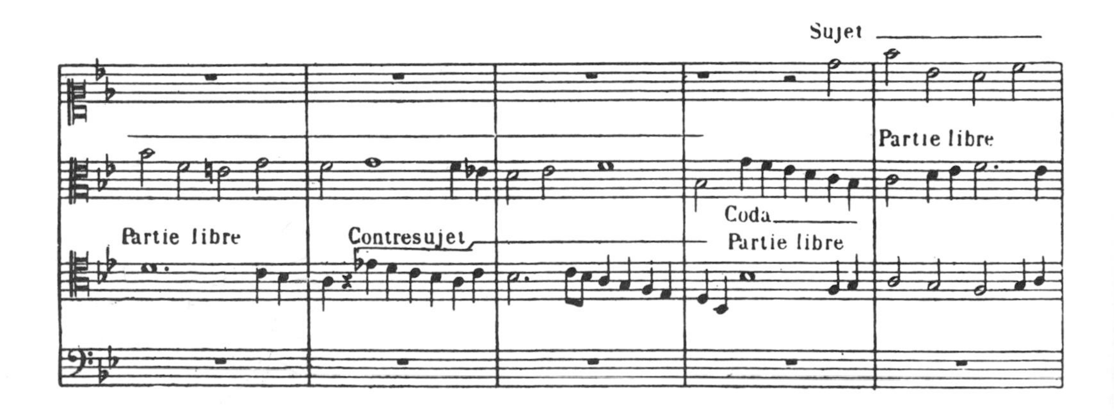

At (*a*) the end of the countersubject is slightly modified to avoid a perfect cadence on the first beat of the succeeding measure. This is occasionally permitted in the scholastic fugue. (N.B. Avoid this.—F.D.)

168. Exposition of a calm and slow subject, having a slow-moving countersubject. By André Gedalge:

169. Exposition of a calm and slow subject, with a quiet, chromatic countersubject. By André Gedalge:

Moderato
Sujet
Coda préparant
l'entrée du Contresujet
Réponse
Contresujet
Sujet
Partie libre
Partie libre
Contresujet
Partie libre
Partie libre
(a)
Réponse
Contresujet
(b)

At (*a*) and (*b*) the augmented fifth produced by contrary chromatic movement on the first beat of each measure is of classic origin. It is frequently used by the masters of the fugue (cf. Bach, Mozart, and Handel, etc.), who always considered it an invertible interval. (N.B. Here we have brought home the recurrent problem of how much liberty to allow. What the masters did in their maturity it not necessarily the best pedagogical practice. I suggest that when the student has attained Bach's skill he permit himself Bach's liberties.—F.D.)

170. Exposition of a calm and expressive subject in instrumental style. Subject by André Gedalge:

171. Exposition of an energetic subject, with a rapidly moving counter-subject. In this exposition, an extended coda between the second and third entries introduces a new figure which is used at once in the free parts. Subject by Onslow:

172. Exposition of a calm and expressive subject in which the countersubject is stated with the first entry of the subject. Subject by André Gedalge:

173. Exposition of a broadly moving subject. The countersubject is again stated with the first entry of the subject. Subject by Massenet:

Contresujet
Partie libre
Coda
Réponse
Partie libre
Partie libre
Sujet
Coda
Partie libre
Contresujet
Partie libre
Réponse
Contresujet

174. Exposition of a fugue with two countersubjects, both heard with the first entry of the subject. Subject by Reber:

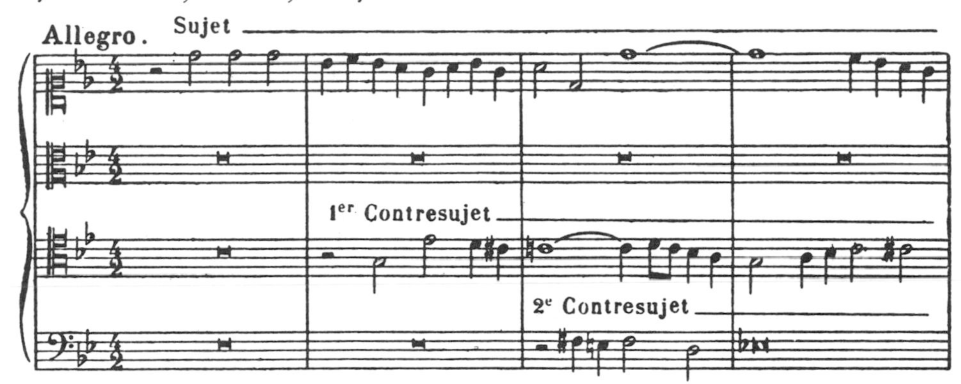

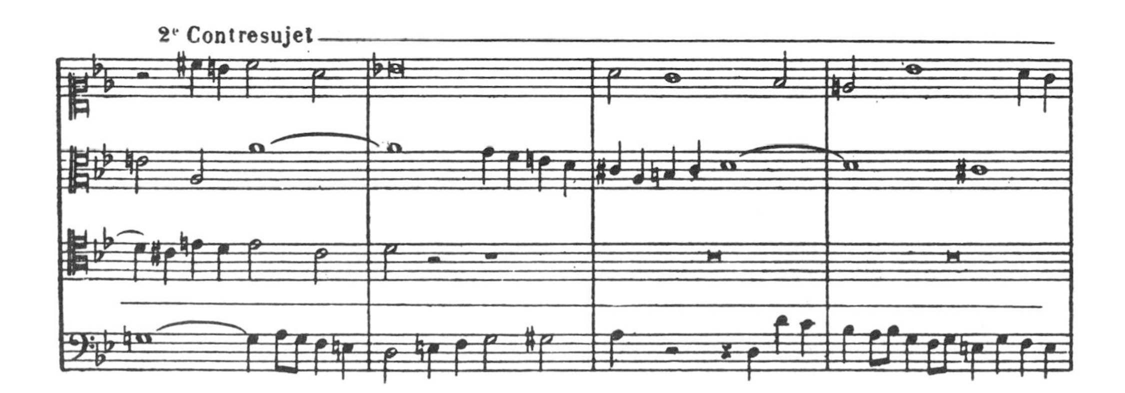

1er Contresujet
Partie libre
2e Contresujet
Sujet
Partie libre
Partie libre
Partie libre
Partie libre
1er Contresujet
Réponse
2e Contresujet

175. Exposition of a chromatic subject with two countersubjects. These are heard successively at the first entry of the answer and the second entry of the subject. For the answer to this subject, see ¶92–¶98. The countersubjects are strongly diatonic. Subject by Cherubini:

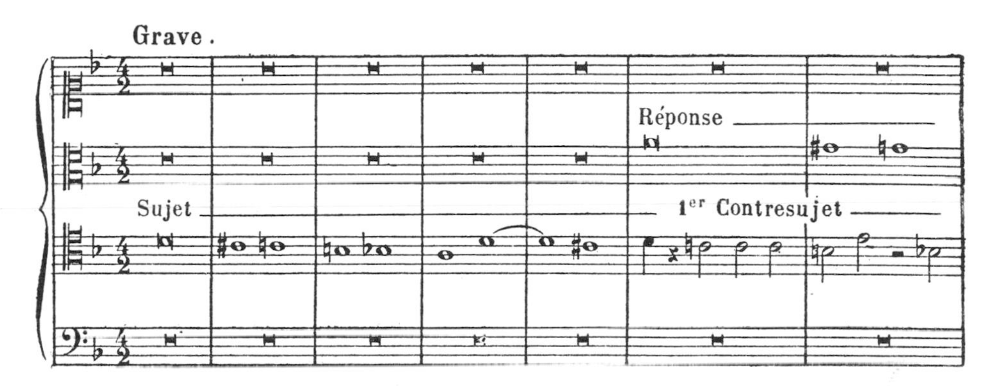

This ingenious exposition is shown as a model of what can be done by a master, not what a beginner should attempt.

176. Exposition of a fugue with three countersubjects. These complicated arrangements should not be attempted by the beginner. Subject by André Gedalge:

In this fugue it has been necessary to add a coda after each entry of the subject, to place in relief the next entry. Note, however, that as each voice constantly sounds either the subject, answer, or one of the countersubjects, monotony is built into the fugue.

VI

THE COUNTEREXPOSITION

Definitions

177. The counterexposition is a second exposition which includes only two entries.

It differs, furthermore, from the exposition by reversing the order of entries; that is, the first entry is that of the answer, the second, the subject. Moreover, in the counterexposition the answer must be sounded by a voice that stated the subject in the exposition, and vice versa.

178. The counterexposition is not absolutely necessary. It cannot be written when the range of the subject does not permit its being placed in a voice for which it was not originally intended.

In general, the counterexposition is only made when the subject is short or lacks sufficient character to make an impression in four entries. (N.B. Many authorities do not agree with Gedalge: To them, the fugue is incomplete without a counterexposition. It is best to write a counterexposition unless the subject is so long as to make it redundant, or unless its range is such that it can only be used in certain voices.—F.D.)

Tonality of the Counterexposition

179. The counterexposition is always written in the principal key of the fugue.

It is separated from the exposition by a short episode also in the principal key. (N.B. Fugal episodes will be discussed in the next chapter.)

Place of Countersubject in the Counterexposition

180. The countersubject may be placed in any convenient part. The range of the countersubject will largely determine the choice.

181. It may be advisable, when a subject is longer than four measures in moderate time, not to write a counterexposition, to avoid needlessly prolonging the fugue. (N.B. See ¶178.—F.D.)

182. The following tables give various arrangements of counterexpositions

which may be used for the successive entries of the answer and subject in two, three, or four parts:

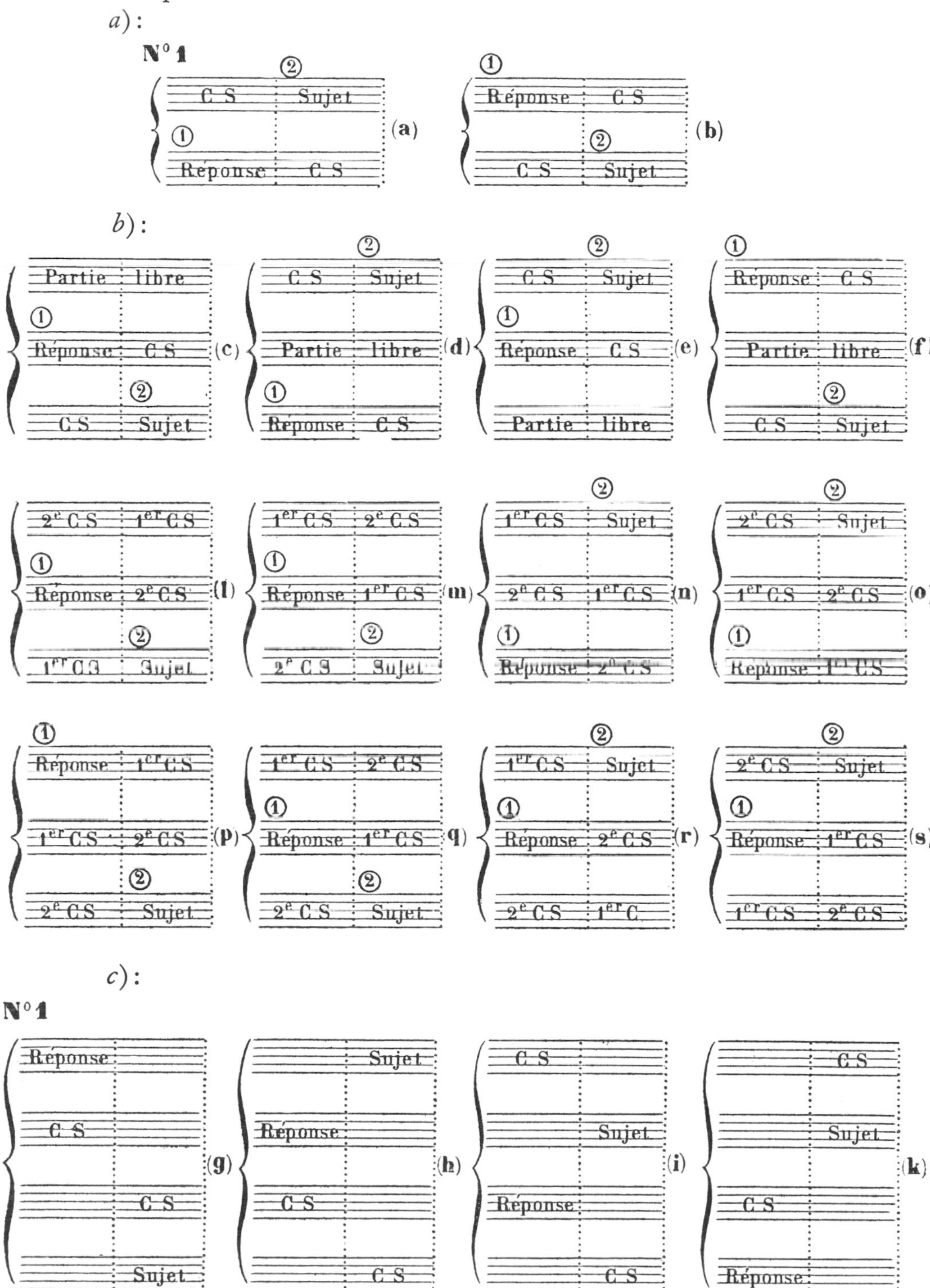

183. Keeping in mind that in the counterexposition the answer and subject must be heard in voices other than in the exposition, comparison of these arrangements with those in ¶145–¶154 will simplify the choice.

184. Exposition, episode, and counterexposition of a subject by Handel:

a) The dissonances formed by direct movement are not permitted in the scholastic fugue.

b) The E in the bass, which can only be analyzed as a passing note in disjoint movement, is forbidden in strict counterpoint.

Note that the bass, which in the exposition stated the subject, sounds the reply in the counterexposition, while the tenor states the subject.

The countersubjects are in the same order as in the exposition.

The First Section of the Fugue

185. With the counterexposition, we reach the end of what is known as the first section of the fugue. It is composed of the exposition, an episode, and the counterexposition. What follows is called the "development" of the fugue.

186. It is of the first importance that the student not begin the following chapter which deals with fugal episodes until he has thoroughly mastered the exposition. The exposition is the most important part of the fugue, not only from the point of view of analysis and writing but because out of it grows the rest of the fugue.

In the succeeding chapters the development of the fugue will be discussed, and in them we will examine the ways in which a fugue expands from the exposition so that it combines both unity and variety.

Exercises

Write at least thirty-six expositions, and continue with their counterexpositions where desirable. Of these, choose the twenty-four that interest you the most. These will be brought forward step by step during the course. In this work, it is useful to have various fugues at different stages of completion.

VII

THE EPISODES

Definitions

187. In examining a musical phrase, it will become apparent that, in general, it presents a symmetry which is brought about by the repetition at various intervals of the same or similar melodic and rhythmic patterns.

The more or less frequent repetition of similar passages necessarily engenders a series of harmonies of similar nature: It gives rise to a more or less regular, more or less complex harmonic sequence.

188. The episodes of a fugue, based on the nature of the musical phrases involved, consist of series of imitations, more or less exact, which derive from fragments of the subject, answer, countersubject, coda, and/or free parts of the exposition. These fragments are combined in such a way as to form an uninterrupted melodic line which connects the various entrances of the subject and answer in the neighboring keys of the subject.

These keys to which a scholastic fugue may modulate are the relative major or minor, according to its mode, and the five keys whose signatures differ by only one accidental from the principal key.

(N.B. In the short episode between the exposition and the counterexposition (¶179), it is often advisable to restrict oneself to material taken from the free parts of the exposition, leaving the rest of the material available for the main episodes of the fugue.—F.D.)

189. If we transpose the same melodic fragment to various intervals, the fundamental harmonies of the original passage will be similarly reproduced, and a harmonic sequence will have been established.

190. It therefore is evident that the episodes of a fugue are built on more or less regular harmonic sequences; the themes of the episodes must derive from the subject, answer, countersubject, coda, and free parts of the exposition; and the episodes must be melodic.

(N.B. It should be emphasized that the fugue is made from its subject. All the elements out of which the episodes are to be composed arise from the subject, directly or indirectly.—F.D.)

Use of Harmonic Sequences

191. Harmonic sequences as such are absolutely forbidden in the scholastic fugue. By this is meant that episodes made up of simple successions of chords forming purely harmonic imitations such as are practiced in harmony lessons have no place in fugal writing.

But this is not the case where one or more simple or complicated harmonic sequences are combined in the harmonic substructure of the episode. Indeed, analysis will show that more or less regular harmonic sequences underlie nearly every musical development, and are inevitable in the composition of a fugal episode.

Quality of an Episode

192. The quality of a fugal episode depends on the choice of motifs or themes; on the melodic line invented with these themes; and on the "working out," that is, the application of contrapuntal and fugal devices to the development of the themes, and the harmonic arrangements that underlie them.

Theme(s) of the Episode

193. A theme of an episode, as has been said, can be taken only from a passage heard in the exposition.

The theme may consist of a simple melodic or rhythmic figure made of a few notes, or of a long melodic fragment. (N.B. It is advisable for the beginner to choose simple melodic and rhythmic elements in order to avoid complicated combinations.)

Episodes are most frequently composed of two, three, or four themes, all extracted from the exposition and combined in simple or invertible counterpoint.

194. The melodic invention shown in combining the elements of the episode depends on the skill and imagination of the composer. The student should constantly turn to the works of Bach, Mozart, Handel, Mendelssohn, etc., to analyze their methods of construction, even though his writing is at present kept under restraint.

Preparation of the Episode

195. Choice of themes is made as follows: Once the exposition it written, all the melodic and rhythmic figures which can be used as combinations of different counterpoints are extracted from it. The subject, countersubject, reply and its countersubject, coda, and free parts are all analyzed, fragmented, and parts of them recombined to form the melodic and rhythmic material of contrapuntal combinations arranged either in direct movement, in contrary movement, in retrograde movement, or, in retrograde contrary movement.

All the above are combined either with or without augmentation or diminution.

Exposition Analyzed from the Viewpoint of the Episode

196. Take, for example, the following exposition from the *Well-Tempered Clavier* of Johann Sebastian Bach:

What follows is a detailed analysis of this exposition.

Fragmentation of the Subject

197. If we consider the subject by itself, we can divide it into the following melodic fragments:

Taking the subject in contrary movement, the following fragments of melody result:

198. The countersubject, similarly analyzed, will furnish the following elements, of which the first two can be considered as variants of the same chromatic phrase:

and in contrary movement:

Further subdivision of these phrases produces the following fragments which may be useful:

(11[a]) ou (14[a])

(11[b]) (14[b])

199. From the free parts, we can take these phrases (Exposition, bar 11, soprano):

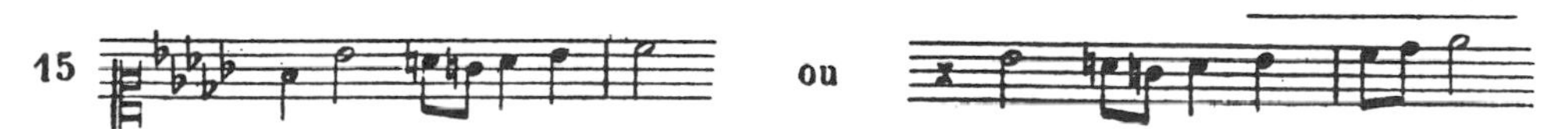

and, in the same voice, bar 13:

16

a purely rhythmic figure which is used by Bach in various forms:

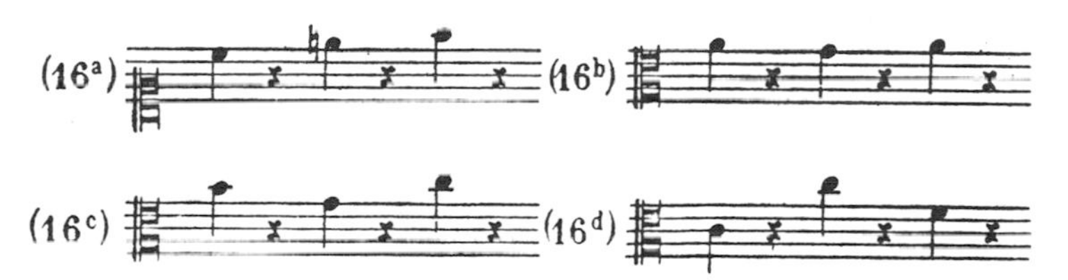

Bach uses it elsewhere in the fugue solely for rhythmic purposes.

These phrases should also be arranged in contrary movement.

In measures 14 and 15 in the soprano, we find two figures similar in rhythm and included in the same melodic fragment:

Both of them derive from the free part, bar 11.

200. The same work should be done on the subject arranged in contrary movement:

and by retrograde and contrary movement combined:

and the countersubject should be subjected to the same treatment.

201. Since the subject which we have chosen is in ternary rhythm, we will not arrange it in augmentation or diminution: Subjects in ternary rhythm do not readily lend themselves to such treatment because of inevitable rhythmic distortion.

(In this fugue, however, Bach uses it once only, with a fragment of the countersubject in augmentation by contrary movement.)

The student should note, however, that augmentation and diminution should always be considered in treating a subject, as they are frequently used with great effect. See ¶251–¶254.

Construction of the Melodic Line of the Episode

202. When the student has assembled the elements available for the development of the fugue, he must choose among them those which he will combine in designing the melodic line of each episode.

As has been said (¶191), this melodic line is always established on a harmonic sequence, or on a series of harmonic sequences.

Take, in this subject,

one of its melodic figures and arrange it on its natural harmonic bass:

203. It is evident that if we remove the upper part we can create all sorts of harmonic sequences, using the bass alone as antecedent. Likewise, whenever such antecedent is heard in the bass we can place above it, at the appropriate interval, the melodic phrase that engendered it.

204. If, moreover, we start with the key in mind at which we intend to end the sequence, we have only to arrange the modulations to the desired key,

and we can be as long or short about it as we wish.

Suppose we want to modulate to the key of B-flat minor; we can arrange the sequence like this:

If a longer sequence were wanted, for instance, to the key of D-flat (fourth degree of the principal key), we could arrange it this way:

205. These sequences, however, are simple harmonic sequences treated melodically. They must be rearranged so that the melodic fragments can be heard in imitation in various voices:

206. So far we have established merely the framework of the episode, that is, the basic harmony, the principal melodic line, and its imitations. Now we have to consider that the other voices must not merely contain simple, harmonic padding, but that all the parts must be treated melodically in simple or invertible counterpoint, and that the melodic figures involved must be taken from the subject, countersubject, or some other part of the exposition.

We must now, therefore, make a preliminary study of the combinations possible from the material available.

207. Since, in the present case, the exposition has not yet been made, we will confine ourselves to the given fragment of the subject (¶202) in constructing an episode.

It can be envisaged in the three following forms:

1) In its entirety:

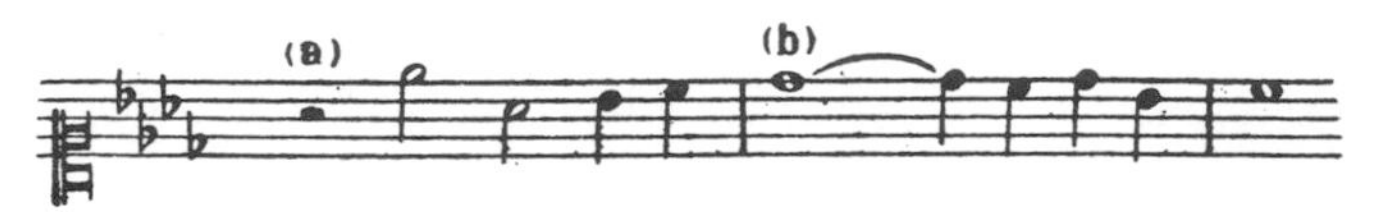

2) By creating a harmonic sequence with the first measure (*a*)

which is invertible with the second measure (*b*).

3) By creating with the second measure (*b*) a sequence which is, likewise, invertible:

Then, to avoid the monotony of the descending sequence, we can end by an ascending sequence (*a*) formed from the second fragment (*b*):

(N.B. It will be noted that in the measure before the last the sequence is no longer regular; minor variations of this sort are always permitted in episodes and are often preferable to absolute regularity, as they prevent the episode from seeming mechanical.)

208. Once this preliminary work is done, and having before us the different combinations of the given fragment that are invertible in three parts,

we can make a plan of construction of the whole episode:

209. The definitive working out of the episode would be like this:

210. In studying the above working out, the pupil should notice particularly the great difference that separates the completed episode from the harmonic sequences that engendered it. Though an impression of the elementary sequence remains, the varied arrangements of the parts succeeds in preventing the dryness and monotony which even so short a sequence would otherwise produce.

However, it will soon be seen (¶216) that the *apparent* use of a simple harmonic sequence can also give a good effect.

Episodes Based on Several Themes

211. In the example we have just studied, all elements were taken from a single fragment of the subject. However, we can likewise combine different figures taken from the subject, countersubject, and/or free parts (¶195). In making a sketch of an episode using these diverse elements, the melodic figure having the greatest length, or that most distinguished in rhythm or expression, is chosen as principal theme. The rest of the material serves as countersubjects, freely treated.

(N.B. Here, in the choice of elements of the episodes, their arrangement, and their relationship with each other, is the first real test of the abilities of the composer.

(Indeed, in the construction of these fugal episodes we come close to the core of musical composition. Although the basic idea—the subject—is given the student, the choices to be made, the alternatives to be explored, the combinations to be invented, the final completion of the episode, all partake of the nature of true composition and have their parallels in wholly original work.

(It is apparent that work must still be done piecemeal. Not until the student has worked his way several times through each of the essential parts of the fugue will he be able to start with a subject and from it construct a complete fugue whose end has been envisaged from its beginning. It is not possible to do this at this juncture, but with each successive exposition the student can plan further ahead, as the parts of previously written fugues are completed. Even so, each decision, each combination, depends on the taste and musicality of the student; for all practical purposes, he is composing.—F.D.)

212. The different themes of the episodes may be written according to the composer's choice, in simple, double, triple, or quadruple counterpoint. The imitations created may be free or exact, canonical, periodic, and in direct, contrary, retrograde, augmented, or diminished movement.

Theme of the Episode Must Be in One Key

213. Under all circumstances the *theme* of the episode, considered as a model of the harmonic sequence, must begin and end in the same key. It must be susceptible of being concluded by a cadence in its own key, even though cadences are almost always avoided by the usual devices of musical writing, as will be shown later.

The modulations imposed by the harmonic sequences are to be made either by notes common to both the last chord of the antecedent and the first chord of the consequent, or by modulating codas. Observe that, if the theme itself modulated, the episode would inevitably take the form of a "circular" imitation, which should be avoided for the sake of the progress of the fugue.

214. Invention, musically speaking, in an episode, is centered more in the creation of the themes than in their handling, since the basic number of combinations of which an episode may be constructed is comparatively small. Examination of the fugues of masters of the form will reveal that episodes, whose variety at a glance seems enormous, actually derive from a relatively small number of fundamental combinations.

These arrangements are based on the application of the rules concerning the various kinds of imitations. Though basically few, they can be almost indefinitely varied by mixing and alternating. (N.B. In this, the part played by the taste and judgment of the composer is paramount.—F.D.)

Arrangement of Imitations in Episodes

215. We have seen (¶209) that, once the theme or themes of an episode have been chosen and harmonized, and the melodic lines fixed, imitations based on them are so arranged that the entry of their principal melody is clearly audible.

These arrangements may be summed up in the following six basic types of combination:

216. *First type:* A different theme is composed for each part, which imitates itself, repeating the theme at different intervals.

This is the manner of a simple harmonic sequence. It can be used in a fugue only on condition that it be melodically interesting; the themes used are generally rather long.

However, such a combination is often used after other types have been heard. It has the advantage of preparing the return of the subject by a sequence of great harmonic intensity. When so used, the melody of the fragment serving as theme is generally short.

Example (Johann Sebastian Bach, *Well-Tempered Clavier*, Fugue XVIII):

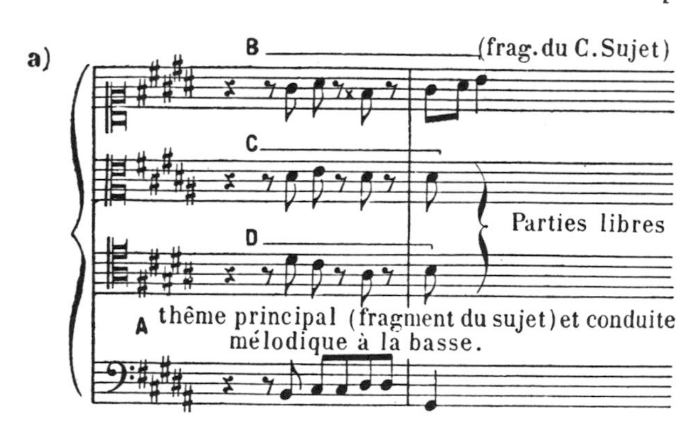

c) DIVERTISSEMENT extrait de la fugue d'orgue de J.S.Bach en Fa ♮ mineur

Working out of these elements:

217. *Second type*: The principal theme is heard in full in only one part. The other parts sound fragments of it. All parts derive from the same theme.

This arrangement, in which, as in the preceding, the harmonic sequence is obvious, differs in that canonical imitations of all sorts may be used, as all parts derive from the same theme. Though difficult to set up, this form of episode has the advantage of lending itself to all sorts of strict imitations.

The D minor organ fugue of Johann Sebastian Bach,

may be studied with profit as almost all of its episodes are constructed along these lines.

Examples:

218. End of exposition; canonical imitation of the principal theme:

At (*a*), Bach permits himself certain liberties of harmony and voice-leading which are to be avoided in the scholastic fugue. The strict rules of pedagogy are frequently broken in the compositions of the masters. Contrary to popular opinion, there is no contradiction implicit in this. The masters were not permitted liberties when they were students. After they had mastered their craft, they were entitled to do as they pleased. So is the student today.

219. Episode on the same theme, but more tightly written, and in three-part canonical imitation:

a) Unison by direct movement is forbidden in the scholastic fugue, as is the use of a neighboring tone on a unison.

b) Neither is the lower neighboring note of a lower part permitted while the same tone is heard as a real note in another part.

220. Principal theme and melodic line in the upper part; from Bach's fugue in B-flat minor which has been examined in ¶196:

Elements of the episode:

Combination of two of the elements to create the principal theme:

Melodic and harmonic outline:

Bach's working-out:

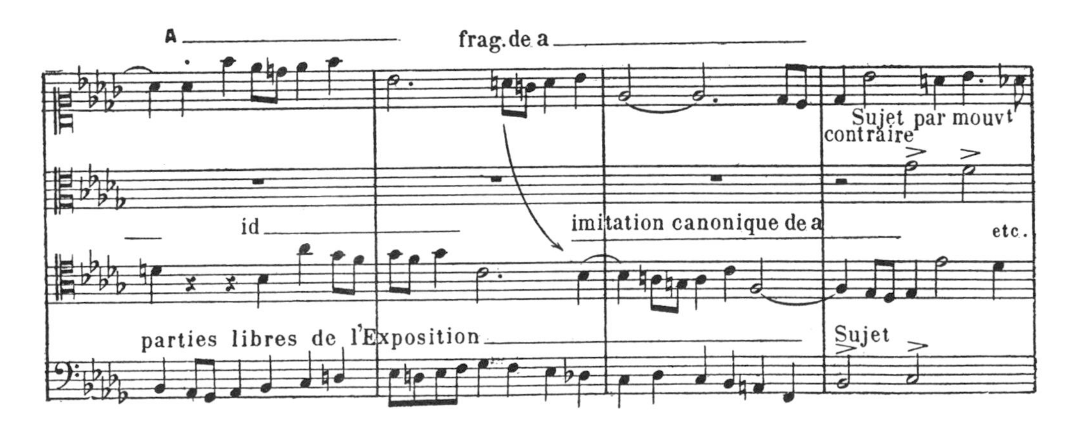

221. Fugue XII from Bach's *Well-Tempered Clavier*:

222. Organ fugue by Johann Sebastian Bach:
Subject:

Elements of the episode:

Melodic outline of the episode:

223. In this episode, note how Bach has avoided the coldness and dryness that would have resulted from the absolute symmetry of the parts if the imitations had been made regularly in each voice, on the same beat. Thanks to his ingenious handling, Bach has been able to make a canonical imitation between the soprano and tenor with the same rhythmic figure in such a way that, while the sequence in the bass ascends, the three parts above it form a descending sequence.

(N.B. For examples of the fatal results of absolute symmetry, the student should examine the "Forty-eight Preludes and Fugues" by Auguste Alexander Klengel, a mid-nineteenth-century German contrapuntist who tried to out-Bach Bach. It is a monument to the fatuity of pure "system-composing."—F.D.)

224. Here, taken from the same fugue (see ¶222), is an episode in five parts. The melodic line is given in its entirety in the upper voice, while the bass makes a free and rhythmic imitation, by augmentation and contrary movement, of a fragment of the subject. The other parts imitate themselves, repeating continuously at different intervals the same melodic and rhythmic figure assigned to each part. (Note that here, as frequently, examples are cited from instrumental fugues whose range greatly exceeds the vocal limits of the scholastic fugue.)

Elements of the episode:

225. *Third type:* Two parts imitate each other, alternately stating the principal theme.

The melodic line of the episode passes alternately between each of two parts. The other parts repeat either fragments of the principal theme or different figures taken from the subject, countersubject, or free parts of the exposition.

a) The following example is from the Bach fugue in B-flat minor which we have examined in ¶196 and ¶220. The numbers placed above the elements of the episode refer to the analysis of the exposition of this fugue given in ¶196.

Elements of the episode:

Melodic and harmonic plan of the episode:

Plan of the working-out:

Bach's working-out of the episode:

226. Episode in three parts, two of which form a canon (Johann Sebastian Bach, *Well-Tempered Clavier,* Fugue XXXI):

227. *Fourth type:* The parts imitate each other two by two.

The principal theme of the episode is accompanied by a second figure which serves as a sort of countersubject. The melodic line remains continuously in the same part, or more rarely, the two groups of voices alternate and sound in turn the theme and its "countersubject."

Examples:

a) Mozart, Piano and Violin Sonata, final fugue:

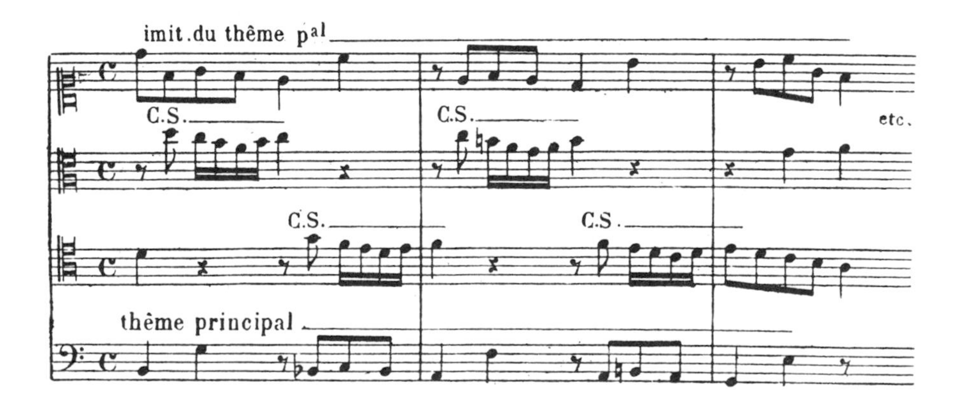

b) Mozart, Quartet in A Major:

c) Bach, *Art of the Fugue,* Number 4:

d) *Ibid.* Another episode on the same theme, differently arranged:

This sort of episode is rarely used alone, as it tends to dryness. It is generally found combined with one or more of the other arrangements given here, or is reserved for very short episodes.

228. *Fifth type:* The principal theme of the episode is imitated in three parts.

The melodic line of the episode passes alternately among three of the parts. The fourth part may imitate itself by repeating continually the same phrase, or it may borrow from the other parts the phrases they sound when they are not stating the principal theme of the episode. Or it may consist of various fragments borrowed from the subject, countersubject, or free parts of the exposition.

Example: Bach, Fugue in B-flat minor (¶196–¶200). Elements of the episode (the numbers refer to fragments analyzed in ¶197):

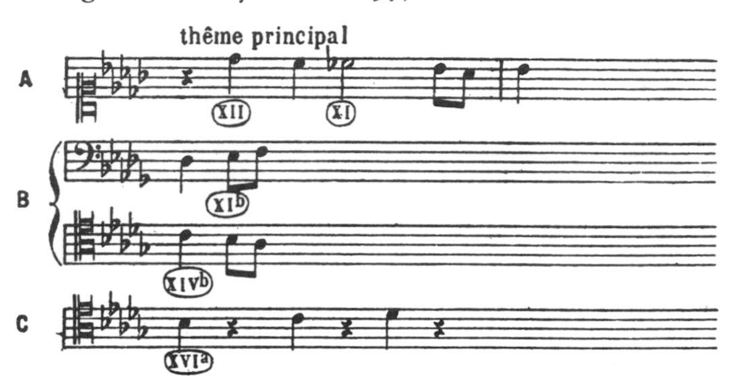

Melodic and harmonic plan:

Outline of working-out:

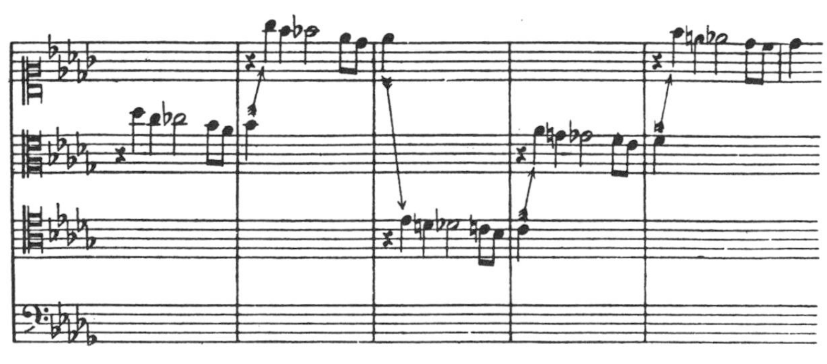

Bach's working-out:

229. The preceding is allied in structure to a canonical episode; however, it is not as strict as a canon. Observe that, if the three themes or figures of which it is composed overrun each other constantly and are, for the most part, written in triple counterpoint, the overrunning is not always made in the same voice as it would be if the canon were regular. In a canon, the phrases would follow in invariable order in all three parts: A, C, B, or A, B, C, etc.

230. Johann Sebastian Bach, *Well-Tempered Clavier,* Fugue IV, in five parts:

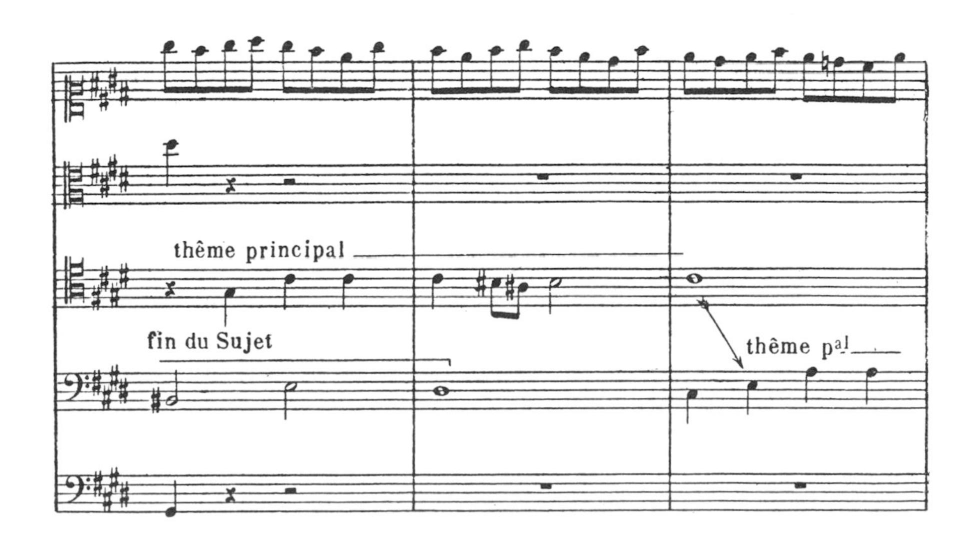

231. *Sixth type:* The four parts imitate each other.

The melodic line of the episode passes successively through all four parts, which, each in turn, present the principal theme of the episode.

This form of episode yields greater richness and greater variety than any of the preceding. It lends itself to all sorts of imitations. The principal theme may be combined with a second or third theme or "countersubject" written in invertible counterpoint.

The arrangement of this sort of episode recalls that of an exposition: all the themes are presented alternately in each part. The difference is that the imitations of the themes of the episode are made at arbitrarily chosen intervals.

Example: Johann Sebastian Bach, *Well-Tempered Clavier,* Fugue XXIV (episode on a single theme):

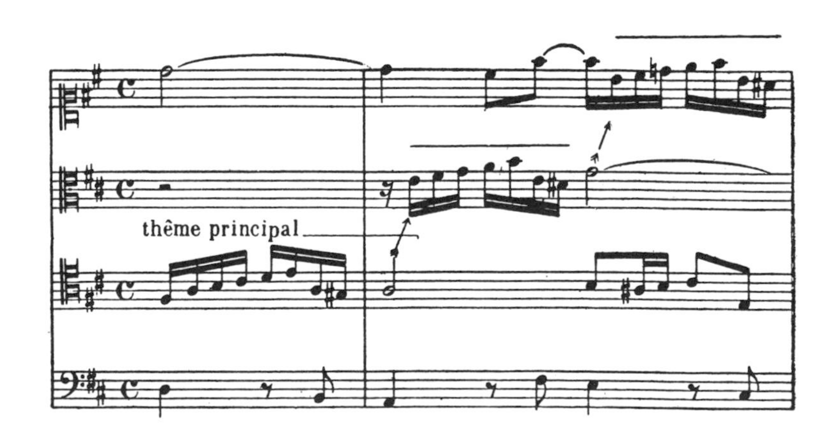

232. George F. Handel, Utrecht Jubilate:

233. Johann Sebastian Bach, Organ Fugue in E-flat:

Episode in five parts:

Canonical Episodes

234. The following episodes are written canonically. In comparing them with other kinds, it is evident that canonical episodes furnish much the greatest interest.

The process of writing a canonical episode will be described in detail below (¶236). Even though the student, before studying fugue, has doubtless familiarized himself with every sort of imitation, we have thought it advisable to repeat in this instance how to construct an invertible canon for use in an episode. The example which we will analyze is in six parts, of which four are in canon. The method is the same for a greater or lesser number of parts.

The canonical form should be used whenever possible as it produces an episode of tighter texture and greater harmonic richness than any other.

Example: Johann Sebastian Bach, Fugue on the Chorale, "Jesus Christus, Unser Heiland" (canonical episode on two themes):

Elements of the episode:

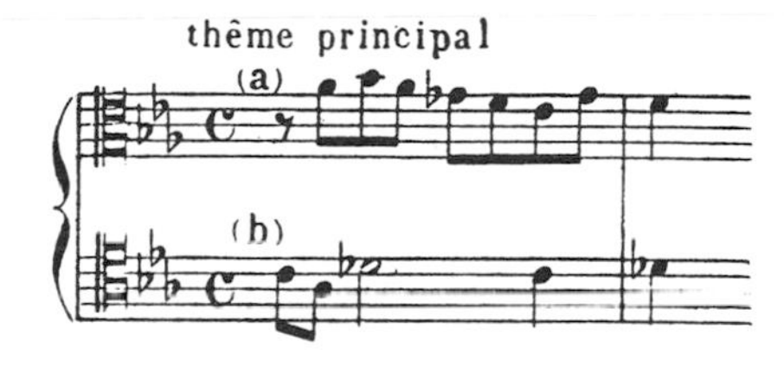

Melodic line:

Plan of working-out:

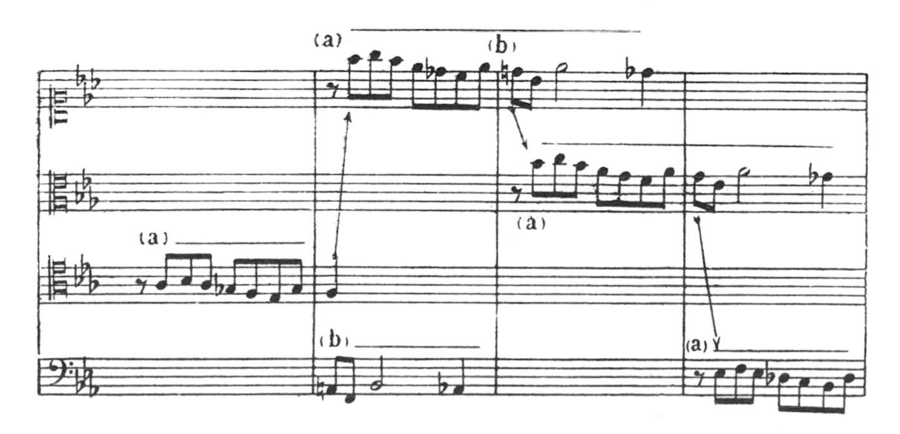

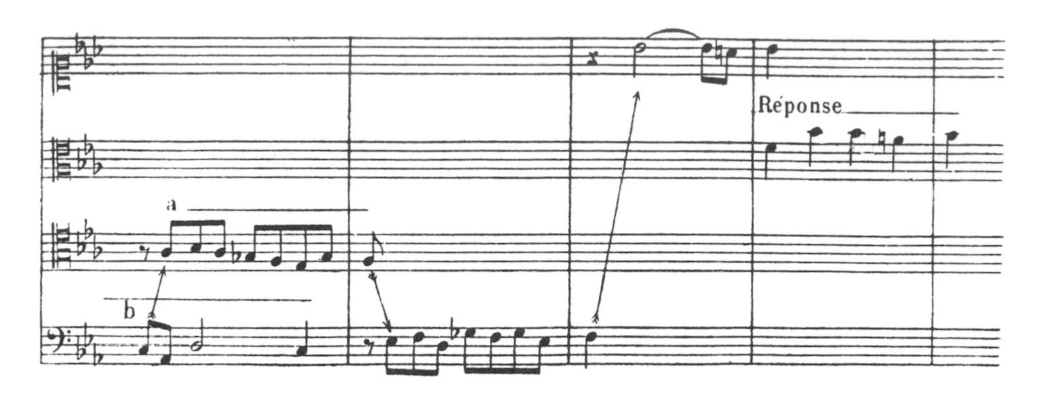

Bach's working-out:

235. Johann Sebastian Bach, *Well-Tempered Clavier,* Fugue XXXVI. Canonical episode on a fragment of the countersubject:

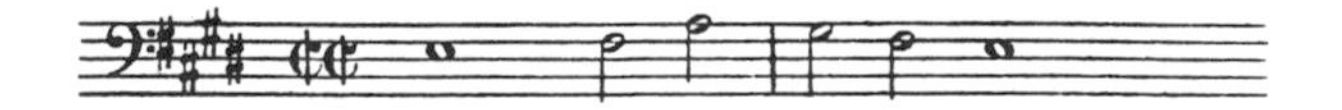

Construction of a Canonical Episode

236. Here is another episode by Bach, in six parts, taken from the "ricercata" fugue in the *Musical Offering*. The subject is:

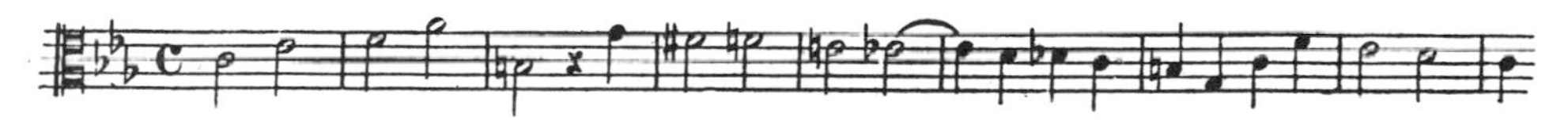

The episode is constructed entirely from the following four figures, combined according to the method used in writing canons. That is, the elements are first arranged so as to produce a complete harmony with each other, invertible or not:

They are then added on to one another, in arbitrary order and at convenient intervals, in such a way as to make a continuous melodic line which forms the principal theme of the episode:

Then, with one or more elements of the melodic line (in this case two, as they are invertible in two parts), the harmonic sequence of this episode is written:

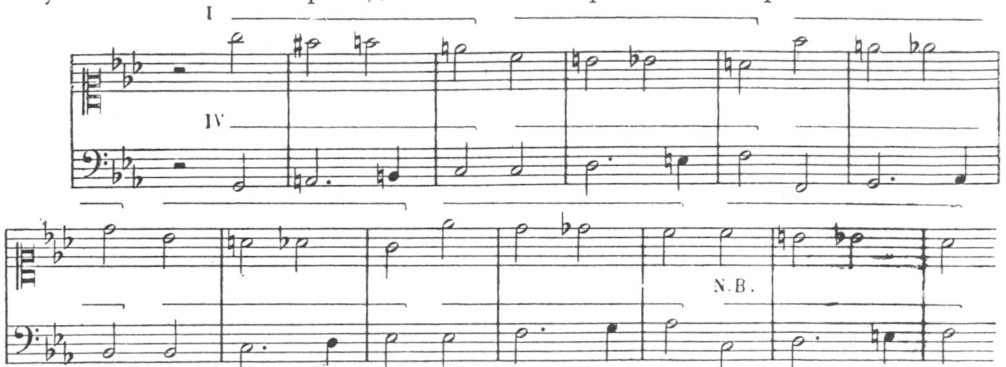

(N.B. In the last three measures, the sequence ceases to be regular.)

237. It is evident that, as the various parts have been harmonically combined in advance, each fragment can be sounded at the same time as the others at an interval determined by whatever has been chosen as head of the theme.

We now have only to arrange the parts as we wish, and the working out will follow inevitably. It there are more than four parts, once a voice has finished sounding the principal theme, it can remain silent or continue with various free imitations.

Of course, when the original combination is not invertible, the elements of which it is made can only be set up in their original harmonic arrangement. If we wish to vary it, the parts must be written in double, triple, or quadruple counterpoint.

238. Here is Bach's working-out:

239. Note in several instances in the above example that various fragments of the principal theme have undergone modifications necessitated either by the register in which they are heard or by the arrangement of the parts. Such modifications are always permitted, provided the phrases are not distorted beyond recognition. However, musical effect must never be sacrificed for the sake of a combination, no matter how ingenious.

Summary

240. On the basis of the above examples, it is apparent that the arrangement of the parts of an episode derive always from one of these combinations:

a) Each part imitates itself.

b) Two parts imitate each other; the others imitate themselves.

c) The parts imitate each other two by two.

d) Three parts imitate each other.

e) All parts imitate each other.

241. Although there may frequently be found in the fugues of the masters episodes that are based solely on one of the above arrangements, such episodes are generally short. In episodes of some length, combinations of these arrangements are desirable. The fugues of Bach, Mozart, and Mendelssohn furnish many examples of such combinations.

Episodes on Successive Themes

242. Moreover, when a long episode is being composed, it may begin with one or more figures taken from the exposition of the fugue, and continued with other elements from the same source. Care must be taken that the themes are skillfully combined so that there is no interruption in the melodic line, and the motifs derive naturally from one another.

The following examples illustrate this more fully. The student is urged to analyze in like manner many other fugal episodes.

243. The following example is from the G major Organ Fugue of Johann Sebastian Bach. The subject is:

244. In this episode, the melodic line (*a*)–(*b*), formed from the principal theme,

alternates between the soprano and alto.

Beginning at (*b*), the theme of the episode changes, and up to the entry of the subject at (*d*), the melodic line remains entirely in the soprano, but in two different arrangements: from (*b*) to (*c*) each part other than the soprano presents a series of irregular imitations, the bass and alto giving rhythmic imitations while the tenor imitates fragments of the principal melodic line.

Beginning at (*c*), the episode is in only three parts; a canon is made by the soprano and tenor, and the bass imitates itself.

245. This example is from Mendelssohn's Fugue for Organ, Opus 37, Number 1:

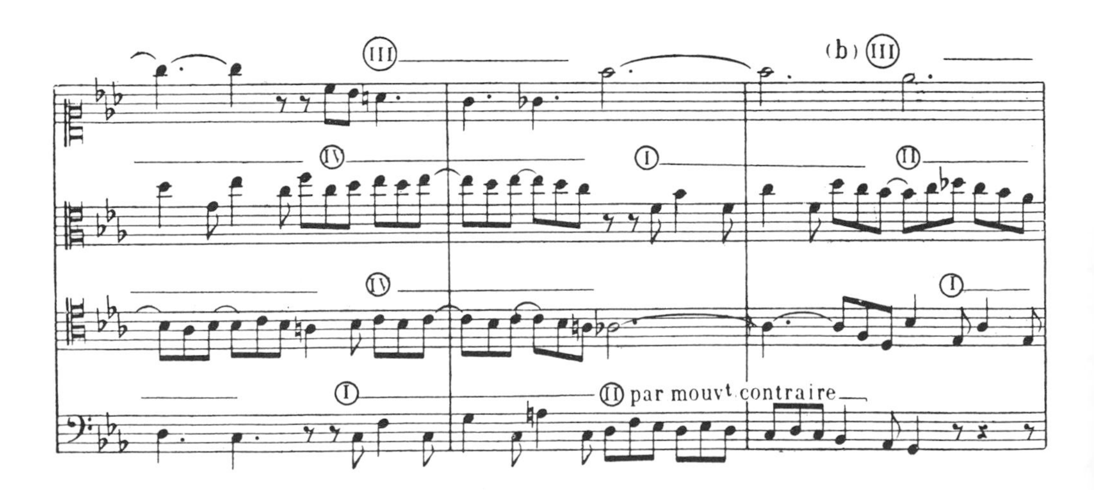

The episode is composed of four phrases. The first, heard in the tenor, is taken from the head of the subject:

This figure forms the principal theme, and gives the melodic line of the episode.

The second phrase, heard at the beginning of the episode in the soprano, is imitated in contrary movement in the bass (end of fourth and beginning of fifth measures).

The third figure serves likewise as an imitation between the soprano and the bass.

Finally, the fourth figure, heard first in the middle of the second measure in the tenor, is reproduced in the third measure in the alto.

In the ensemble, from (*a*) to (*b*) the parts imitate each other two by two, while from (*b*) to (*c*), that is, up to the entry of the subject at the fourth degree, each part imitates itself.

Note that in the final measures of the episode the imitations of the second and third figures are purely rhythmic, and the melody of these figures is distorted. This is permitted even in the scholastic fugue, in which episodes are frequently composed entirely of rhythmic imitations.

246. Quoted below are other, unanalyzed examples. These are to be analyzed by the student, who will find more material in the preludes and fugues of Bach and Mendelssohn, and in the quartets and symphonies of Haydn, Mozart, and Beethoven, where he will find practical application in musical composition of the devices used in fugue. We will return, moreover, in a special manner to this latter point, which, in the last analysis, is the principal reason for the profound study of fugue.

a) Johann Sebastian Bach, *Well-Tempered Clavier,* Fugue XLI:

b) Johann Sebastian Bach, Organ Prelude in C minor:

Although this episode (*b*) is not taken from a fugue, it is so characteristic of the fugal process that it is included here. The melodic coda which ends it is more developed than is customary in the scholastic fugue, but a coda of this sort could be logically applied to any fugue. It would find its place at the end of any intense and expressive episode where it would serve to make more salient the entry of the subject in a new key.

c) R. Schumann, Third Fugue on the name "Bach":

In this example (*c*) the entries of the different themes are insufficiently pointed up; the ensemble is overstuffed and heavy, and derives rather from a harmony exercise than from contrapuntal writing. This episode must, therefore, be considered not as a model of contrapuntal writing but as a model of melodic line. As in the preceding example, it ends on a coda which forms a cadence reintroducing the subject. But while in Bach's work the coda is distinctly melodic, here the appeal is harmonic, since the parts, arranged note against note, form a sequence of strongly marked chords.

d) Mozart, Quartet in A major:

USE OF CONTRARY MOVEMENT

247. We have said that all the elements of an episode can be imitated in contrary movement: this imitation is frequently used in the arrangements studied above.

Contrary movement can be used concurrently with direct movement, as in the following examples.

a) Mendelssohn, Organ Fugue, Opus 37, Number 3. The principal theme of the episode is:

which, in contrary movement, is:

The melodic plan of the episode is:

In the working-out, the parts imitate each other two by two, one pair presenting the theme in direct movement, the other in contrary movement:

b) André Gedalge, *Four Preludes and Fugues for Piano,* Number 2. Subject:

Episode in three parts:

248. In some instances, all the elements of the episode can be presented in contrary movement.

This arrangement is used infrequently, since it lacks the advantage of contrasting movement and therefore offers less interest. Nevertheless, it is found in Bach's works in several instances where the theme in contrary movement retains sufficent distinction to serve as the basis of an episode.

The following is taken from Bach's B-flat minor fugue cited above (¶196–¶200, ¶228). In it, all elements, both principal and accessory themes, appear in contrary movement. Reference should be made to ¶197, in which the phrases from which this episode is made are analyzed, to clarify the illustration:

Use of Retrograde and Contrary Retrograde Movement

249. The combination of retrograde and contrary retrograde movement is seldom used in fugue. Few subjects lend themselves thereto, either because of the change of rhythms or because the themes in retrograde movement lose all musical character. Nevertheless, when the subject is usable in this manner, certain interesting examples arise.

Example: André Gedalge, *Four Preludes and Fugues for Piano,* Number 3:

a) Direct and retrograde movement combined; canonical episode in two parts:

b) Direct combined with retrograde and contrary retrograde movement:

250. The two episodes above have as theme the subject in its entirety. This is not permitted in the scholastic fugue.

Use of Augmentation

251. The use of augmentation is infrequent in fugal episodes. Later (¶328), we shall see that this device is much more frequently used in the stretto section, where it often produces striking results.

The following example (*a*), in six parts, is taken from the already cited fugue in Bach's *Musical Offering*. Here, the highest part sounds a phrase in augmentation which, between the second soprano and alto, is presented in imitations at its original speed, and which is likewise taken up in a sequence in the bass.

a)

b) Johann Sebastian Bach, *Well-Tempered Clavier,* Fugue VII:

Use of Diminution

252. Diminution is much more frequently used in episodes, as it tightens the phrase and permits more closely spaced entries of it. In the stretto, however, augmentation is of particular value since, when the subject permits it, the presentation of the subject and answer simultaneously with the subject augmented is available.

Augmentation and Diminution in Contrary and Retrograde Movement

253. The themes, treated in augmentation or diminution, can likewise be presented in contrary, retrograde, or contrary-retrograde movement. In the following example, a diminished theme is heard at the same time in direct and contrary movement.

Mozart, *Two Fantasies and Fugues for Piano,* Four Hands, Number 2. Subject:

Theme of the episode in diminution:

Theme in diminution and contrary movement:

Double Augmentation and Double Diminution

254. Also to be cited are episodes based on imitations in double augmentation and double diminution. These are most frequently found in fugues written on a chorale, where the use of these devices derives from the inherent character of such fugues.

This example may be considered as in either simple or double augmentation, depending on which of the phrases, (*a*), (*b*), or (*c*), is taken as the principal theme.

Example: Johann Sebastian Bach, *Ach Gott und Herr*:

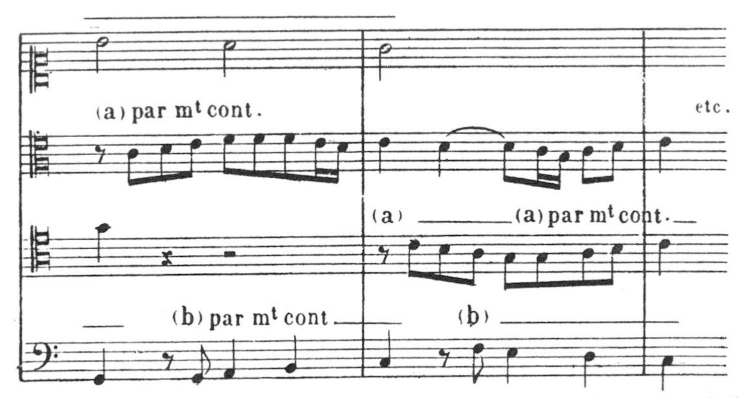

255. Herewith we end the study of the technique of the episode. Later, in discussing the musical composition of the fugue, we will have occasion to consider the choice of themes of the episodes, their preferential order, and what means to take to conceal the process of construction. The better the student is trained in the technical aspects of the fugue, the less will his craft be apparent. Moreover, he will be able to give freer rein to his imagination. And he will accomplish more with less effort.

Summary

256. Certain conclusions should be made from the preceding examples. It may have been noticed that the entries of the parts are frequent, and such entries are preceded by rests, to make them stand out. In consequence, all parts do not sound at the same time. It frequently happens that the episodes of a four-part fugue are largely written in three parts—not the same parts throughout, to be sure, but in three parts at a time, each part becoming silent in turn. (N.B. It is of the first importance to "let the air in" by silencing one or another of the

parts. Otherwise, the texture of the fugue would be suffocatingly dense.—F.D.)

257. Entries must always be made by a phrase taken from the subject, countersubject, or free parts of the exposition. They must never be mere harmonic filling.

A part is never silenced without a reason. If it drops out, it must be so treated that, taken alone, it would be capable of making a cadence, perfect or otherwise.

258. The sequences on which an episode is based should be established logically, that is, in such a way that they arrive naturally at the desired key if by a modulating sequence. If non-modulating, they should bring the episode to a close that is arranged appropriately for the next entry of the subject in the requisite new key.

259. When an episode is constructed of two or more different sequences, care should be taken to end on those producing the most closely written imitations.

260. To sustain the musical interest of the fugue, all parts must be treated melodically, in a style compatible with the subject. Careful attention must be given to the highest part, and the bass must never have the character of a simple harmonic bass. Furthermore, all the parts should combine to give the impression of a clear and continuous melodic line.

Exercises

Continue the construction of your fugues by writing their first modulating episodes. These should be arranged to modulate into the appropriate keys given in ¶265, below. Each subject, answer, and their countersubjects must first have been fragmented, as in ¶197–¶200.

(N.B. The order of the chapters is changed hereafter from the original. Chapter VIII which follows was Chapter X.—F.D.)

VIII

THE MODULATIONS OF THE FUGUE

261. The first section of the fugue ends with the counterexposition, or with the exposition if no counterexposition is written. The developments which constitute the second section follow immediately. These developments consist of episodes which periodically progress to the subject, answer, and countersubject.

262. To avoid the monotony resultant from the constant repetition of the original key, the subject is heard in a different key each time it reappears. But, just as melodic and rhythmic unity are given the fugue by limiting its constituent elements to material derived from the exposition, so tonal unity is achieved by limiting its modulations to the neighboring keys of the principal key of the subject.

Neighboring Keys

263. The neighboring keys of any key are:

a) In major:

The minor key on the second degree.
The minor key on the third degree.
The major key on the fourth degree.
The major key on the fifth degree.
The minor key on the sixth degree.

b) In minor:

The major key on the third degree.
The minor key on the fourth degree.
The minor key on the fifth degree.
The major key on the sixth degree.
The major key on the seventh degree.

264. The exposition, the counterexposition, and the first and last strettos must always be made in the principal key of the subject. This rule is invariable.

Order of Modulations

265. The scholastic fugue modulates in the following order. The episodes must therefore be planned to modulate to, or permit the entrance of the subject at the keys indicated:

In major, the first modulation is made to the sixth degree (minor) of the principal key, in which the subject is heard followed by the answer, which leads the fugue to the key of the third degree (minor).

By means of an episode, modulation next is made to the fourth degree (major) where only the subject is heard, as the answer would bring the fugue back to the principal key.

In a short episode, or with no transitional passage, if possible, modulation is next made to the key of the second degree (minor) in which a single entry, either of subject or answer, is made.

A new episode, more developed than the others, follows. During it, the subject may be heard at the key of the dominant. It is followed by the first stretto, in the principal key.

This may end on a pedal point on the dominant, which may be linked directly to the stretto, or may be separated from it by a short passage which is generally in the key of the dominant.

266. In minor, the number of episodes and the manner of ending on a stretto is the same as in major. The order of modulations is different:

The first episode leads to the subject in the key of the third degree (major), where the answer brings about modulation to the unaltered seventh degree (major).

From there, modulation is made to the fourth degree (minor), and the answer is heard at the sixth degree (major).

Finally, an episode in which the subject is heard in the key of the dominant leads to the first stretto.

Length of Episodes

267. While no arbitrary rule can be laid down concerning the proportions of the episodes, an approximation may be given according to the length of the subject and exposition.

If we take 4 to 6 measures as the average length of the subject, then the exposition should contain a minimum of 16 to 24 measures.

In proportion, the following lengths may be given to the different episodes. The table here given for the major mode is applicable (with modulations to the appropriate keys) to the minor mode as well.

Parts of the Fugue	*Number of measures varying approximately* *from*	*to*
Exposition	16	24
Episode	4	8
Counterexposition	8	12
First Modulating Episode	8	12
Subject at the Sixth Degree	4	6
Answer at the Third Degree	4	6
Second Modulating Episode	10	16
Subject at the Fourth Degree	4	6
Transition	2	4
Subject or Answer at the Second Degree	4	6
Third Modulating Episode	14	20
	—	—
Total to First Stretto	78	120

268. These dimensions may be regarded as extremes within which the student may arrange the different parts of the fugue. With strettos of proportionate length, the entire fugue would run to between 120 and 170 measures. A fugue of this length would probably seem neither truncated nor overdeveloped.

269. Arbitrary though they may be, these proportions (and the order, number, and choice of modulations) are requisite to the scholastic fugue. Obviously, the fugues of Bach, Handel, Mozart, or Mendelssohn will not yield exact examples of these arrangements; not one of their fugues abide by these rules. However, guideposts are necessary to the beginner, and, although no special value attaches to the proportions and modulations given, they are useful in organizing the work.

Subject in the Opposite Mode

270. The subject must not modulate from the major to the minor mode of its original key, and vice versa. That is, a subject in A minor may not appear in A major. Change of mode is, however, permitted in the related keys that are in another mode from the subject.

271. (Nor must the answer be written when a subject, in major, modulates to the third or fifth degrees, or when a minor subject modulates to the fifth or unaltered seventh degrees. This is because such answers would modulate into keys from which it would be difficult to return to the principal key.)

(N.B. The above paragraph is placed in parenthesis because many authorities disagree with Gedalge. Actually, such answers are written with impunity.

Return to the principal key is left to the ingenuity of the student.—F.D.)

272. Note, however, that certain subjects lend themselves badly to transposition into the opposite mode in any key whatever. A subject may be unmusical or unrecognizable when transposed from major to minor or vice versa.

273. These difficulties arise generally from the creation of intervals of difficult intonation or of dubious tonality brought about by the change of mode. A subject so transposed may be difficult to harmonize as well as unmusical melodically.

274. The best way to deal with these cases is to consider any alteration of a note of the subject, actual or implied in the harmony, not as chromatic but as tonal, that is, as taking the subject momentarily into another key.

When the subject, so interpreted, is transposed to the opposite mode, a faithful version of the subject will result if the relation of the keys in the new mode is the same as their relation in the original.

Example: Subject in its original mode, A minor:

ton de la médiante
par rapport à la♮min. dominante de la

Subject transposed to its relative major (C major):

In this example, we consider that the subject in its original mode has, for our present purposes, modulated momentarily to the mediant. When transposed to its relative major, the corresponding fragment is considered as in the key of the mediant of the relative major.

275. Here is another example of this sort. The subject is in E-flat major:

Subject transposed to the relative minor (C minor):

The following example, theoretically, is more complex (subject in C major):

Transposed into its relative minor, it would take this form if we follow the method just discussed:

and not the following, which, at first glance might appear exact, since all its intervals coincide, note by note, semitone by semitone:

If, however, we are guided by the harmonic relation of the different degrees of the subject in its original mode, the first solution will be seen to be the right one, as in it the harmonic relationships of the keys correspond exactly, in the opposite mode, to those in the original.

Obviously these modulations are theoretical. The subject does not actually pass through these keys.

276. These examples may serve as a warning to the student when he composes his own subjects that he take care that they be able to fit either mode.

Moreover, in choice of subjects for his scholastic fugues, the student should avoid those of the nature just described. Any subject whose mode is not strongly marked should be avoided.

277. More examples relating to modulating episodes will be found in Chapter XII.

Exercises

Continue the writing of modulating episodes leading to the appropriate entries of subject and answer. Follow freely the table in ¶267.

IX

THE STRETTO

Definitions

278. In the exposition, the entries of subject and answer are always arranged so that one is not heard until the other has finished. If, however, the answer is introduced before the completion of the statement of the subject, a stretto is formed.

279. The name "stretto" (the past participle of the Italian *"stringere,"* "to tighten") is applied to any combination in which the answer enters nearer to the head of the subject than in the exposition.

280. Moreover, the name "stretto" is given to the entire last section of the fugue in which, as we shall see, each stretto is made progressively nearer the head of the subject. The next chapter will be devoted to a study of the stretto section of the fugue as a whole. Here, we will discuss the construction of the individual strettos which combine to make up the stretto section.

281. In the construction of a stretto, it will be seen that, first, its indispensable elements are the head of the subject and the head of the answer, and second, it is composed of symmetrical successive entries of the head of the subject and the head of the answer.

282. Moreover, close combinations of the head of the countersubject of the subject with the head of the countersubject of the answer are used in a similar way, and are likewise called "strettos."

Canonical Strettos

283. There are four basic types of strettos:

I. The theme of the subject continues in full while the answer is being heard. This is called a "canonical stretto."

Example:

284. The following combination can be made in any number of parts:

Arrangement of Voices

285. The order in which the voices enter is in no way fixed, but depends on the wish of the composer, the exigencies of the harmony, or the sound desired. The preceding stretto could just as well have been arranged like this:

Entries at the Unison

286. The following arrangement is less good because the last two entries are made at the unison, which is to be avoided:

Here, the unisons prevent the distinct audibility of each entrance, and thereby destroy the effect of their proximity.

Inverse Canonical Strettos

287. When the canonical combination is begun by the answer, it is also called a "stretto."

Example:

More particularly, this sort of combination is called an "inverse canonical stretto." It may be combined, like the canonical strettos of the subject, in any convenient number of parts.

Incomplete Canon

288. II. Here, the theme of the subject cannot be continued in its entirety during the entry of the answer. The subject must, therefore, be either modified, ended, or interrupted, in which case a similar phrase is substituted for the interrupted part. The subject should be continued, unmodified, as far as is musically possible.

Example:

Sujet
Contre Sujet
Stretto
Partie libre
Partie libre
Réponse
Sujet
Contre Sujet modifié
Sujet
(Rép.interrompue)
(Sujet interrompu)
Contre Sujet modifié
Réponse

289. Note in the above example:

a) The entries are equidistant; subject and answer are heard every two measures.

b) The subject and answer have only been interrupted when it was impossible to continue them.

c) The fourth entry gives the answer in its entirety. This is usually the case when the stretto permits four entries; interruption of subject and answer is in the first entries.

However, as will be discussed later, complete statement in the final entry is compulsory only in the first, last, and next to last strettos that make up the stretto section of the fugue.

Note in the above that, each time the subject or answer is interrupted, it is filled out either by the countersubject, modified or not according to the necessity of the moment, or by phrases extracted from the countersubject.

Interruption of Subject and Answer

290. III. The subject is of such a nature that it can in no way be continued at the entry of the answer.

In this case the subject must be interrupted so that the answer can be heard. The part occupied by the subject is, therefore, continued either by imitating at another interval the interrupted fragment of the subject, or by sounding the countersubject or phrases taken from the subject or countersubject. Under no circumstances should material be used which was not heard in the exposition. However, melodic or rhythmic forms deriving from this material may be used if it is impossible to reproduce them exactly.

Example (subject by César Franck):

b) Inverse stretto, more condensed than the above:

In the third measure of example (*a*), in the tenor, there is an instance of the sort of modification that may be made in the subject or answer to improve the musical effect. Here, the A of the answer should be A-natural (third measure, third beat). But it is better to flat it to avoid a sense of false relation with the A-flat in the preceding measure.

Close, Unitonal Stretto

291. In a close stretto in four parts, modulation at each entry must be avoided. The parts should be arranged, melodically and harmonically, so that the ensemble of the entries emphasizes a single tonality, and not sudden alternations between the keys of the first and fifth degrees.

Remember that from the correct handling of a multitude of similar details arises what is called "métier," that is, skilled craftsmanship.

Harmonic Concord of the Entries

292. It is of the greatest importance that the entry of the answer on the subject, and vice versa, only be made when the first note of the entry produces a harmony concordant with that which precedes it. It is essential that the subject is not quitted on a phrase which implies harmonies distant from the head of the answer. If possible, entry should be made on a note common to both harmonies, or at least on a note of a common chord.

Free Strettos

293. IV. These strettos are made from a combination of subject and answer, canonical or otherwise, at intervals other than the normal fifth above or fourth below.

They may also be made from combinations of subject and subject, or answer and answer, all treated at various degrees. Detailed analysis of them will be found in ¶302.

Method of Setting up Strettos

294. The following are examples of the analytical procedure necessary to establish the various strettos of the subject. It will be recalled that, in the exposition, the answer enters only after the subject has been stated in full.

Example:

295. Now, if we compare subject and answer, it will be seen that the latter can be made to enter at various distances from the head of the subject, and that its entrance need not interrupt the subject. By trial and error, we can find the places, starting from the last measure, where the answer will go.

By this process of investigation, beat by beat, and measure by measure, we can arrive at a number of combinations that form canonical strettos. Examples:

a)

Each of these combinations forms a canonical stretto of the subject and answer, complete in two parts.

(N.B. Note that the apparent 6/4 chords in these examples can be obviated by the addition of an appropriate part below them [¶297]. Observe, also, that repeated notes are treated as if they were suspensions.—F.D.)

296. More frequently, the subject cannot continue while the answer is being sounded, and the canon is, therefore, incomplete. This can be illustrated by use of the same answer at another place on the same subject.

Example:

It is obviously impossible here to continue the subject at the same time as the answer.

SUPPLEMENTARY HARMONIC PART

297. Certain subjects do not lend themselves to harmonic strettos, or can only do so by means of a supplementary harmonic part (¶295). The melody of this part should derive from the head of the subject.

298. Other subjects are only capable of producing canonical strettos if the answer is heard first. (See Inverse Canonical Strettos, ¶287). Others may lend themselves to both inverse and normal strettos.

Here are two inverse canonical strettos made from the subject given in ¶294. Note that they can only be used if the first is in at least three parts, and the second in four parts with the answer in the bass and the subject in the soprano:

It should be understood that the parts added here are for the purpose of indicating the possible harmony of the passage, and that alternatives exist.

299. The following subject, by Johann Sebastian Bach, is capable of producing both normal and inverse canonical strettos, complete in two parts:

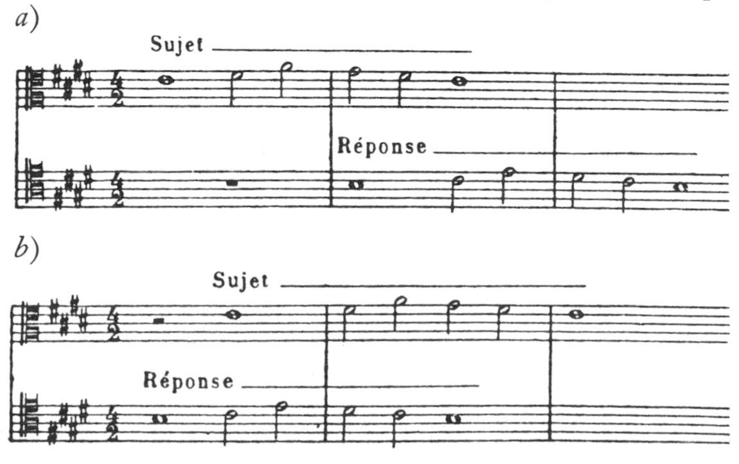

300. In addition to canonical and inverse strettos with the answer, a subject may be able to produce canons with itself at various intervals (¶293). Every subject (and answer) should be analyzed from this point of view, by trying it in canon at every interval and at all distances from the head of the subject or answer.

Frequently the latter, because of the changes brought about by mutation, differs sufficiently from the subject to lend itself to special canonical combinations.

301. Continuing our analysis of the subject in ¶294, we find that it affords the following additional canons:

a) Canon with the subject at the fifth below:

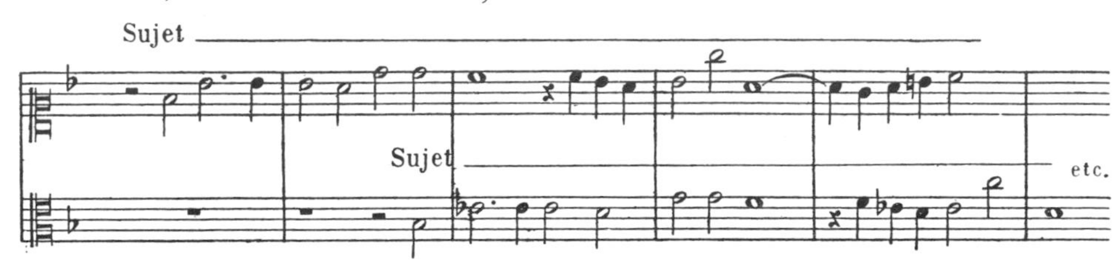

b) Canon with the subject at the octave above:

c) Canon with the subject at the seventh below:

d) Canon, answer with answer, at the sixth below:

e) Canon, subject with answer, at the sixth above:

302. Regarding the above strettos, it should be pointed out that:

1. Since the answer may enter at any harmonically practicable distance from the head of the subject, its strong and weak beats need not necessarily coincide with those of the melody of the subject, as was the rule in the exposition.

2. Canons at various intervals necessarily imply that modulation to related keys and, briefly, to distant keys, is permitted in the stretto.

3. Sometimes frequent changes of accidentals may be necessary, (¶301, last measure of the subject in [*b*] and [*c*]).

4. Stretto (*e*) in ¶301 is on the off beat. Formerly, theoreticians attached the utmost importance to this form of stretto, and considered it absolutely indispensable to a fugue since it is the most closely knit possible. With modern subjects it is seldom practicable, but when opportunity arises it should be used.

303. All strettos hitherto cited have been in two parts. The same analysis should be made in three and four parts, and in more if the number of voices permits. Very few subjects, however, admit of being so handled.

Equidistant Entries

304. In strettos of more than two parts, the voices must enter at a distance equal to that which first separated the answer from the head of the subject when it entered in the stretto.

This rule holds absolutely in the first and last strettos. In others, entries at variable distances are tolerated.

305. When the subject and answer cannot be canonically combined in four voices—and this is nearly always the case—the subject must be quitted at the first entry of the answer.

In this event (see ¶288–¶292), the part occupied by the subject continues in a counterpoint which resembles, as much as possible, the omitted fragment, to avoid giving the impression of a sudden stoppage of the theme in that part. If this is impractical, the countersubject should be used in a similar attempt to combine it with the answer. This part of the fugue requires considerable work and ingenuity.

Preparatory Arrangements of a Four-Part Stretto

306. To establish a four-part stretto of the subject studied in ¶294 above, we turn again to the combinations which we have established in two parts.

The following plans serve to indicate ways of preparing four-part strettos, and are not to be considered final. All of them are in the principal key of the subject. In view of their number, it is doubtful that all could be used. Nevertheless, it is essential that preparatory work of this nature be always as complete as possible. (N.B. One never knows what might turn up. The greater the number planned, the greater the choice.—F.D.)

Here, then, are arrangements in four parts of the examples given previously:

1. (¶295 *a*):

2. (¶295 *b*):

Sujet
Réponse
Sujet

etc.
etc.
Réponse

3. (¶295 *c*):

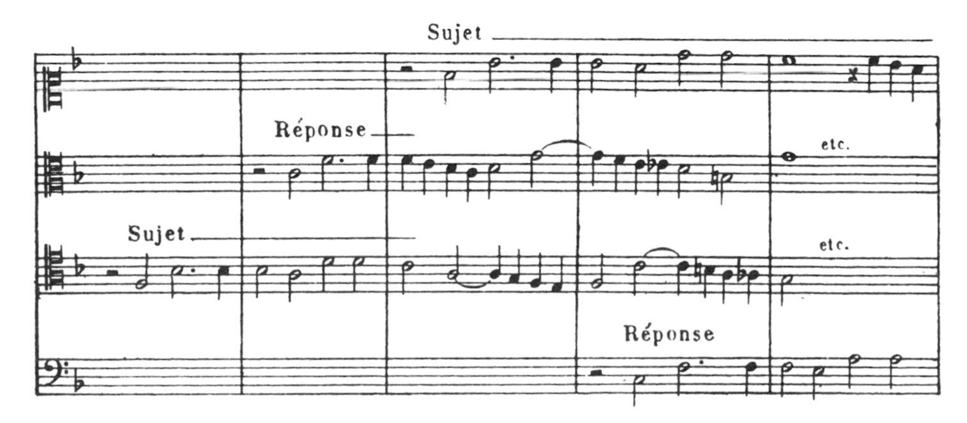
Sujet
Réponse
etc.
Sujet
etc.
Réponse

4. (¶295 *d*):

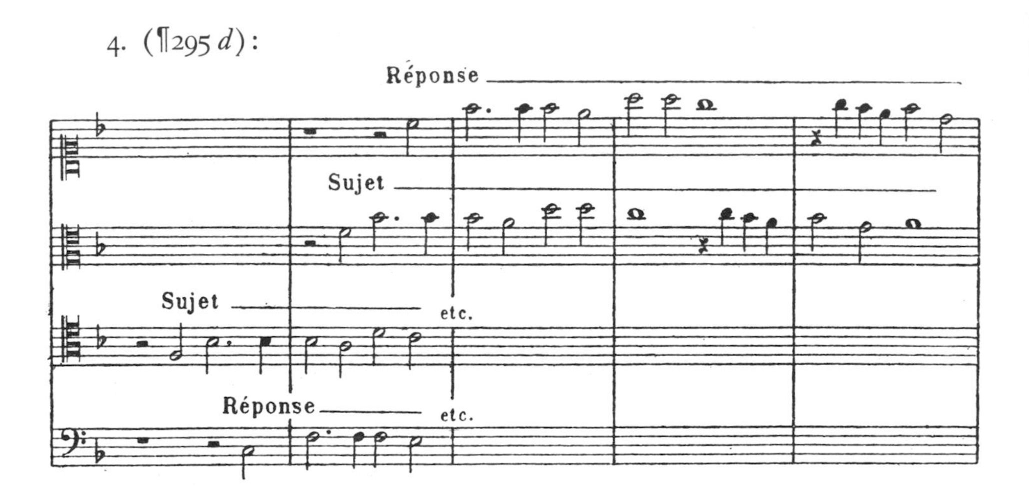
Réponse
Sujet
Sujet
etc.
Réponse
etc.

5. (¶296):

Sujet
etc.
Réponse
Sujet

6. (¶299 *a*):

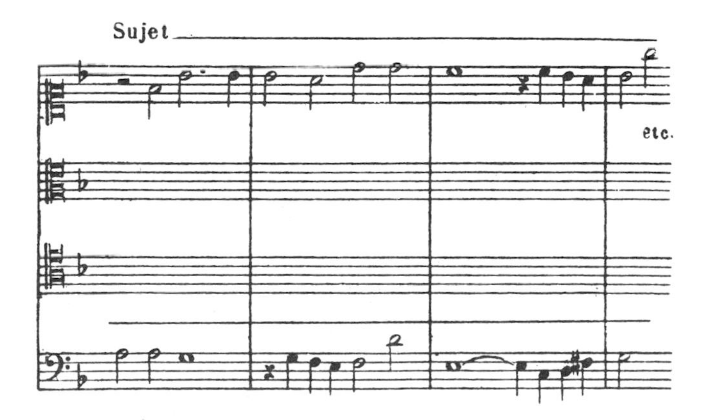

7. (¶200 *b*):

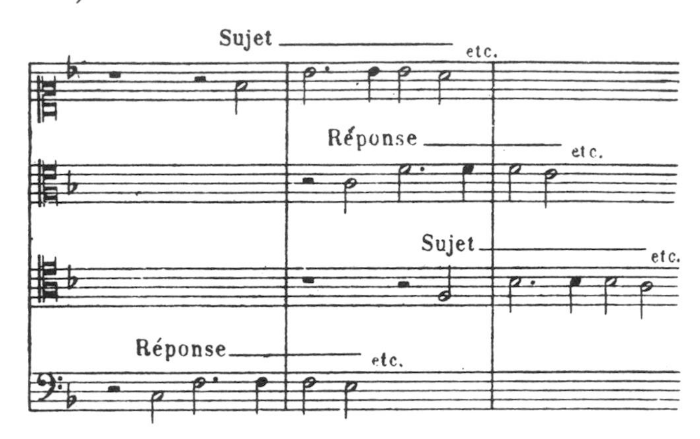

Interruption of Subject and Answer

307. All the strettos given in ¶306 are considered canonical strettos, or true strettos, even though the entries are not always complete. From this we conclude:

In a stretto, the successive entries may include only the first measure, or even the first notes of the subject or answer, always excepting the last entry where the subject or answer must be heard complete.

308. In practice, strettos other than the first and last are generally treated freely, so as not uselessly to prolong the fugue. This is especially the case when the subject is long, or when it is incapable of generating different canonical strettos in several parts.

Asymmetrical Entries in the Stretto

309. The examples that follow show how the preparatory arrangements in ¶306 may be made in strettos having non-equidistant entries.

Here is an inverse stretto; it is the working-out in four parts of the example given in ¶299 (*b*):

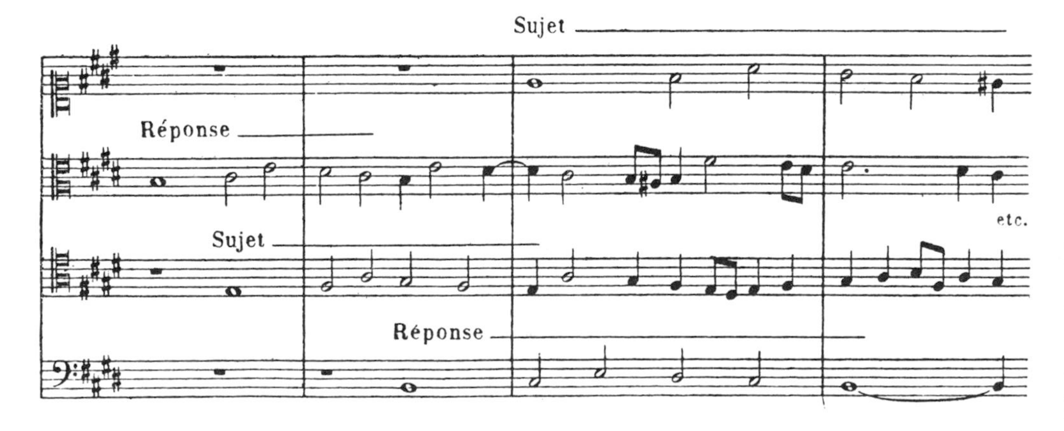

310. In this case, though there is asymmetry in the ensemble, the entries are made two by two at equal distances. This is the preferred arrangement when writing asymmetrical strettos.

It will be seen later that numerous examples of this sort of arrangement are to be found in the works of Bach, Handel, Mozart, and Mendelssohn, who use it as a special sort of fugue.

311. The following stretto, developed from the stretto given in ¶301 (*e*), on the off beat, shows how tightly the subject and answer may be woven together in the different parts. Strettos of this tightness are generally reserved for the ending of the fugue:

312. In the above example, the bass could have presented the answer without any change, but it appeared advisable to modify it at the third measure to get a more logical final cadence.

Indeed, if the working out of the canon in four parts were strict from the third measure on, its tonality would be carried into B-flat major and G minor:

Note that in this canon, arranged with unvaried intervals in all the parts, it was necessary on two occasions to flat the E of the answer in the alto.

By this, modulation was made to the key of the subdominant. Therefore, to end the fugue properly in its principal key, the entire canon should have been transposed a fourth lower or a fifth higher. In the next chapter it will be shown how such arrangements can be serviceable in bringing about the pedal point on the dominant which immediately precedes the conclusion of the fugue.

Classification of Strettos

313. The name "stretto" is generally reserved in the scholastic fugue for close imitations, canonical or not, of the subject and answer at their normal intervals (the fifth above or the fourth below) in neighboring keys as well as in the principal key. All other combinations of this sort are called "canons" or "close imitations."

Strettos of the Countersubject

314. However, the comparable work that must be done with the countersubject also passes under the name of "stretto." The various strettos and canons that the countersubject may give in four parts, either alone or combined in the strettos of the subject and answer, must be investigated. Procedure should be based on the above examples.

Combined Strettos of Subject and Countersubject

315. Interesting combinations may be worked out by introducing the countersubject into the strettos of the subject and answer. This can be done either by presenting it in one part during the successive entries of subject and answer in the others, or, which is most desirable, by means of a double canon with the canon of the subject.

Note that this is feasible only with short subjects and, therefore, short countersubjects. Examples follow:

a) Johann Sebastian Bach, *Well-Tempered Clavier,* Fugue XXXIII:

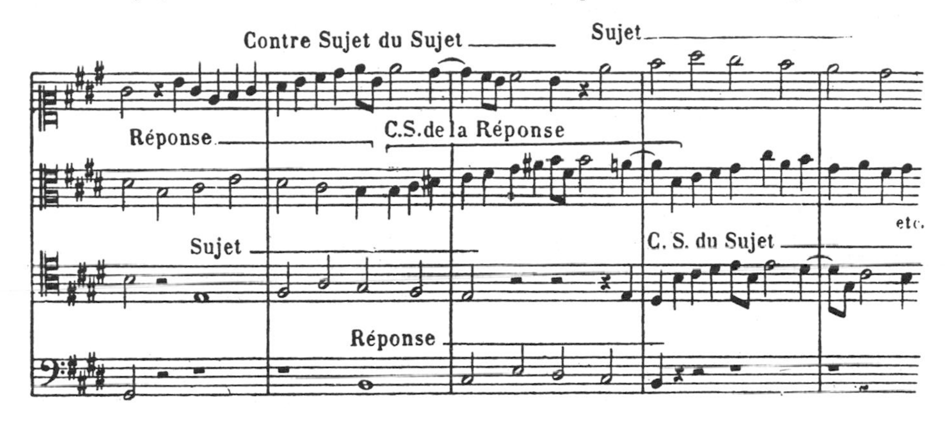

b) *Ibid.,* Fugue IV:

316. In example (*a*) above, the countersubject of the subject is heard in its entirety on a canon of the answer and the subject; it ends at the third entry, while the countersubject of the answer which began on the third beat of the second measure is being heard. If Bach had written the two last entries at the same distance as the first two, that is, half a measure apart, he would have had to interrupt the countersubject of the answer.

Example (*b*) illustrates a combination of close stretto of the subject with stretto of the countersubject. It may be considered typical, and should be consulted when constructing a stretto with the heads of the subject and the countersubject. Note the canonical stretto of the subject in which imitations of a fragment of the countersubject are likewise canonical.

Stretto in Contrary Movement

317. The subject may be taken in contrary movement, as may the answer and the countersubject, to construct strettos in contrary movement. Examples follow:

a) Johann Sebastian Bach, *Well-Tempered Clavier,* Fugue XLVI—Stretto in Canon in Contrary Movement at the Seventh below.

b) *Ibid.,* Fugue VIII—Canon in Three Parts at the Octave.

318. In (*a*) above, the two parts not involved in the canon are not written haphazardly, but are designed to participate intimately in the ensemble of the stretto. All the phrases of which they are composed are taken from the subject or other fragments of the exposition treated in real or rhythmic imitation.

Note at I in the soprano, imitation on the off beat with the subject; at II, fragment of the subject in direct movement; at III, fragment of a free part of the exposition; at IV, rhythmic imitation of the end of the subject; at VIII, rhythmic imitation of the end of the subject in direct movement.

The tenor begins at V by a rhythmic imitation of the third measure of the subject. At VI it presents a rhythm that the soprano takes up at IV in contrary movement; at VII there is a rhythmic imitation of the second phrase of the subject in direct movement.

(N.B. Instances of this sort of fine craftsmanship could be cited throughout the works of Bach, Mozart, etc. It is this sort of workmanship that gives coherence, unity, and variety to their greatest achievements, whether in fugue or in free composition. In fact what was said in ¶246 cannot be repeated too often: It is in their masterpieces in free style that we see the practical application of the devices of fugal composition. And in that resides the main reason for the profound study of fugue.—F.D.)

Stretto in Direct and Contrary Movement

319. A stretto may also be written in contrary movement in some parts and in direct movement in others. Examples follow:

a) Johann Sebastian Bach, *Well-Tempered Cluvier,* Fugue XLVI—Canon at the Sixth below in Contrary Movement:

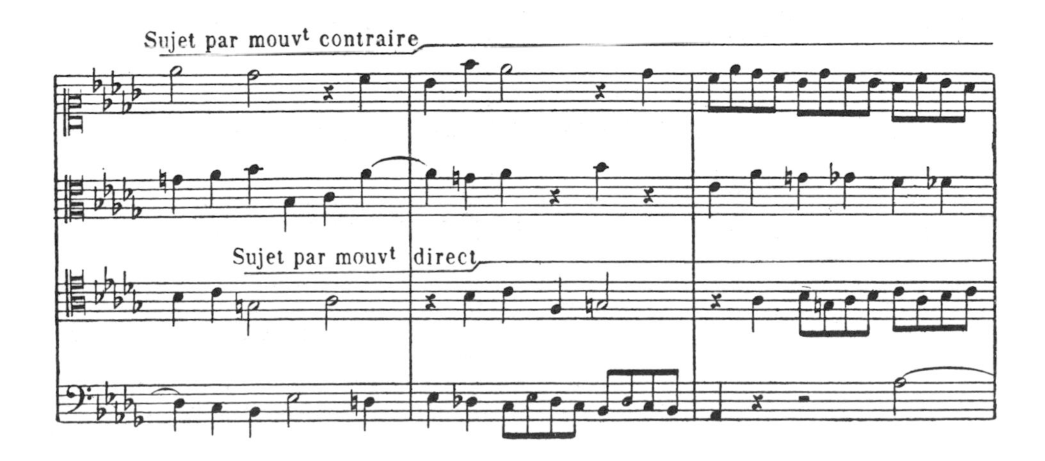

b) Johann Sebastian Bach, Organ Fugue in C Major—Subject in Contrary, Answer in Direct Movement:

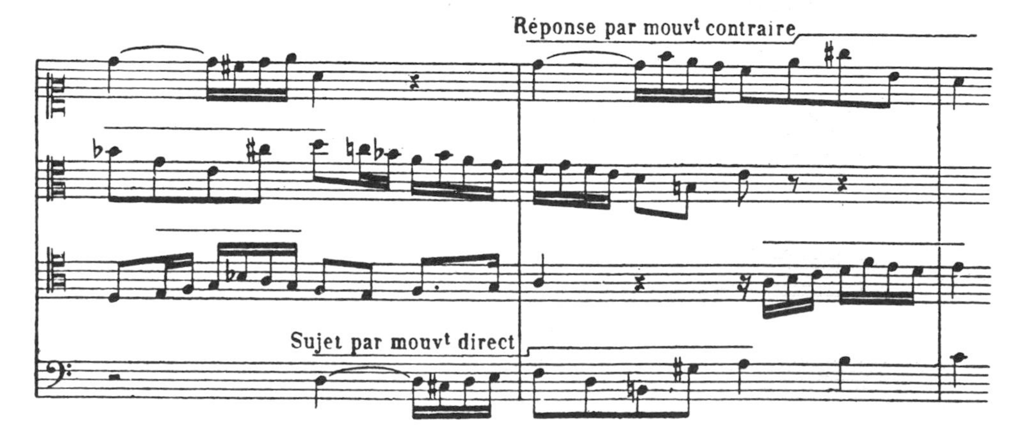

320. The same remarks as in ¶318 may be made about the writing of these examples. In analyzing example (*a*), the student should refer to ¶196 and following.

In (*b*), it will be noticed that the four entries are alternately equidistant, two by two.The first part of the stretto is composed of combinations of the subject in contrary movement with the answer in direct movement. One fragment,

which repeats continually, and is heard successively in all the parts, consists of a distortion of the answer in either direct or contrary movement.

Stretto in Diminution

321. Use of diminution is frequent in strettos. Not only do most subjects lend themselves to diminution, but the device has the further advantage of bringing about extremely closely spaced entries even if the subject is heard in its entirety.

It is used in both direct and contrary movement.

322. The following from a Bach fugue already cited, Fugue XXXIII of the *Well-Tempered Clavier,* affords an excellent example of a stretto in which all the parts are treated in diminution:

323. However, more variety can be given to a stretto by placing phrases in diminution in opposition to the original values of the subject, and, further to increase the contrast, by simultaneously employing both direct and contrary movement.

The sixth fugue in Johann Sebastian Bach's *Art of the Fugue* presents a series of strettos based on combinations of this sort, of which the outline is given below.

The student should write out the entire fugue in four parts, the better to analyze its construction both from the special point of view of this paragraph, and from that of the style of writing and the general management of the parts.

It is quite certain that very few fugal subjects will lend themselves to as many combinations. However, it frequently happens that this sort of analysis uncovers potentialities in subjects that are not visible at first sight.

The subject of Bach's fugue in its original form is as follows:

a)

b)

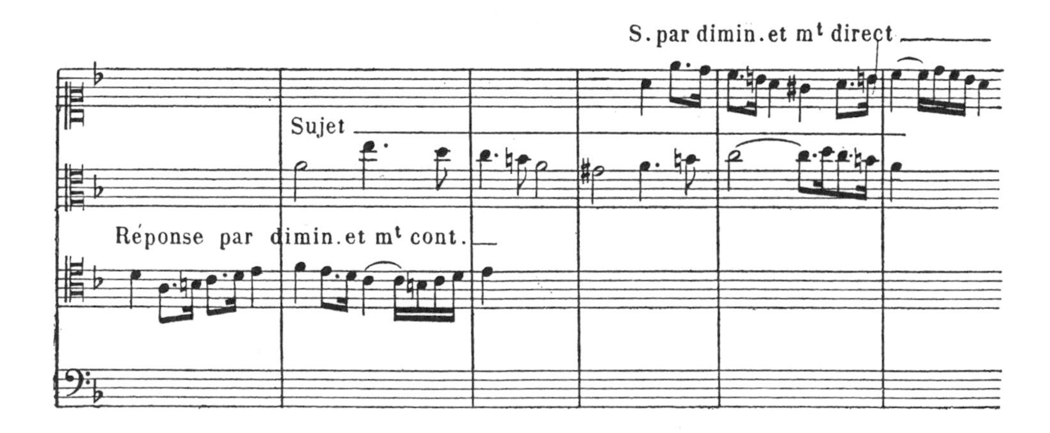

c)

S. par dimin. et m^t cont.
Sujet
S. par dimin. et m^t cont.
etc.

d)

Sujet par m^t cont.
S. par dimin. et m^t cont.
S. par dimin. et m^t direct

e)

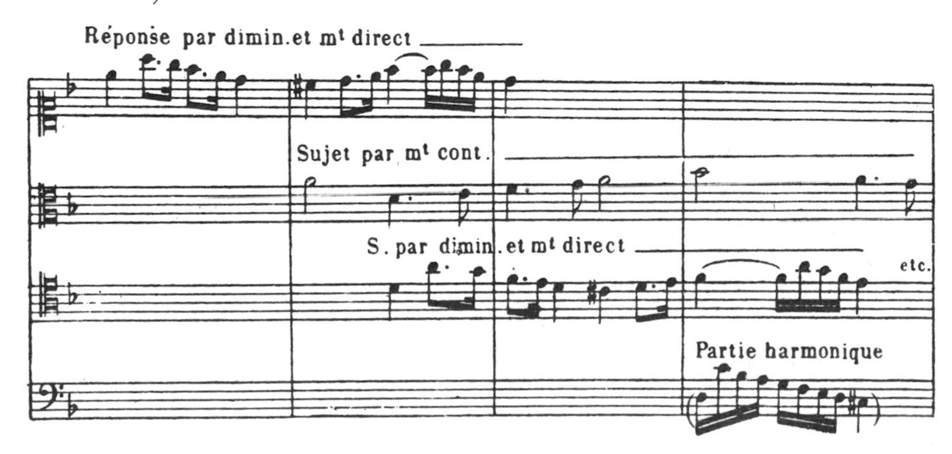
Réponse par dimin. et m^t direct
Sujet par m^t cont.
S. par dimin. et m^t direct
etc.
Partie harmonique

f)

Sujet par m^t cont.
S. par dimin. et m^t direct
etc.
S. par dimin. et m^t direct
(notes harmoniques)

g)

Sujet par m^t contraire
S. par dimin. et m^t direct
Réponse par dimin. et m^t direct

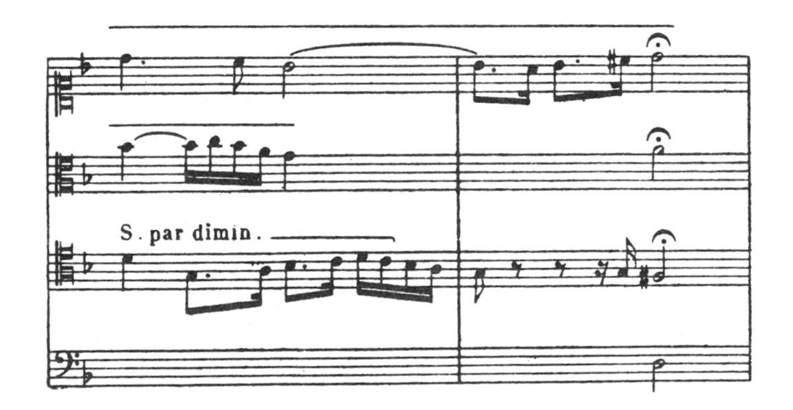
S. par dimin.

324. In these examples we have extracted the elements of the strettos and have eliminated the subordinate parts, the better to illustrate the procedure and to show the student how to investigate combinations of this sort. We have confined ourselves to giving, when necessary, the fundamental harmonies used by Bach.

325. The student should, by this time, have had sufficient practice to make his own analysis of the examples in ¶323. However, here are a few of the more interesting points in these remarkable combinations:

In examples (*a*), (*b*), and (*c*) the subject is intact. In (*a*) the diminished subject forms a canon in direct and contrary movement in diminution with the subject in its original form.

Example (*b*) begins with the answer in diminution. In (*c*), the canon formed by the diminished subject is in contrary movement with the original subject.

Examples (*d*) and (*e*) show, respectively, the opposite of the arrangements in (*a*) and (*b*). Whatever was in direct movement in the first is in contrary movement in the second, and vice versa.

The same relationship exists between examples (*c*) and (*f*), save that the canons do not begin at the same distance from the head of the subject, and are not at the same interval.

Finally, example (*g*) reproduces at different intervals the same arrangement as (*f*). In (*g*) the tenor sounds the head of the subject in diminution in the penultimate measure.

Stretto in Augmentation

326. As opposed to diminution, the effect of augmentation is to separate the entries. Therefore, it is used in the stretto solely as a contrasting element designed to make more effective the sudden entries of the subject in different parts, either in its original form or in diminution.

327. Because of the nature of augmentation, it can generally be used only in one part, or, at most, in two, and in that case only when the augmented subject lends itself to a double canon with the original, which seldom happens. In using augmentation there is always the danger that it may detract from the musical interest of the fugue by slowing it up or relaxing it—a capital defect at the intended climax of the fugue.

328. In certain strettos the augmented subject can be combined only with close imitations of the heads of the subject and answer in their original form.

The subject analyzed in ¶295–¶298 is capable of making the following combinations of this sort:

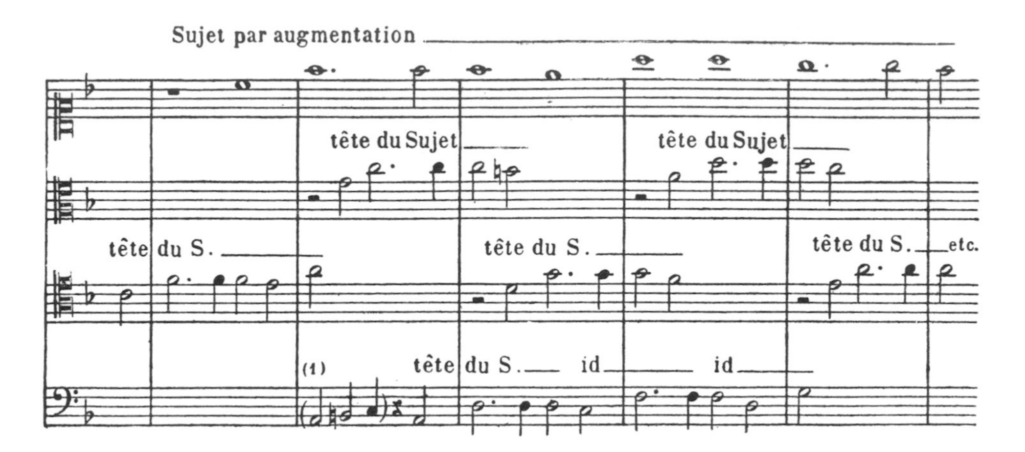

329. It can be seen that an infinite number of this kind of arrangement can be made according to the devices that are feasible, such as modifying the subject and answer, use of diminution with contrary or retrograde movement, etc.

Canonic Stretto in Direct and Contrary Movement, and in Augmentation

330. When the subject permits it, one can, while the subject is presented in augmentation, make canons in the other parts in direct or contrary movement using the subject or answer in their original values. The works of Bach, Mozart, Handel, etc. offer many examples of this sort. Here are two, taken from Bach:

a) *Well-Tempered Clavier,* Fugue XXVI:

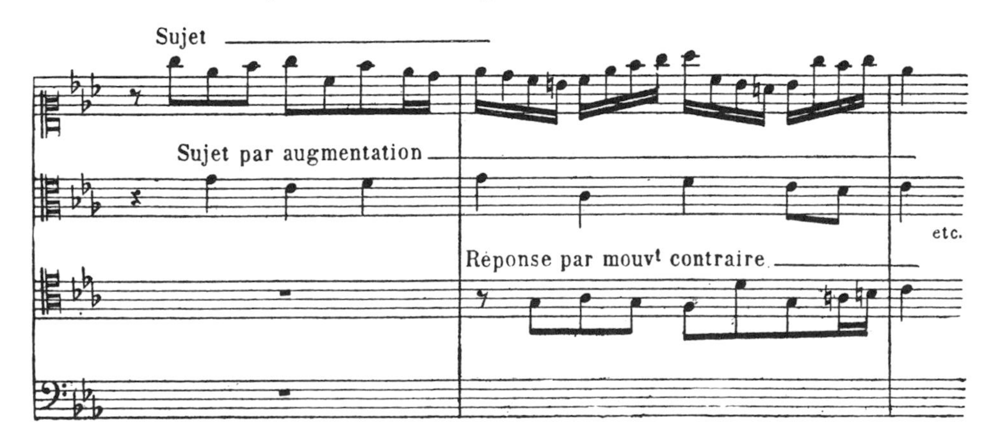

b) Fugue for Organ in C major:

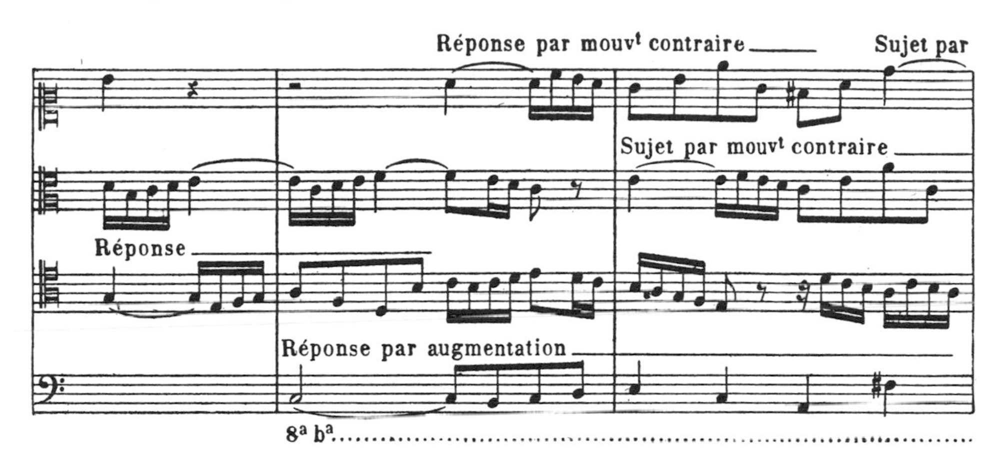

Stretto in Combined Augmentation and Diminution

331. The seventh fugue of the *Art of the Fugue* is based entirely on the use of augmentation of the subject combined with either the subject in its original form or the subject diminished in direct or contrary movement. This fugue should be copied into four vocal parts, and studied as a whole. Here are several fragments of it.

It is made on the following subject:

a)

Sujet augmenté
Sujet(par mouvt contraire)

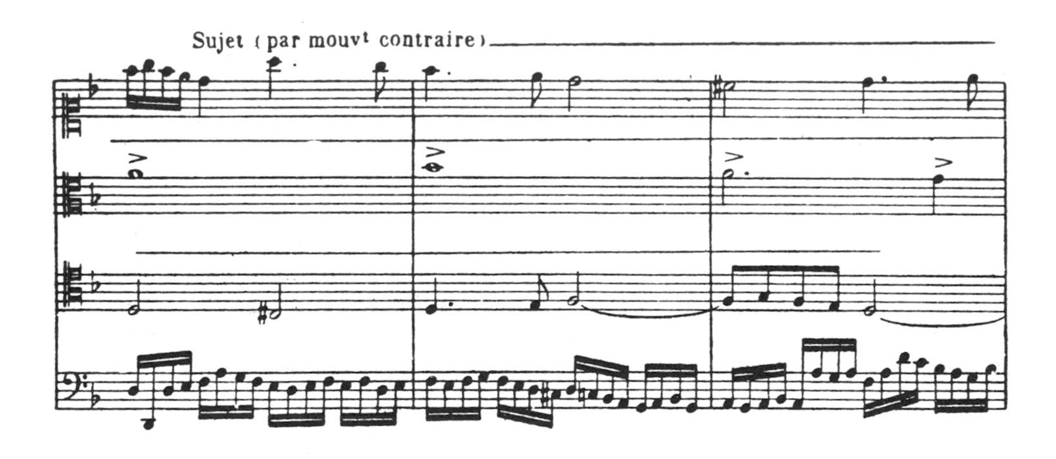
Sujet (par mouvt contraire)

Sujet diminué
etc.
Sujet diminué
etc

b)

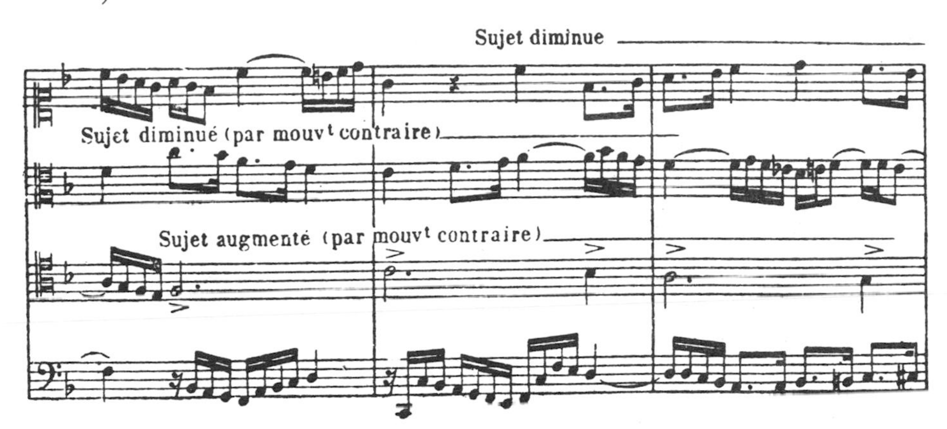
Sujet diminue
Sujet diminué (par mouvt contraire)
Sujet augmenté (par mouvt contraire)

Sujet diminué (par mouvt

Sujet diminué (par mouvt contraire)
etc.
contraire)

In (*a*), the augmented subject is accompanied in two parts by a canon at the octave with the original subject; the fourth part is borrowed entirely from the diminished subject.

In (b), three parts present strettos and fragments of the subject in diminution, while the subject is treated in augmentation in contrary movement.

Stretto in Retrograde Movement

332. Of all the devices possible to a stretto, retrograde movement, either direct or contrary, is employed least frequently, as few subjects can undergo it without becoming completely unrecognizable.

This sort of combination, wherever used, may be treated in the same way as the preceding.

The examples given in ¶249 may be taken as strettos in which the subject is heard simultaneously in its original form, and in direct and contrary retrograde movement.

333. All the combinations that can enter into the stretto section are described above. Although, in most cases, all cannot be used, they should be investigated with the greatest care before writing the fugue.

334. Before showing how to proceed with previously discussed material in the construction of the stretto section of a fugue, we must take up another contrapuntal device which is more or less obligatory in the scholastic fugue. This is the organ point or pedal point.

Exercises

The student should now investigate all possible canonical combinations necessary to the construction of strettos. He should make a complete working analysis of the material of each fugue. This should comprise:

a) Subject fragmented in direct, contrary, diminished, augmented, and retrograde movement, etc.

b) Answer similarly treated.

c) Countersubjects of subject and answer treated likewise.

d) Canonical imitations investigated between: subject and answer; subject and subject; answer and answer; countersubject and countersubject of the answer; countersubjects with themselves; all of these at every interval.

The amount of material available by this method is enormous. Its choice and arrangement will demonstrate the gifts of the composer.

X

THE PEDAL POINT

Definitions

335. The "pedal point" of the fugue takes its name from the harmonic device on which it is based. It consists of sustaining during a number of measures the same note in one of more parts.

336. The pedal point may be single or multiple. It is generally made on the dominant or tonic, although, in exceptional cases, it may be made on any degree of the scale.

Harmonic Rules Governing the Pedal Point

337. The harmonic rules governing the pedal point are the same in fugue as in harmony: it can only begin and end on a consonance; it must enter as a consonant part of a harmony, and can only be quitted as if it were a consonance. (It may, of course, be ended in the bass when dissonances, prepared or otherwise, exist in the upper voices, assuming it originally was part of a consonant harmony.)

In certain cases, the pedal point on the dominant may terminate when it forms a prepared dissonance, normally resolved.

As soon as it is heard, the pedal point becomes a note foreign to the harmonies of all the other parts, and, in consequence, can form any number of unprepared dissonances with them.

Role of the Pedal Point

338. One of the great advantages of placing the pedal point on the tonic or the dominant is that this enables the composer, while affirming the principal key of the fugue, to sound at the same time various neighboring keys. It therefore binds tighter the threads of the fugue and revives its interest.

339. This property of the pedal point permits its use as preparation for the first entries of the stretto section if it be placed immediately before the first stretto, as we shall see in the next chapter. In this situation, it is almost always heard in the dominant. The pedal point on the tonic, however, is always reserved

for the conclusion of the fugue.

340. The order of frequency in which the pedal point is placed in the different parts is, first, the bass, where it is called the "inferior" pedal point; second, the highest part, called the "superior" pedal point; third, an inner part, called the "inner" pedal point.

Double Pedal Point

341. The pedal point may also be doubled, either in the same part (generally the bass), or in the two outer parts. In the latter case, the pedal point of the tonic and the dominant may be used simultaneously, or either may be doubled.

Place of the Pedal Point

342. The arrangement of the other parts may be varied in conformity with the place in the fugue where the pedal point is first heard. If the pedal point is placed before the stretto section, it may take the place of an episode, or the episode may proceed on the pedal point. If it is used at the end of the stretto section, it will introduce various close strettos, canonical or otherwise.

343. As the pedal point is the part of the fugue in which the greatest liberty is permitted, it is impossible to formulate strict rules for it. The ways of treating it depend on the ingenuity of the composer. It should, however, be said that all the kinds of episodes hitherto studied, as well as strettos, may be used with a pedal point.

344. The important thing is that it be brought in musically and naturally. The listener must be made, somehow, to feel it coming. Although this is impossible to define, it does pave the way, when properly handled, for the end of the fugue if on the dominant; if on the tonic, it sets forth the conclusion itself.

345. Without laboring this point, to which we will return later, we will give a few models of the different kinds of pedal points.

The following pedal point on the dominant is an example of an episode constructed on a pedal point in which each part imitates itself. It is, moreover, one of the kinds of combination most frequently used, as it permits the closest diatonic or chromatic harmonic sequences as preparation for the close contrapuntal arrangements of the stretto.

Example—Episode Introducing the Pedal Point—Johann Sebastian Bach, *Art of the Fugue,* Fugue VIII:

346. In the following, a free stretto in three parts is established on the pedal point in the dominant. It ends, like the preceding, in a sequence in which each part imitates itself.

Example (Felix Mendelssohn, Organ Fugue, Opus 37, Number 3):

347. Here is an admirable example of a pedal point on the tonic on which a double stretto in direct and contrary movement is constructed. This is the ending of Bach's great Organ Fugue in C major which we have already cited on several occasions.

It will be noticed that though the fugue is written in four voices, the pedal point is treated in five. This additional voice is likewise permitted in the scholastic fugue to create a more ample sonority at the end of the fugue. Furthermore, the different combinations of strettos may require a fifth part.

In certain cases of the double pedal point, six-part writing is both necessary and permitted temporarily in a four-voiced scholastic fugue. Examples will be given later.

348. The end of the G major organ fugue by Bach, also previously cited, presents an example of pedal point on the tonic in the highest part which is joined in the last three measures by another pedal point on the tonic in the bass.

Ornamented Pedal Point

349. Sometimes, instead of sustaining a single note, the pedal point repeats it rhythmically, or in a melodic pattern that repeats at regular intervals. This is called an "ornamented" pedal point.

The rhythm or pattern is always borrowed from a characteristic figure in the subject or countersubject, or an analogous rhythm or pattern.

350. The following are diverse models which have been varied according to the inclination of the composer. In (*a*), the inner pedal point on the tonic is rhythmically ornamented by the leading note. In (*b*), the pedal point in the bass presents a rhythm analogous to that of the principal theme. In (*c*), the pedal point is on the second degree of the principal key; it is first ornamented by its upper neighboring note, and, at the second measure, by a trill. In (*d*), the alternation of the tonic with notes of the scale in sixteenth notes is frequently used in fugues for piano and organ. In (*e*), a rhythm alternates with that of the principal figure. In (*f*), the pedal point is complex: It is, at first, double, one sustained, the other ornamented with a rhythm taken from the countersubject; then it becomes an inner pedal point. In (*g*), the pedal point imitates the rhythm of a fragment of the subject.

a) Johann Sebastian Bach, Organ Fugue in C major:

b) Johann Sebastian Bach, Organ Prelude in F minor:

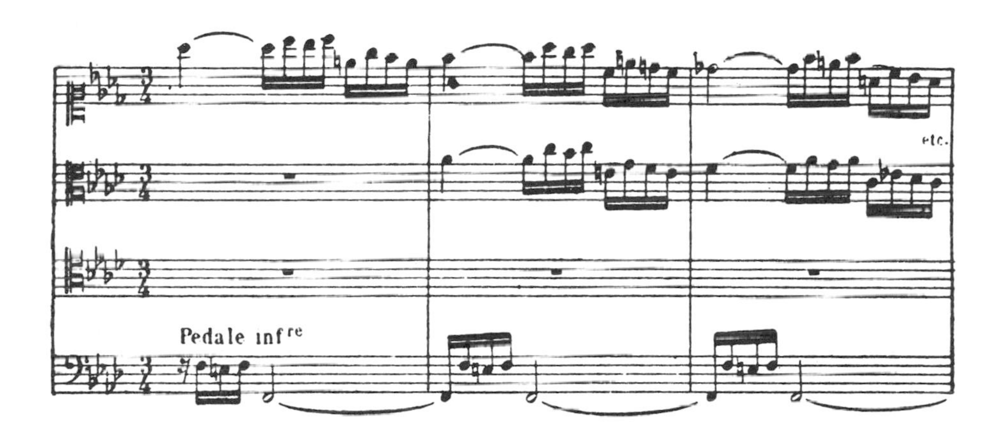

c) Johann Sebastian Bach, Organ Fugue in D minor:

d) Johann Sebastian Bach, Organ Fugue in B minor:

e) *Ibid.,* Prelude:

f) Robert Schumann, Sixth Fugue on the Name of "Bach":

g) Felix Mendelssohn, String Quartet, Opus 81:

Multiple Ornamented Pedal Point

351. In Bach's Organ Passacaglia in C minor, there is an interesting arrangement of ornamented single, double, and quadruple pedal points forming rhythmic imitations. This passage, though not, strictly speaking, fugal, is given to draw the student's attention to the possibilities of ornamented pedal points.

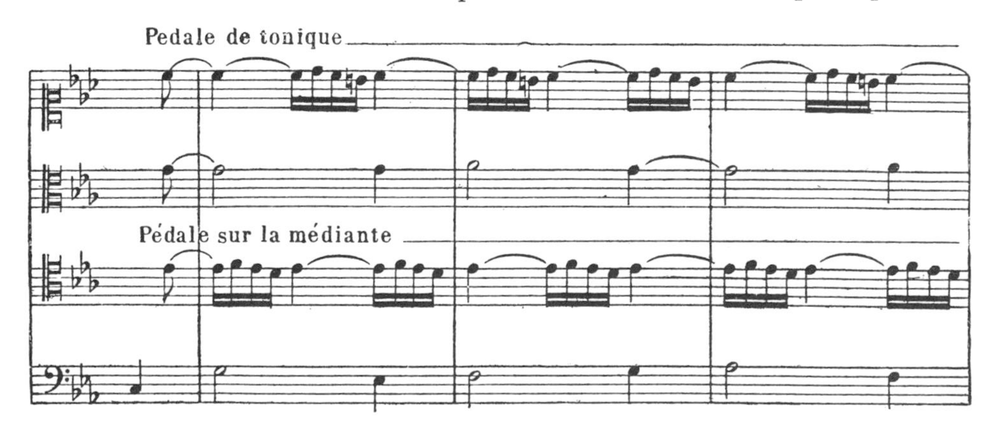

352. An interesting combination, applicable to the scholastic fugue though not written in strict style, is found in the fugue of Beethoven's Ninth String Quartet, in which the pedal point enters successively in the three upper parts:

353. The student should analyze carefully the plan of the melodic and harmonic line of themes, and the arrangement of imitations in the above, proceeding as before in his analysis of episodes and strettos.

354. With this, we conclude our analysis of the elements of a fugue.

Exercises

Continue to bring forward the construction of the fugues already started, which by now should number several dozen. Material should be brought up to the beginning of the stretto section, and should be fully analyzed and strettos tentatively arranged. However, it would be wise to wait until after the next chapter, on the stretto section, before continuing further, as, in it, the arrangements of strettos and pedal points are more fully explored.

XI

CONSTRUCTION OF THE STRETTO SECTION

355. In the stretto section of the fugue, only the first and last strettos should present the same general arrangement.

356. Both must belong to the principal key of the fugue; they must both be composed of four entries, of which the last alone must sound the principal theme (subject or answer) in its entirety.

However, the first and last strettos differ in the arrangement of the entries of the principal theme: these must be closer in the last stretto.

357. All the other strettos that make up the stretto section vary according to the nature of the subject. The modulations and number of entries are not fixed.

358. Theoretically, the stretto section should be composed solely of an uninterrupted succession of canons of the subject and answer, canons that become more and more condensed as the fugue approaches its end.

In practice, it is rarely thus. Few subjects lend themselves to numerous canonical combinations, and, therefore, other devices must be used to supplement this lack.

359. The different ways of constructing a stretto section may be summarized as follows:

I. Canonical entries of subject and answer continue without interruption.

II. Strettos of subject and answer are connected by strettos of the countersubject(s).

III. Strettos of the subject and answer are connected by episodes.

Each of these will be studied separately.

360. I: Canons of the subject and answer continue without interruption.

a) A first stretto, composed of four entries, is written as explained in ¶283 and following.

b) Immediately after the first stretto, a second is begun, followed without interruption by a third, and so on to the end of the fugue.

To avoid monotony, the successive entries may modulate to neighboring keys. The principal key, however, should always be kept in mind when setting up these modulations, lest one stray too far.

Example—Johann Sebastian Bach, *Well-Tempered Clavier,* Fugue I:

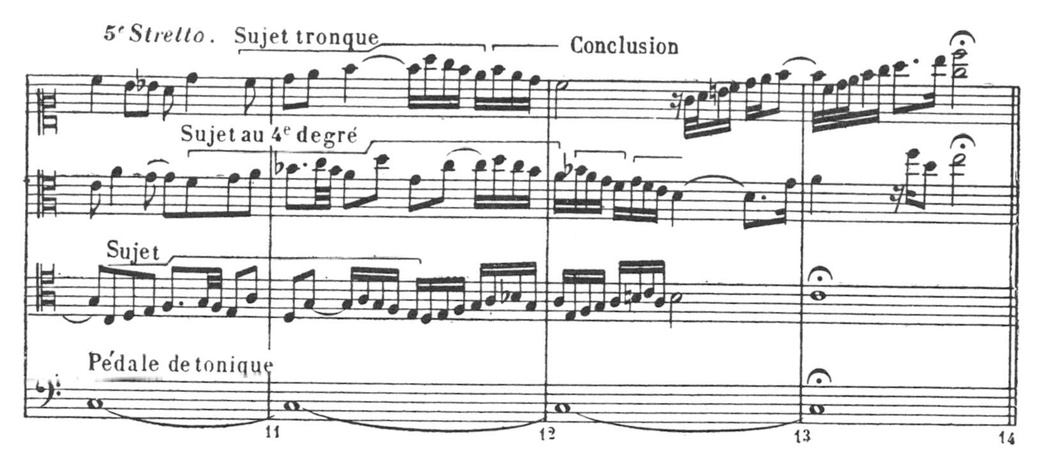

361. Always remember that, as we have repeatedly stated, examples borrowed from the works of the masters do not follow all the conventions of the scholastic fugue. They are, therefore, to be regarded not so much as models as the best examples of writing in the fugal style.

What should be avoided by the student are the empty formulas, full of banalities, which are often encountered in the scholastic fugue, and which have nothing in common with art. Even in using the stiff and conventional framework of the scholastic fugue we ought to make music, for that should always be the goal of the musician.

362. In the above example of Bach, the following rules of the scholastic fugue are broken:

a) The first stretto consists of a single entry of the subject, followed by three of the answer.

b) The four entries are at unequal distances from the head of the subject.

c) The last stretto has only three entries instead of four.

d) The strettos follow no order in the closeness of the entries.

363. In fact, analogies with the scholastic fugue are few in number in this example. They are limited to the short pedal point on the dominant (measures 7 to 8), separated by two entries from the pedal point on the tonic on which the fugue ends.

Nevertheless, this example should be profoundly considered. It is a perfect model of the *style* of the stretto, and the perfection of style should inspire the student in his work, even as he avoids the liberties of writing and form that Bach could permit himself, but which would be out of place in a classroom.

Alternate Strettos of Subject and Countersubject

364. II: The strettos of the subject and answer are separated by strettos of

the countersubject(s).

On the completion of the first stretto of subject and answer in four compulsory entries, the first stretto of the countersubject is made, which is followed immediately, in a neighboring key, by the second stretto of the subject. This second stretto is in two parts, canonical or otherwise. It is followed by another stretto of the countersubject and a third stretto of the subject, and so on to the end of the fugue.

365. The D-Major Fugue from the second book of the *Well-Tempered Clavier* is interesting and instructive in this connection. Here it is, complete and transcribed for four voices:

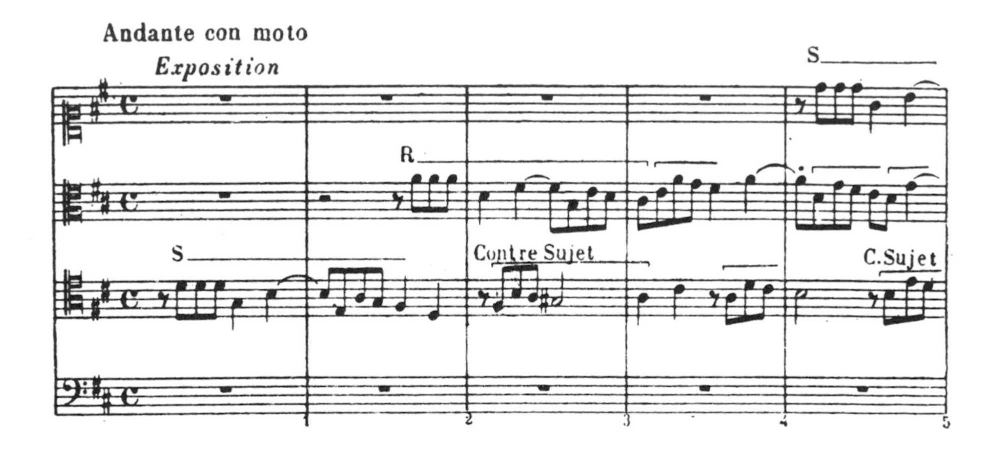

Rép. au 6e degré
Divertiss! II
1er Stretto (inverse)
Sujet
Réponse
11
12
13
14
15

Divertiss! III (2e Stretto du C.S.)
16
17
18
19
20

2e Stretto au 6e degré
R
C.Sujet
S
S
R
21
22
23
24
25

3e Stretto de la Rép.
Divert! IV
(3e Stretto du CS)
R
R
R
26
27
28
29
30

4e Stretto (du Sujet)
Divertiss! V
S
S
S
31
32
33
34
35

4e Stretto du C.S.
S
36
37
38
39
40

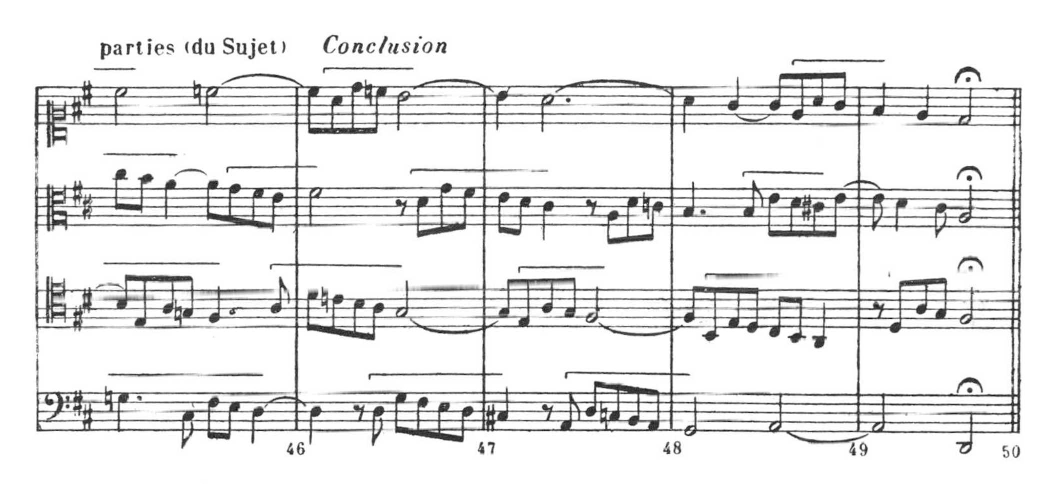

366. It should be noted at once that the countersubject of this fugue, which, moreover, is not written in invertible counterpoint, is taken from a fragment of the subject:

Since Bach has given it the character and function of a true countersubject, we should not consider it otherwise. The student should apply in the scholastic fugue the processes used by Bach in a freer style, taking into account the rules and principles of the scholastic fugue.

The construction of this fugue is clear enough for the student to make his own analysis.

367. Here, to compare, is another stretto on a subject whose possible com-

binations have already been studied at length (¶294 and following). Subject by André Gedalge:

2e Stretto (canon du Sujet au 3e degré)
S
S

2e Stretto canonique du C.S.
C.S.
C.S

3e Stretto canonique du S. au 2d degré
R
S

4e Stretto du Sujet (combiné avec le C.S. et le S. par augmentation)
S. augmenté
S
fr. du C.S.
S
S
S
fr. du C.S
C.S
S

Pédale sur la dominante
C.S
S
S
cresc.
dimin
S
S

S
S
S

368. By comparison with the analysis in ¶294 and following, it is apparent that by no means all the combinations of which this subject is capable have been used. It could have been more tightly written, using strettos of the subject and answer, and without making use of canons of the countersubject. The first stretto would have been improved had it been written in the form given in ¶306 (*b*), instead of by interrupted entries. And the last stretto would have had more interest had it been written as in ¶312–¶313. We have given it as above because it affords an interesting example of student's work.

Further analysis should be made of the above, and other strettos written on the same subject. The student should be guided by the analyses in Chapter IX.

Episodes of the Stretto Section

369. III: The strettos of the subject and answer are linked by episodes.

Whenever—and this is most frequently the case in the scholastic fugue—the subject does not lend itself to a number of canonical combinations sufficient for the uninterrupted succession of strettos of the subject or countersubject, it is customary to link the available strettos by episodes.

370. These episodes are combined in the same way as those that precede the stretto section, save that the themes must be short, and must be taken from the head of the subject, answer, or countersubject. Moreover, they must be written in canonical style, recalling that of a stretto; at least they must present continual overlapping entries of the various themes.

371. In these episodes one is free to use all the devices of direct, contrary, and retrograde movement, diminution, and augmentation. But it should be kept in mind that "the briefer the better" is the rule for these episodes. If too long, they would nullify the climactic interest of the stretto section, as the recurring entries of subject and answer would be too widely separated.

372. Moreover, consideration of the vast number of possible combinations of contrapuntal devices will show that in most cases it is not necessary greatly to rely on these episodes, since the over-all length of the stretto section need be no more than thirty to forty measures.

373. Here is another stretto from a scholastic fugue which includes two episodes based on the following subject and countersubject:

Stretto:

Réponse
6
7
8
9
10

14

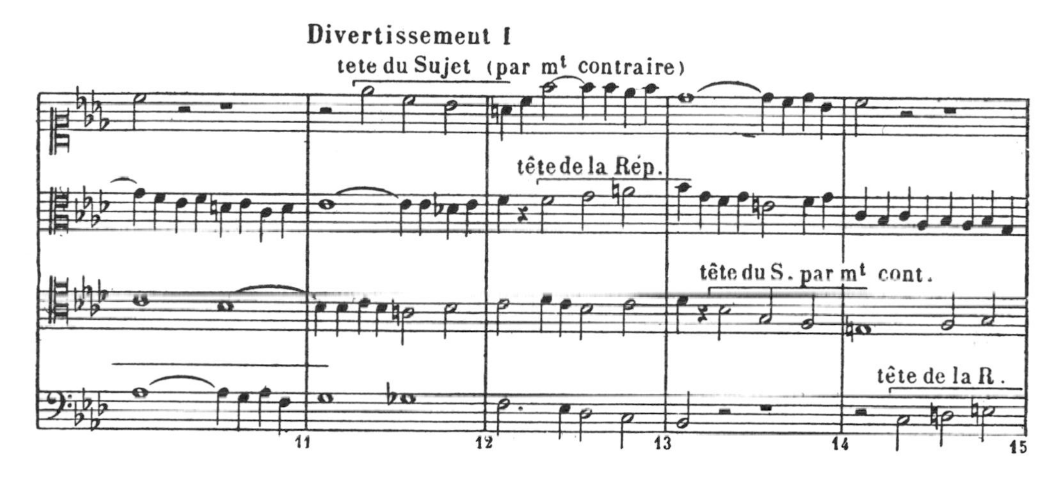
Divertissement I
tete du Sujet (par m^t contraire)
tête de la Rép.
tête du S. par m^t cont.
tête de la R.
11
12
13
14
15

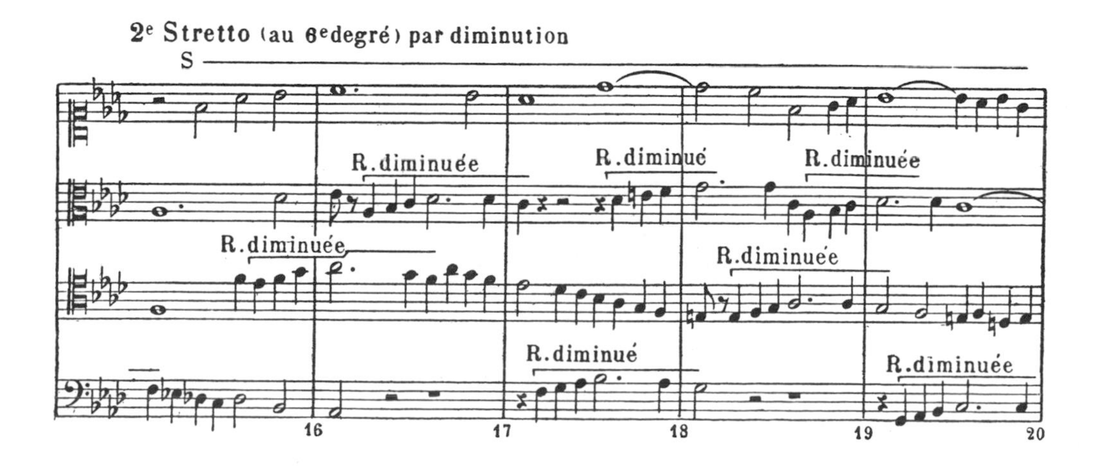
2e Stretto (au 6e degré) par diminution
S
R. diminuée
R. diminué
R. diminuée
R. diminuée
R. diminuée
R. diminué
R. diminuée
16
17
18
19
20

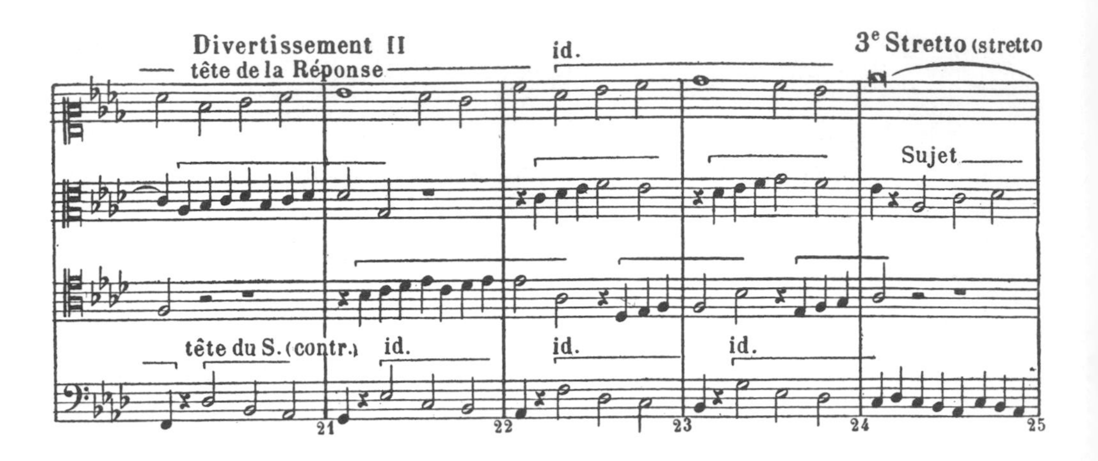
Divertissement II
tête de la Réponse
id.
3e Stretto (stretto
Sujet
tête du S. (contr.)
id.
id.
id.
21
22
23
24
25

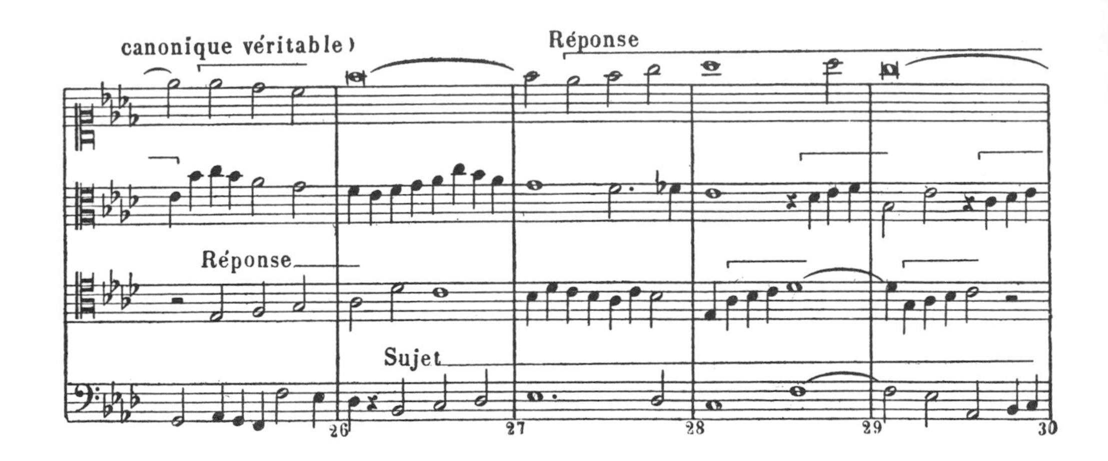
canonique véritable)
Réponse
Réponse
Sujet
26
27
28
29
30

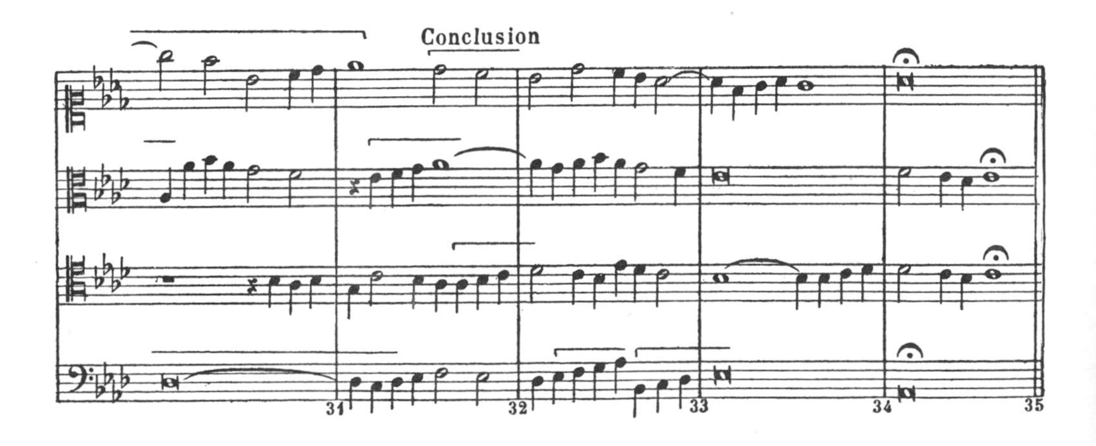
Conclusion
31
32
33
34
35

Linking Episodes and Strettos

374. Analysis will show that the episodes of the preceding stretto are made in the same way as the episodes in the development section of the fugue. They differ only in the brevity of the themes, and in that they are written more compactly.

The melodic plan of the first episode (beginning at the twelfth measure) may be analyzed as follows:

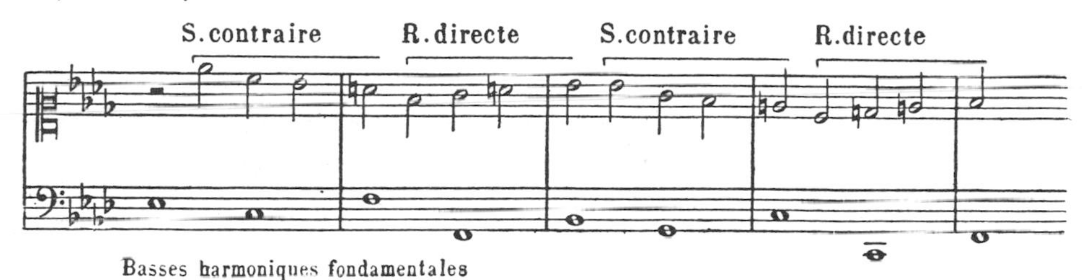

The four voices imitate each other, and the free parts are taken from the countersubject.

375. In the second episode, the melodic line is made by the soprano; the alto and tenor imitate each other, and the bass imitates itself. Note that in this episode:

> *a*) The alto and tenor present imitations of the head of the answer in diminution, imitations identical to those on which the preceding stretto was based.
>
> *b*) The melodic line of the episode continues without interruption into the third stretto, in a way that brings in naturally the fourth entrance of that stretto. Moreover, the free parts continuously imitate the head of the subject and answer in diminution, and in direct and contrary movement.

376. The phrases of an episode in a stretto should be combined in such a way that the episode may be followed directly by a stretto, canonical or otherwise, free or strict. This procedure binds together this part of the fugue. The effect is even better if a short episode presenting the head of the subject in contrary movement is linked to a stretto in direct movement.

The following stretto on the subject

affords an example of an episode arranged in such a way. Similar to a stretto in contrary movement, this episode brings in naturally the second stretto of of the subject which seems to continue it.

1er Stretto
R
S
R
S

1er Divertissement en forme de Stretto par mt contraire
S.contraire
2e Stretto au 6te
S.contraire
S.contraire
S.contraire
S

degré
2e Divertissement
R
S

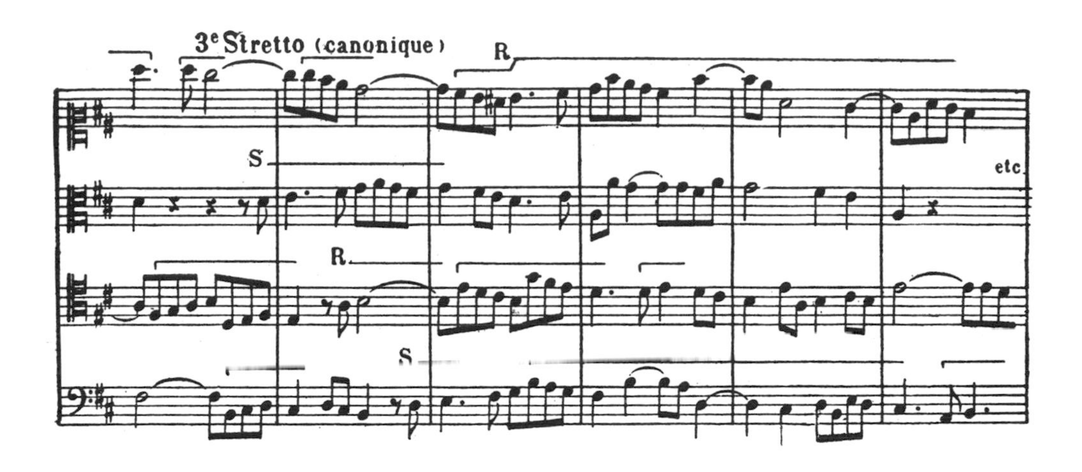

CONSTRUCTION OF THE ENSEMBLE OF THE STRETTO SECTION

377. In a general way, the construction of the stretto section of a scholastic fugue may be summed up as follows:

a) *First stretto,* composed of four entries, canonical or not; the fourth entry alone must sound the entire principal theme, accompanied or not by the countersubject. The first stretto is always in the principal key of the subject.

b) *First episode,* or stretto of the countersubject, of no less than two entries leading to a

c) *Second stretto* of the subject, which must contain only two entries, nearer the head of the subject and in neighboring keys.

d) *Second episode*: Short and compact, or a second stretto of the countersubject, more closely written than the first.

e) *Third stretto* of the subject, which, if the last, must be in four entries written still closer to the head of the subject, and in the principal key of the fugue. The last entry must be complete.

This final stretto may be preceded by a pedal point on the dominant, and heard over a pedal point on the tonic; or it may separate the pedal point of the dominant from that of the tonic; or it may begin on a pedal point on the dominant and end on that of the tonic.

In any case, it is advisable to conclude the fugue either on or immediately after the pedal point on the tonic.

Inverse Stretto

378. It was at one time the rule in the scholastic fugue to precede the final pedal point by an inverse stretto, that is, a stretto that begins with the answer. The advantage of this is that the fourth and last entry consists of the subject, which being in the principal key and not, like the answer, in the dominant, reaffirms the tonality of the fugue at its ending. Many authorities still strongly recommend this arrangement. (N.B. So do I.—F.D.)

Analysis of a Stretto Section

379. We shall now analyze an entire stretto section, written for a scholastic fugue. The subject of this fugue offers but little musical interest. Precisely for this reason it will serve to show what can be made of a subject, provided that it lend itself to those combinations without which no fugue is possible.

First we give the exposition of this fugue:

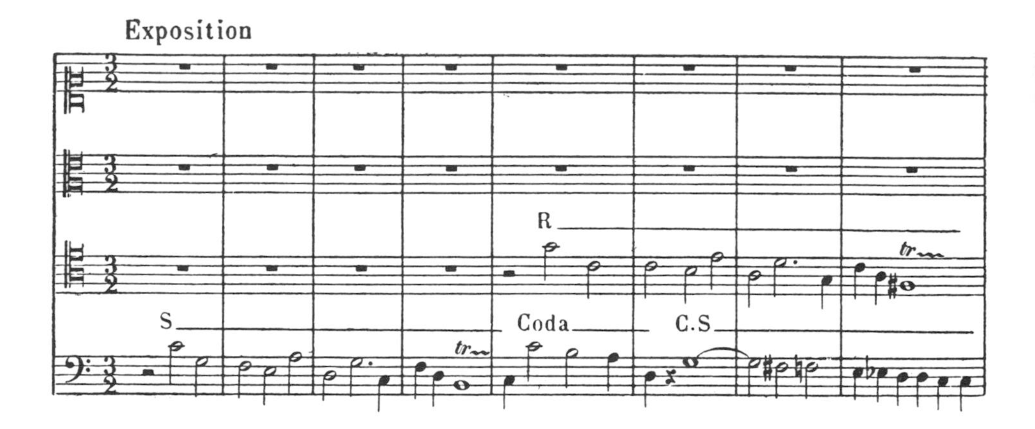

Stretto:

1er Stretto

S
R
fr! du C.S
S
fr! du C.S
1
2
3
4
5
6

R
1er Divertissement
tr
tête de la R.
tête de la R
fr! de la Coda
7
8
9
10
11
12

2e Stretto (canon à l'8ve de
Coda par mt contraire
R
tête de la R.
tête du S. par
tête de la R.
tête de la R.
R
Rép. par dimin.
13
14
15
16
17
18

la réponse
3e Stretto au 3e degré
(canon du S. et de la R. à l'8ve)
tr
dimin. cont.
S
R
tête de la R. dimin. cont.
19
20
21
22
23
24

4e Stretto (canon de la Réponse à la 5te supre)
S. dimin.
R
R
25
26
27
28
29

2e Divertissement
5e Stretto (canon de la Rép. à la 6te et à la 2de supre)
R
tr
tête du S. dimin. cont.
R
Sujet diminué
R
30
31
32
33
34

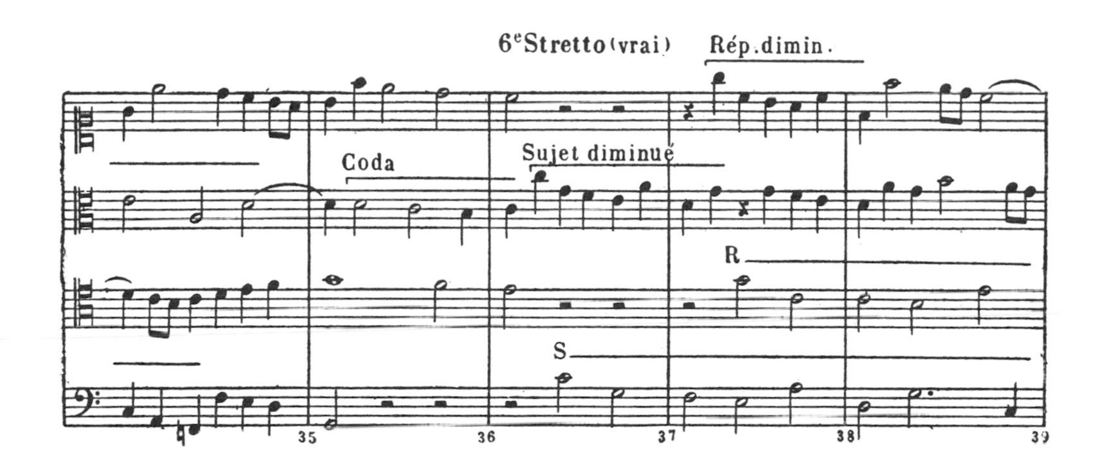
6e Stretto (vrai)
Rép. dimin.
Coda
Sujet diminué
R
S
35
36
37
38
39

fr! du C.S.
S. dimin.
fr! du C.S.
S. dimin.
tête du S.
tête du S.
R
S. dimin.
fr! du C.S. par mt cont.
40
41
42
43
44
Pédale de dominante

tête du S.
S. dimin.
tête du S.
S. dimin.
tête du S.
S. dimin.
fr. du C.S.
tête du S.
S. dimin.
45
46
47
48
49

380. If the exposition of this fugue be compared with the first stretto, it will be seen that they differ not only in arrangement of the entries, which are closer in the stretto, but also in the writing of the parts. In the stretto, these are made of fragments of the countersubject in close imitation.

The first stretto must not resemble the exposition. If it did, the fugue would seem to begin over again.

381. A first episode begins at the tenth measure of the stretto section. Its elements are borrowed from the head of the subject and the coda. The equidistant entries of the principal theme,

are made measure by measure, the tenor and alto imitating each other while the two other parts imitate each other in contrary movement. This episode, based on a non-modulating sequence, modulates abruptly to the key of the dominant at the seventeenth measure, where the second stretto begins.

382. The second stretto, formed by a canon at the octave of the answer, is in two parts. The other two parts either sound the answer in diminution, (bass, measure 17) or the head of the subject and the reply in diminution and contrary movement (alto and bass, measure 18 and 19).

The third stretto, closer by one beat than the preceding, presents in the key of the third degree a canon of the subject and answer at the octave, between the alto and tenor voices.

The fourth stretto is based on a canon of the answer at the fifth above. This canon is between the bass and the tenor, at the same distance as the preceding.

383. The second, third, and fourth strettos follow each other without interruption. An episode of two measures, formed of phrases that reproduce fragments of the subject in diminution, serves as a transition to the fifth stretto. This begins in three parts: the bass and alto present a canon which is ended on a cadence to the principal key, leading to a sixth canonical stretto of the subject and answer. Within this stretto, an identical canon, save that it is in diminution, is given to the two upper parts.

384. The pedal point on the dominant, on which this sixth stretto ends at the forty-second measure, is more complex. It sets forth simultaneously:

a) The subject in diminution.

b) The head of the subject in original values.

c) Fragments of the countersubject in direct and contrary movement.

All this may be interpreted as a developed but compact episode whose melodic line up to the end of bar fifty is as follows:

385. Without going into details concerning the musical composition of this stretto, we may remark that this part of the pedal point is composed of two groups of four measures, similar melodically and harmonically.

386. At the fifty-first measure, a double pedal point (above and below) begins, on which there is a stretto of the countersubject in canon at the octave, while the bass states the subject of the fugue. The pedal point leads to the tonic by a broken cadence at the fifty-seventh measure, and sustains a compact episode made of imitations of the head of the subject, while the melodic line, begun at the fifty-first measure, continues in two parts in the soprano.

387. The pedal point on the tonic ends at the sixty-second measure, and after a seventh stretto of four close entries of the subject and answer, of which only the head is heard, the conclusion of the fugue is reached by a perfect cadence.

388. In making an analysis of this stretto, the student will observe that it includes no elements other than those furnished by the exposition. It becomes apparent that, to one who knows how to use all the devices of counterpoint, a theme may be developed musically even though it apparently presents little musical interest.

389. Even in this stretto, lengthy for a scholastic fugue, not all possible combinations of the subject have been used. The student should investigate other possibilities for a stretto that are inherent in this subject.

Exercises

The student should now begin to assemble the stretto sections of the several dozen fugues which he is to complete. Procedure should be based on the two preceding chapters. Special attention is directed to ¶294–¶303.

XII

THE MUSICAL COMPOSITION OF A FUGUE

Musical Qualities of the Fugue

390. The primary and essential characteristics of a well-written fugue are, first, continuity of writing and, second, unity of style.

391. To assure the first of these essentials, certain theorists have forbidden the perfect cadence during the course of the fugue, reserving it for the conclusion alone. This is unwarranted, and is based on erroneous reasoning.

392. Evidently, if the fugue be misunderstood as merely an ensemble of elements designed to bring the subject by modulation into various keys, there would be created an artificial structure whose joints would have to be carefully concealed by devices well known to musicians.

But continuity of writing cannot be assured by the avoidance of perfect cadences alone; the slightest pause in a work of the kind which we have just mentioned would give the effect of a definite ending, which must be avoided in the course of the fugue.

393. However, if the fugue be considered in its true light as the development of a musical idea, an entirely different approach to the writing of a fugue is brought about, for the development of a musical idea consists in building with the rhythms and melodic patterns of which the theme is composed a series of new melodic and rhythmic forms that derive naturally and logically from one another.

394. From this correct viewpoint, the fugue will appear, once the exposition is ended, as the development of a single musical idea by the uninterrupted creation of new forms derived from that idea. It may be considered as a long episode, having many melodic forms and closer and closer imitations that lead back periodically to the original theme in the principal or other keys.

395. All the great masters envisaged the fugue in this way, and it is in this respect that their fugues differ from the majority of scholastic fugues. The latter are too often mere artificial assemblages of bits and fragments, written without melodic consistency, and denuded of color or feeling or style. Whereas, the fugues of the masters combine unity of style with variety of melodic forms, all

of which progress to a predetermined climax.

In the minds of the masters, the fugue was a vehicle for the expression of ideas, not a process for the display of formulas.

(N.B. No one could disagree with this lucid description of the ideal kind of fugal writing. However, the student should remember that fugues of the sort that Gedalge here describes are the fruit of much hard labor which, at its inception, cannot be other than formalistic and stiff. Moreover, the writing of scholastic fugues is not done primarily in order to write other fugues; rather, scholastic fugues are studied as prototypes of all kinds of musical composition. See ¶246.—F.D.)

Continuity of Writing and of Melodic Line

396. Continuity of writing in a fugue may be accomplished by observing this sole principle:

Never silence all parts at the same time.

However, a more essential matter is the continuity of the melodic line.

This may be acquired by taking care in the handling of transitions, and, above all, by making sure that the subject, at its every appearance, logically continues the episodes that preceded it. Likewise, by aid of the free parts that accompany the subject, the episodes should proceed naturally from it. In other words, the episodes should be joined around the subject, one beginning when the other finishes, as the following example (Johann Sebastian Bach, Organ Fugue in C minor) will show.

a) End of Exposition, First Episode:

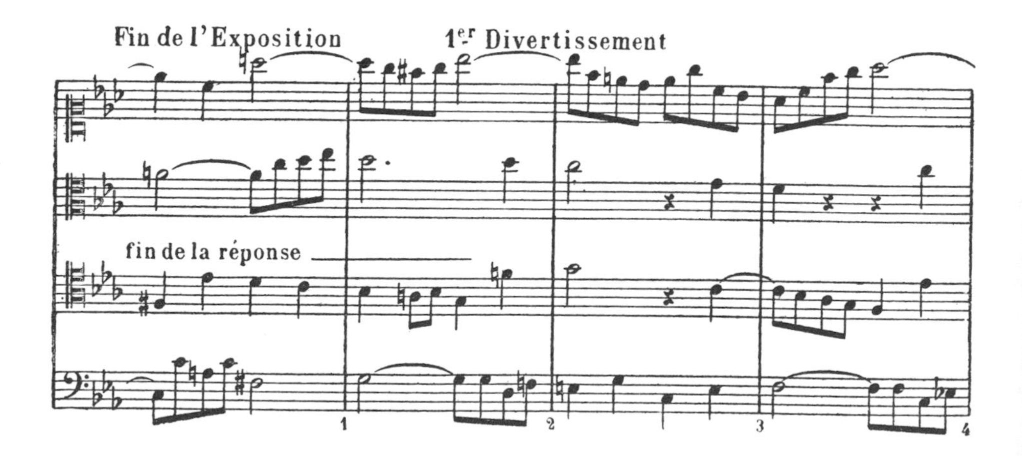

S
5
6
7
8

2e Divertisst
9
10
11
12

13
14
15
16

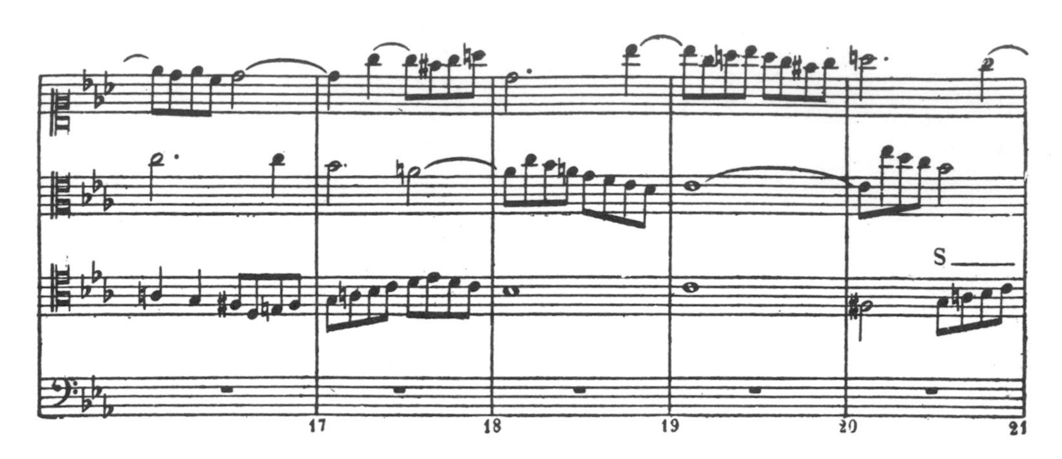
S
17
18
19
20
21

3e Divertissement
23
24
25
26

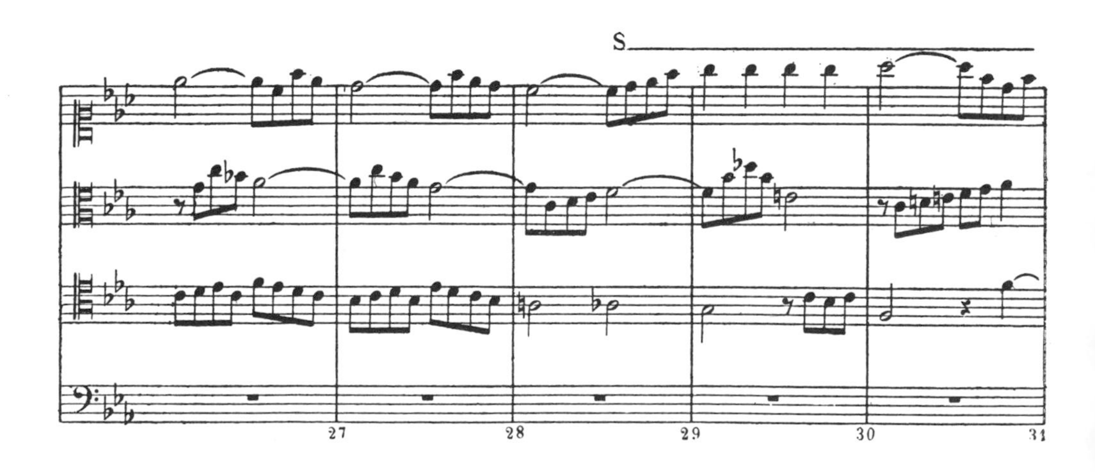
S
27
28
29
30
31

b) Same Fugue:

397. In example (*a*), from the eighth to the eleventh measures, at the entry of the subject the soprano and tenor continue the dialogue which they began in the preceding episode. Note the expressive harmony, first beat of the tenth measure, on which the bass is silenced.

In the twelfth bar, the tenor and alto announce the melody of the next episode, which thus begins before the subject is ended.

On a dialogue which, between the soprano and alto, continues the second episode, the subject is taken up by the tenor, with a modification in the head of the subject. This same phrase serves in the twenty-fifth measure as a passage to the tenor, in order to bring in the principal figure of the third episode, at the end of which the soprano similarly takes up the head of the subject.

398. The episode with which example (*b*) begins continues without interruption at the end of the third measure where the subject re-enters in the bass, and likewise in the seventh measure where the tenor sounds the answer. There is in the ninth measure an admirable 6/4 chord, though it must not be forgotten that, however inspired, it is not permitted in the scholastic fugue. (N.B. This again raises the apparent, but only apparent, contradiction which the ignorant have used for years as a club with which to attack the scholastic fugue. "If it is done by Bach, why not in the classroom?" they ask. The answer is: "The pupils are not Bach."—F.D.)

Use of the Perfect Cadence

399. It is not essential that all fugues be constructed without a cadence. In many cases it is advisable momentarily to conclude at the end of some melodic episode. In such cases the perfect cadence may be discreetly used. Its use, however, is limited by the following conditions:

a) The subject must enter either shortly before or immediately after the end of the cadence, so that the melodic line is not interrupted.

b) The subject, following a cadence, must enter on a note that is consonant with the final harmony of the cadence.

400. In any event, the perfect cadence may be used each time the musical sense permits or demands it, just as punctuation is used in writing. The following examples will serve to demonstrate this.

401. These examples (very free for a scholastic fugue, and not to be followed literally by the beginner—F.D.) will show that after a perfect cadence it is sometimes unnecessary for the subject to enter in the same key or even in the same mode fixed by the cadence. The transition, however, must be logical and natural, and the new key had better be in close relationship with that preceding it. Examples follow:

a) Johann Sebastian Bach, Organ Fugue in C major:

b) Johann Sebastian Bach, *Well-Tempered Clavier,* Fugue XXVI:

c) *Ibid.,* Fugue I:

d) *Ibid.*, Fugue IV:

402. At (*a*), the entry of the subject is made on the last note of, and in the key of the cadence. At (*b*), the cadence is on the dominant of the subject. At (*c*) and (*d*), the subject begins in minor immediately after a cadence in the major mode. The study of Bach's fugues reveals many ingenious ways of avoiding monotony and of keeping alive continuously the interest of the fugue.

403. In the scholastic fugue the subject must not enter on a dissonance, even though prepared, after a cadence. This prohibition applies to all entries of all parts in a scholastic fugue. Entry may be made only on a consonance.

Example:

The fragment (*a*) in the above example should be corrected as in (*b*) below, or in some like manner:

The subject, in this case, enters in a key and on a chord foreign to that fixed by the cadence. (N.B. Better avoid this.—F.D.)

404. When the subject begins on the dominant and progresses to the tonic, either directly or by passing through various scale tones, even the formula of the cadence may be used to advantage when the cadence is completed at the moment when the subject sounds the tonic or the mediant.

Example (Johann Sebastian Bach, Organ Fugue in G minor):

405. This procedure is likewise applicable to a subject that, beginning on the dominant followed by the tonic, proceeds to the seventh degree, this latter being considered as the third of the dominant key.

Example (Johann Sebastian Bach, Organ Fugue in C major):

406. Sometimes a subject that begins on the tonic can be introduced by a perfect cadence that ends an episode. This is done particularly when the next episode is based on a different theme than that which precedes the subject.

Example (Johann Sebastian Bach, Organ Fugue in C major):

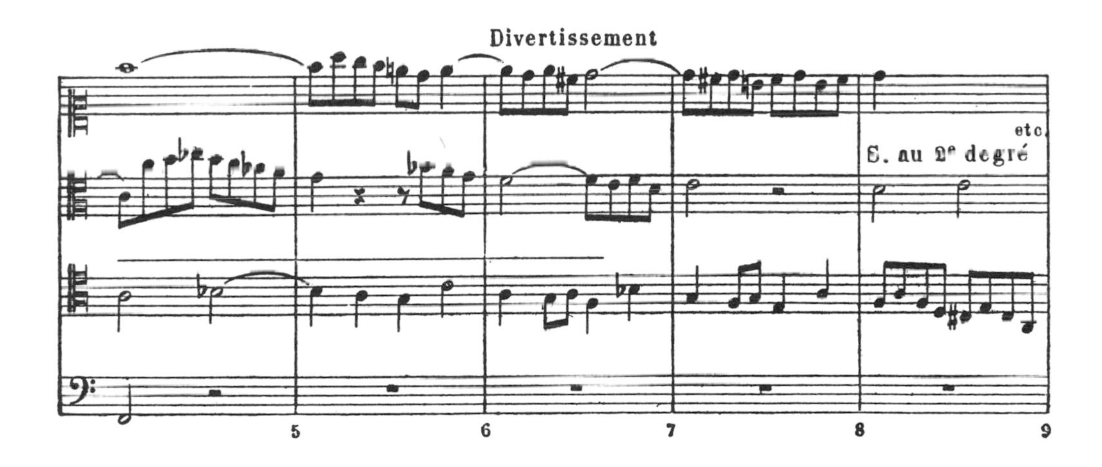

In this example the perfect cadence is averted by the use, in the soprano, of the B-flat at the end of the first measure which prepares the key of F major in which the subject is to be heard. However, the perfect cadence in F does not end until the second measure of the subject, which enters on the formula of the cadence (measures four and five).

407. Use of the perfect cadence is also justified during an episode which is to be continued with a different theme than that on which it began.

Example (Johann Sebastian Bach, Organ Fugue in G major):

Here the cadence, which in the second measure was averted by means of a retard placed on the third beat, is made halfway in the third measure. Note that this device brings out in marked relief the new melodic figure which serves as theme for the next part of the episode.

408. Under the same condition, that the melodic continuity of the fugue be not interrupted, the perfect cadence is sometimes used to begin an episode after the end of the entry of the subject.

The following example begins and ends on a perfect cadence; here, the use of these cadences is justified by the length of the subject and by the profoundly expressive character of the melody, which have enabled Bach to compose this fugue as a sort of repetitive opposition between the subject and the episodes that surround it. This arrangement, little used in the scholastic fugue, gives the impression of a charming and melancholy dialogue.

Example (Johann Sebastian Bach, Organ Fugue in A minor):

409. The perfect cadence, however, should only be used when it is clearly motivated by the melodic sense of the parts; there are fugues in which it may occur many times, and others in which its use is not justified at all. No rule can be formulated; only the logic and good sense of the composer will serve as guides. Analysis of Bach's fugues will improve one's judgment.

The fugue in A minor from which the above example is taken is an excellent illustration: there are in it numerous perfect cadences, each of which is necessitated by the expressive character of the passage which produced it, or by the distinction which it brings to the passage that follows it.

410. However, in the exposition, perfect cadences must be avoided. There all the entries should form an uninterrupted chain, and the least break in the melodic continuity and writing of the parts must be avoided. The exposition must be considered as an indivisible entity which is only ended at the completion of the fourth entry.

Style of the Fugue

411. The style of the fugue is more than the ensemble of the various opera-

tions necessary to construct a fugue. If this were not true, all fugues would be alike. Actually, the style of the fugue is implicit in the style of the subject. One must be careful not to write the same fugue on different subjects. There is enough leeway, even in the strict form of the scholastic fugue, to express different subjects differently.

412. The sole differences between a vocal fugue and an instrumental fugue are those owed to the range of the instruments and the difficulties of intonation of various intervals which an instrument can surmount but a voice cannot. In every case, unity of style may be assured by observing this principle: make the fugue from its subject.

Expressive Role of the Countersubject

413. The first necessity of unity is the establishment of the sentiment and character of the subject. Beyond indications of mode and speed, which have only a vague and general value, it is the countersubject that fixes the character of the subject. If the role of the countersubject were only harmonic, it could be replaced by any adequate counterpoint. The countersubject, however, must bring out the character of the subject, not only from the viewpoint of harmony and rhythm but as a means of expression.

414. The countersubject, as we have stated, must contrast with the subject without contradicting it. Bach's instrumental fugues afford some magnificent examples of this.

415. Consider, for example, the subject of the Organ Fugue in E minor:

The indications to be gathered from its mode and tempo are extremely vague. Such a subject could lend itself to many ways of expression.

But, when the countersubject enters at the first entry of the answer,

no further doubt is possible. The countersubject, by its expressive character, impresses an absolutely definite quality upon the subject, and takes a preponderant role in establishing the style and development of the fugue.

The fugue as a whole—if it is to be as it should be: the development of a musical idea set forth in the subject and defined by the countersubject—must take from them not only its rhythms and harmonies but its style. New rhythms and melodic figures may be introduced, provided they partake of the same character, or, if they contrast, that they accentuate the characters of the subject and countersubject.

416. Generally speaking, a slow subject will be benefited by an animated countersubject more than would a light and rhythmic subject. However, when a livelier countersubject is combined with a serious subject, care must be taken that its melody is appropriately expressive, lest it seem to parody the subject.

The combination of both a lively subject and a lively countersubject would result in confused writing, and would make the fugue less effective. No precise rules governing this problem can be formulated. However, it may be helpful to repeat: The countersubject should contrast with but not contradict the subject.

Free Parts

417. The free parts heard in the exposition must likewise contribute to fixing the character of the subject: they must not be conceived as unimportant parts or mere harmonic filling, but, rather, as non-invertible countersubjects, modifiable at will. In no case may they ever contradict the style of the subject.

Unity of Style Equals Unity of Expression

418. Since the entire fugue is potentially contained in the exposition, the unity of style of the latter fixes that of the fugue, and we may infer that "unity of style is synonymous with unity of expression." It is, nevertheless, possible to introduce new elements into the fugue without destroying its unity—elements both rhythmic and melodic, so long as they do not contradict the expressive character of the fugue.

419. Whereas each episode is most frequently constructed on a different figure, fugues exist in which all episodes are founded on the same melodic or rhythmic phrase. (This is to be avoided in the scholastic fugue, in which each episode should be written on a different theme.)

Examples exist in Bach in which all episodes are based on the same theme. In the D Minor Organ Fugue, various combinations of this theme are presented:

Fugue XII of the *Well-Tempered Clavier* is likewise developed entirely around the rhythmic figure:

These episodes should be arranged in four voices in open score and carefully analyzed by the student.

Character of the Episodes

420. If unity of style produces unity of expression, much care must be taken in choice of phrases destined to be used in the different episodes. The choice, it will be recalled, must be made as soon as the exposition is finished. All imitations and other contrapuntal devices which the exposition may afford are investigated; all combinations that lack distinction or may weaken the expressiveness of the fugue are set aside. Then a general melodic plan for the fugue is established in conformity with the instructions given in Chapter V on the preparation of episodes. Especial attention should be given, while working out the episodes, to arranging the parts so that the subject is linked intelligently with them each time it re-enters.

421. Melodic invention cannot be reduced to an exact rule. Nevertheless, there are devices used by the masters that are worth calling to the student's attention. These all serve to enhance the musical idea, to make its development more intense and more interesting, and to give a melodic unity to the fugue.

One of these methods consists in treating a theme as a harmonic sequence, then momentarily abandoning it, and again taking it up in a like sequence in another key.

Here is a striking example from one of the episodes in Bach's Organ Fugue in C Minor. A first sequence, composed of two similar figures, A and A′,

modulates from E-flat to B-flat, and from B-flat to F minor; a second sequence, having a concise antecedent, B,

brings back by a series of modulations the first sequence, heard this time in G minor, which is repeated in full up to the return of the subject in the principal key of the fugue:

422. Analysis will show that the interest of this episode lies in the skillful employment of elements that are extremely simple in themselves. Note, moreover, that one has only to omit the repetition of the first sequence to realize that all the spirit and warmth of the episode springs from its reintroduction before the entry of the subject.

Here is Bach's working-out. We first give it (I) as a plan of execution, and then (II) in its final form in four parts.

I:

II:

423. Deftness is essential in work of this sort. The accessory themes and figures should afford an interest no less great than the principal theme of the episode. Frequently the original sequence may be rearranged at its second hearing to avoid monotony and repetitiousness. A comparison of the example we have just seen with the fragment below taken from a fugue by Franz Schubert will show the defects of the latter. (N.B. Schubert was aware of his need of contrapuntal training, and, a few weeks before his untimely death, had arranged for lessons with Simon Sechter. The latter lived to ripe old age, became the most noted counterpoint teacher of his time, and, literally, composed a fugue every morning before breakfast.—F.D.)

424. Here, unlike the episode by Bach, there is no thematic development, but simply a repetition made by transposing to the fifth below the first A in the sequence. This is a tautology, and the effect of monotony and dryness is accentuated by the full repetition at the second expression of the theme of the arrangement made at first hearing. As the correspondence of the parts is the same, it sounds the same; there is no effect of a developing idea, but rather a formula that is repeated, a sort of pseudo-melodic harmonic sequence.

425. One particular reason for the difference between the two fragments is that in the example by Schubert there is, strictly speaking, no real melodic line produced by the movement of the parts, but merely a suite of formulas. Bach, however, using even simpler musical forms, was able to make from them a living and varied melodic line.

426. Likewise, depending on the quality of the opening phrase, a single harmonic sequence can give rise either to a series of uniform and dull formulas or to a melodic line full of life and charm.

Here are two examples, one from Schubert's fugue, the other from Fugue III of the *Well-Tempered Clavier*. Both are constructed in the same way: each part imitates itself (¶216), and both have analogous harmonic sequences. The first is but a formula. The second is alive, developed in a precise, elegant, firm melodic line. Yet the point of departure is the same in both; the means used are similar. One can only conclude that the difference between them is attributable to the quality of the musical materials employed. (N.B. Gedalge has omitted reference to the difference in rhythmic interest between the two. Schubert permits three measures in identical rhythms in each part. Bach takes care that his are varied, elastic, and contrasting. Rhythmic variety is of the utmost importance, and should be uppermost in the student's mind.—F.D.)

Schubert:

Bach:

427. Too much attention cannot be devoted to Bach's endless variety of procedure—the methods he uses to bring back the subject during or after an episode, and the art by which he can in every instance combine musically the most diverse elements into one expressive whole.

We have already examined (¶440 and following) methods for arranging the return of the subject in reference to cadences. We now show, by an example from his E Minor Fugue for organ, how, in an episode notable for profundity of sentiment, Bach has known how to reserve the most expressive part of his melodic line for the entry of the subject.

The musical method is, of course, indissolubly linked with the musical idea. Thus, in examining one, sight should not be lost of the other.

428. Without dwelling on the intrinsic beauty of this fragment, it is noteworthy that Bach proceeds by a series of contrasts, a method worth calling to the student's attention.

The episode is composed essentially of two sequences, (A) descending and

(B) ascending. The latter anticipates the key in which the subject is to reappear by repeating the same figure thrice in succession in the same cadence, but in different arrangements, and, consequently, with different effect. This apparent monotony places the entry of the subject more strikingly in relief: At the moment when all parts combine to increase the intensity of expression, the melodic line is at its highest point and the subject and countersubject return. From here the intensity can only decrease, and diminishes for two measures, after which, at the ending of the subject, a new episode begins.

429. Here we pass over the border from the devices of writing to actual composition. *It is the value of the musical ideas rather than the dexterity with which contrapuntal and other devices are manipulated that determines the quality of the fugue, as it does of all musical composition.* In principle, therefore, the fugue should always be formed in the mind, before it is written. (N.B. Hardly applicable to the beginner struggling with assembling the elements of a fugue on a given subject. But ultimately true.—F.D.)

430. Moreover, the fugue should be written as the work of a musician and composer. Each part must be written from that standpoint, and be the object of like care and workmanship. The stretto section, in particular, requires sound judgment and musical sense. The basic principle for the beginner should be: Never sacrifice music to empty artifices of counterpoint.

Various Ways of Linking the Stretto Section

431. In the scholastic fugue, the stretto section may be joined to the first part of the fugue in these ways:

a) By linking the first stretto directly to the last episode.

b) By making an averted or broken cadence, with a pause marked by a pedal point between the stretto and the episode.

c) By placing a pedal point on the dominant before the stretto section, linking it directly or separating it from the stretto section by a hold.

432. Whatever arrangement is adopted, the last episode should by its closely knit construction prepare for the stretto in such a way that the latter will give the impression of a logical continuation, rather than a repetition of the exposition, or an interruption in the musical sense of the fugue.

Role of the Pedal Point

433. In Chapter X (¶388 and following) we examined in detail the various aspects that a pedal point can assume in the musical composition of a fugue.

Harmonically, the pedal point affords the advantage of grouping chords of the most distant keys on a note of the principal key without loss of the sense of tonality. Likewise, it permits the assemblage of all the principal melodic elements of the fugue in distant keys, in a condensation which intensifies the expressiveness of the fugue, and, consequently, brings it a new vigor as it approaches its conclusion.

Employment of the Pedal Point

434. Moreover, the pedal point logically finds its place near the conclusion, that is, before the stretto section—which may be called the "peroration" of the fugue—or immediately after it.

435. The pedal point on the tonic at the end of the stretto either concludes the fugue or is followed by the final cadence, either perfect or plagal.

436. Having assigned a logical place for the pedal point, we must now examine it from the standpoint of the musical composition of the fugue.

Importance of the Pedal Point

437. The importance, that is to say, the length and musical quality, of the pedal point varies for many reasons. The masters sometimes use none; sometimes they use more than one; some are short, some long. Choice is up to the composer. The important thing is to avoid disproportion in any part of the fugue.

438. In the scholastic fugue, the places most generally assigned to the pedal point are, as has been said:

a) Pedal point on the dominant at the end of the episode immediately preceding the stretto section.

b) Pedal point on the tonic at the end of the fugue.

These arrangements may be varied by placing a pedal point on the dominant at the end of the fugue and following it by a pedal point on the tonic. But the above arrangement is preferable.

439. The musical elements used in writing a pedal point must vary according to its location in the fugue. Without trying to formulate precise rules for musical creation, certain methods may be indicated by the student to serve as bases for his first attempts.

Composition of the Pedal Point

440. The pedal point on the dominant, heard before the final stretto, may be introduced in the following ways:

a) When the episode has arrived at the highest point of an ascending sequence.

b) When the episode has arrived at the lowest point of a descending sequence.

c) When neither extreme has been reached.

441. In the first two instances, the climax of the sequence, ascending or descending, having been reached, it may be advisable to proceed on the pedal point with an episode in which the sequence is the opposite of that just made. This sequence may be composed of the same elements as the preceding, but in inverse order. Examples follow:

a) Pedal Point Entering during an Episode at the Highest Point of an Ascending Sequence:

b) Pedal Point Entering during an Episode at the Lowest Point of a Descending Sequence (Max d'Ollone, Fugue on a Subject by Gounod):

442. When the pedal point intervenes during a descending or ascending sequence, it is normal not to interrupt the sequence but to continue it on the pedal point; and, when the extremity of the sequence has been reached, to resume inversely.

Example (J. Boulay, First Prize Fugue, 1897, on a Subject by Dubois):

443. These are three typical arrangements of an episode leading into a pedal point. The student should at first be guided by these models, and should later vary their methods. In any event, he should never proceed unless guided by some definite plan.

Linking Pedal Point and Stretto

444. The ways of arranging the connection of pedal point and stretto are so various that no rule can be given save that the student should arrange the transition with logic and a sense of proportion. Examples follow:

a) Ch. Koechlin, Fugue on a Subject by Gedalge:

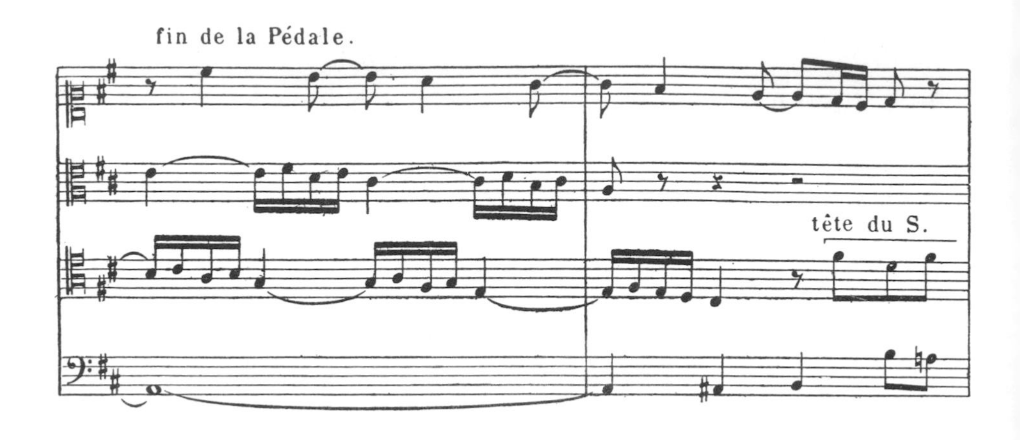

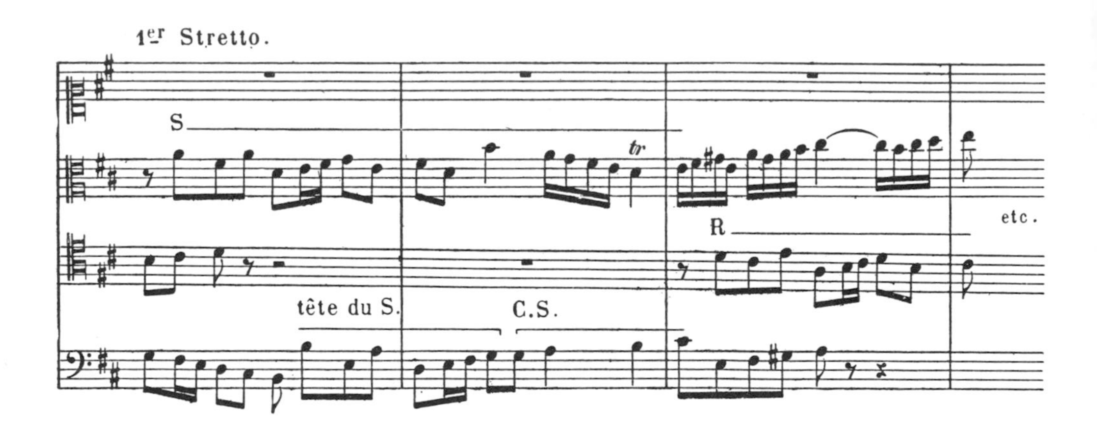

b) Max D'Ollone, Fugue on a Subject by Massenet:

c) H. Rabaud, Fugue on a Subject by Massenet:

d) F. Halphen, Fugue on a Subject by Gedalge:

e) A. Savard, Fugue on a Subject by Massenet:

445. If no pedal point is written before the first stretto, the latter can be joined directly to the episode that precedes it by arrangements analogous to the foregoing. In any event, the episode before the stretto should be compactly written.

446. Bach occassionally permits a statement of the subject immediately befor the first stretto. The following example is taken from his G Major Organ Fugue:

447. This example shows how, even when the subject is heard at the second degree, the parts can be drawn progressively together to approach the character of a stretto.

This episode, constructed in canonical form from a fragment of the subject, is closely allied by the pattern of its bass to the phrases heard immediately before it in close imitation in the three lower parts. The theme of the episode, stated by the tenor in the fifth measure of the example, is always presented so that the melodic sequence designed to lead up to the entry of the subject (measure eight) may be readily perceptible.

Melodic Arrangement of the Stretto Section

448. As has been stated, this section is constructed of a series of increasingly closer entries of the subject and answer. These entries must be combined so that their ensemble gives the impression of an uninterrupted melodic line, and not of a succession of juxtaposed, separate melodic fragments. At best, absence of melodic line produces incoherence; at worst, monotony, caused by the more and more closely spaced entries of the head of the subject.

449. A plan of the ensemble of the stretto section should, therefore, be drawn up, much as the plan of the episodes. Care should be taken that the entries become progressively closer, the closest reserved for the last. If the arrangement be properly calculated *in advance,* incoherence and monotony can be avoided.

450. Some of the fugues in the *Well-Tempered Clavier* should be arranged in parts and analyzed, notably numbers I, IV, VIII, XX, XXVII, XXIX, XXXIII, and XLVI. Here the strettos do not follow the exact specifications of the scholastic fugue, but they furnish invaluable examples of organization and construction.

Pedal Point on the Tonic

451. The same procedures indicated in ¶434–¶444 in discussing the pedal point on the dominant before the stretto apply to the pedal points on the dominant and tonic at the end of the stretto section. The sole difference is that, in the latter case, the part-writing must be in the character of a stretto. (See the examples given in Chapters X and XI.)

Conclusion of the Fugue

452. The fugue should end either on a pedal point on the tonic, or immediately afterward, and always on a perfect or plagal cadence. No rules govern the ending. It is, of course, necessary not to prolong it pointlessly; the student should not hesitate to sacrifice various combinations if they merely add length. On the other hand, the fugue should not be ended if something remains to be said. The judgment and musical sense of the composer must guide him here.

Exercises

453. For the student's convenience, here is a table showing minimum length and essential parts of the scholastic fugue, which, by now, should be largely arranged, at least in skeletal form. It completes the table given in ¶267, and

like it, is written for the major mode. In minor, appropriate modulations must be made. The strettos are the minimum required. No attempt is made to limit the development of the fugue. The table is not a mold but a model.

Parts of the Fugue	*Number of measures varying approximately* from	to
Exposition	16	24
Episode	2	8
Counterexposition	8	12
First Modulating Episode	8	12
Subject at the Sixth degree	4	6
Answer at the Third degree	4	6
Second Modulating Episode	10	16
Subject at the Fourth degree	4	6
Transition	2	4
Subject or Answer at the Second degree	4	6
Third Modulating Episode	14	20
Pedal Point on the Dominant	2	8
First Stretto—Four Entries	10	18
First Stretto of Countersubject—Two Entries	2	6
Second Stretto, Subject and Subject—Two Entries	4	8
Second Stretto of Countersubject—Two Entries	2	6
Third Stretto, Inverse—Four Entries	6	12
Pedal Point on the Tonic	4	16
Total	106	194

XIII

GENERAL SUMMARY

Order and Arrangement of Work in Writing a Fugue

454. Once the subject is chosen, the student should proceed as follows:

a) Work out the answer.

b) Choose the countersubject.

c) Investigate and establish the possible strettos and canons that the subject, answer, and countersubject(s) furnish with each other and with themselves.

d) Analyze the subject, answer, and countersubject(s) and fragment them to determine what melodic and rhythmic phrases can be extracted from them in direct, contrary, and retrograde movement, and in augmentation and diminution.

e) Write the exposition.

f) Fix the melodic elements of each episode, and the harmonic and melodic line of the entire fugue.

g) Write the strettos.

h) Work out in definite form that part of the fugue between the exposition and the first stretto.

Examining the Answer

455. To determine the correct answer:

a) Harmonize the subject with its natural, fundamental harmonies; keep in mind that, from the special viewpoint of the answer, the dominant of the subject when heard in the first melodic movement or at the end of the subject must always be considered as the first degree of the key of the dominant.

b) In case of doubt, choose that answer which, while complying with the rules, least distorts the subject.

c) Indicate by appropriate numerals the degrees occupied in the scales of the first and fifth degree by all the notes of the subject; the answer is made by the analogous interval in the scale of the fifth or first degree, respectively.

The Countersubject

456. Choice of the countersubject is made as follows:

a) Determine exactly the fundamental bass of the harmony of the subject.

b) Take, as framework of the countersubject, the most suitable among the notes of the harmonies that are invertible with the subject. Remember that subject and countersubject must serve mutually as good harmonic basses.

c) Use as many suspensions (prepared dissonances) as possible.

d) Give the countersubject an entirely different form than the subject. Bear in mind that the countersubject establishes the exact emotional character of the subject. Although differing rhythmically and melodically, it must supplement rather than contradict the subject, and must form a precise melodic phrase.

e) Never seek the countersubject primarily with the answer. Work first with the subject, and, if necessary, modify the countersubject to suit the answer.

Investigation of Strettos and Canons

457. To establish strettos and canons:

a) Seek at every interval the canons that may be furnished by the subject with itself and with the answer.

b) Do likewise with the countersubject and the countersubject of the answer.

c) Establish any invertible canons of the subject and countersubject, or answer and countersubject.

d) If the subject does not lend itself to canonical strettos, outline the strettos in which the subject must be interrupted to permit the entry of the answer. In such cases, melodic phrases taken from the subject and modified if necessary should be continued after its enforced interruption.

e) Seek canonical or other combinations of the subject and countersubject in augmentation, diminution, and in contrary, retrograde, and contrary-retrograde movement.

Writing the Exposition

458. To write the exposition:

a) Emphasize the parts in which the subject and countersubject are heard. Give less importance to the free parts.

b) Avoid too great a number of different patterns. Remember that the figures introduced in the exposition all participate in the further development of the fugue, rhythmically, melodically, and expressively.

c) Each voice must sound, alternately and successively, the subject and answer.

d) A short coda is necessary when the answer cannot enter immediately after the last note of the subject, and vice versa.

e) The subject or answer should enter as soon as possible after the statement of the preceding entry, provided it does not disturb the rhythm of the subject or answer.

f) The exposition must be written entirely in the keys of the tonic and dominant.

g) Avoid the perfect cadence in both the exposition and the counter-exposition, and in the phrases leading into the ensuing episode.

Melodic Line of the Fugue

459. Sketch the melodic line of the fugue:

a) Subdivide the subject and countersubject into melodic and rhythmic fragments.

b) Reserve the use of the head of the subject and countersubject for the stretto.

c) Combine the fragments in various ways, and utilize as well material from the codas and free parts of the exposition.

d) Reject any figure that is not of musical interest.

e) Investigate at all intervals the various canons and imitations to which the fragments may lend themselves. Group these methodically according to their comparative expressiveness, and according to the closeness and intensity of the canons which they afford. Arrange them so that they lead to a logical climax or series of increasing climaxes.

f) Establish for each of these phrases a simple harmonic bass, susceptible of making a series of harmonic sequences that modulate logically into neighboring keys.

g) Settle in advance the modifications of rhythm and motion that each phrase is to undergo, and determine their function and the importance to be assigned to them in the fugue.

h) When all this is done, make a melodic sketch of each episode, being sure that it can readily be harmonized in four parts. This will inevitably be the case if the harmonic sequence involved has been established on a proper bass.

i) Classify the episodes. Separate them by the parts of the fugue in which the subject and answer are heard in various keys. Write these latter parts in definitive form, the episodes alone being sketched in, forming links to join them to the first stretto.

Stretto Section

460. To write the strettos:

a) The plan of the entire stretto section is based on elements of the first part of the fugue.

b) The first and last strettos must comprise four entries; the others may be made in two.

c) In the stretto section passing modulations may be made to neighboring keys, but it is wise to return frequently to the principal key in which the first and last strettos must be made.

d) In the first stretto, avoid giving the impression of repeating the exposition of the fugue. The closer entries of subject and answer are, of course, of primary importance in achieving this. The free parts, those heard with the answer as well as with the subject, should be arranged so as to maintain the tonality as much as possible in that of the principal key.

e) The stretto section generally ends on a pedal point on the tonic.

Perfect Cadence

461. The perfect cadence may be used in any part of the fugue except the exposition, on condition that it does not induce an interruption of all the parts at once.

Interruption of the Parts

462. A part may never be silenced unless for a musical reason. It must always be quitted in such a way that, taken alone, it could be harmonized by a cadence.

(N.B. This is of the greatest importance in part-writing. The parts are not simply inserted or withdrawn for conveniences of harmony or rhythm. Each part should state a musical phrase.—F.D.)

Movement of the Parts

463. The parts should move so as to produce individually clear, complete melodic lines. All the parts are to be treated in a melodic, not harmonic, manner.

464. As the fugue draws near its climax, each episode should be more condensed. Likewise, individual episodes should be more closely written at the end

than at the beginning.

465. (When a subject lends itself to so many canonical episodes that there is no room for all of them in the stretto section without making it disproportionately long, some may be used in the earlier parts of the fugue, reserving the closest combinations for the stretto itself.)

(N.B. I have placed the above in parenthesis because I do not agree with it. A better plan would be to make two or more fugues on a subject offering such a plethora of canonic possibilities. This would afford excellent practice in writing different fugues on the same subject.—F.D.)

Entries

466. No part should ever enter merely for harmonic purposes.

Each entry should be preceded by a rest long enough clearly to mark it.

Consecutive entries of subject and answer must never be made in the same voice.

Two successive groups of entries in different keys should not be made in the same order of the parts.

Ending of the Fugue

467. When the interest of the fugue is exhausted, its ending should not be prolonged needlessly. No attempt should ever be made to tack on "agreeable" or novel harmonies or other far-fetched effects.

468. Make the fugue from its subject. The character of the fugue must suit the character of the subject. And all the elements of the fugue should grow out of the subject.

469. Expressiveness, not agitation or speed, gives warmth and intensity to a musical idea.

470. Never forget:

a) A fugue, even a scholastic fugue, is a piece of music.

b) Time spent in studying fugue from the sole viewpoint of combining notes is wasted.

c) Practice in writing fugues is only useful if it be undertaken for the purpose of learning the art of developing a musical idea.

That is what I have tried to show in this work.

471. As a further guide for the student, I will now show him how, once the exposition of the fugue is completed and its elements analyzed and established, he may make a general plan embracing the fugue as a whole, by which he may be enabled readily to express its melodic and harmonic course.

The elements of this work having been studied in succession in the previous parts of this treatise, it should be useful to assemble them now, and to apply them to the composition of a fugue. The method indicated below is recommended to all students. It will facilitate their work, and permit them to arrange their ideas logically. (N.B. Before continuing, the student should complete the fugues which he has been writing piecemeal. Then he will have acquired sufficient skill to take a new subject and work it directly into a complete fugue, as set forth immediately below.—F.D.)

Composing the Fugue as a Whole

472. Before writing the fugue, plan:—

a) Melodic and harmonic scheme.

b) Draft of its fulfillment.

c) Working out.

It is assumed that all preliminary work such as investigation of counter-subjects, strettos, canons, analysis of the exposition as a source of themes of episodes, etc., has been completed.

(The numbers placed before the fragments of themes in the episodes refer to the corresponding numbers placed under the same fragments in the exposition.)

Exposition (Subject by André Gedalge):

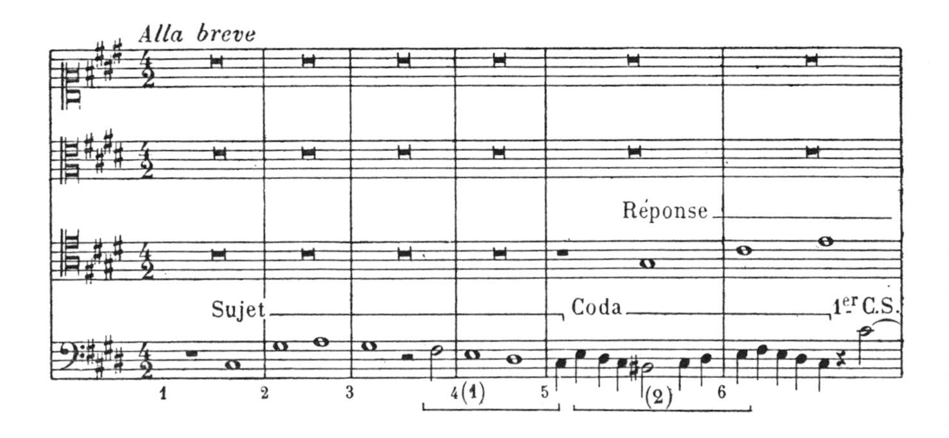

Réponse
Coda
1er C.S.
Partie libre
2e C.S.
12
(7)
13
(8)
14
15
16

Sujet
Coda
1er C.S.
Partie libre
2e C.S.
7
(3)
8
(4)
9
(5)
10
11
(6)

Eléments du 1er DIVERTISSEMENT
A) THÊME PRINCIPAL formé d'un fragment du Sujet(1) et de la Coda(2)
(1)
(2)
B) 1er THÊME ACCESSOIRE fragment du 1er C.S. (4)
(4)
C) 2d THÊME ACCESSOIRE progression mélodique tirée de la partie libre(6)
(6)
1er DIVERTISSEMENT
Plan MÉLODIQUE et HARMONIQUE du Divertissement
Basses harmoniques
Plan d'EXÉCUTION
1er DIVERTISSEMENT
RÉALISATION
A
B
C
17
18
19
20

Rentrée du Sujet
au relatif majeur
2e C.S.
(2)
Sujet
1er C.S.
Sujet
etc.
ton relatif majeur
2e C.S.
Sujet
1er C.S.
21
22
23
24
25
Réponse
1er C.S.
Réponse
1er C.S.
26
27
28
29
30

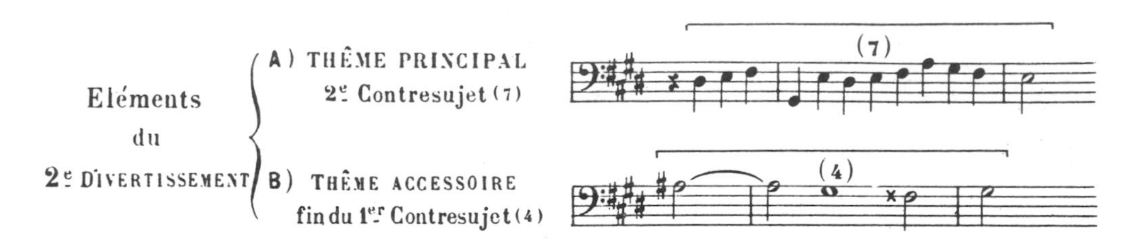
Eléments
du
2e DIVERTISSEMENT
A) THÊME PRINCIPAL
2e Contresujet (7)
B) THÊME ACCESSOIRE
fin du 1er Contresujet (4)
(7)
(4)

2e DIVERTISSEMENT
Plan MÉLODIQUE
et
HARMONIQUE
du
2e Divertissement
A
A
B
B
A
A
Plan
d'EXÉCUTION
du
2e DIVERTISSEMENT
B
B
A
A
RÉALISATION
31
32
33
34

A
A
A
B
A
B
A
B
A
B
35
36
37
38
39
Ton de la sous dominante
Sujet
1er C.S.
2e C.S.
Sujet
1er C.S.
2e C.S.
40
41
42
43
44

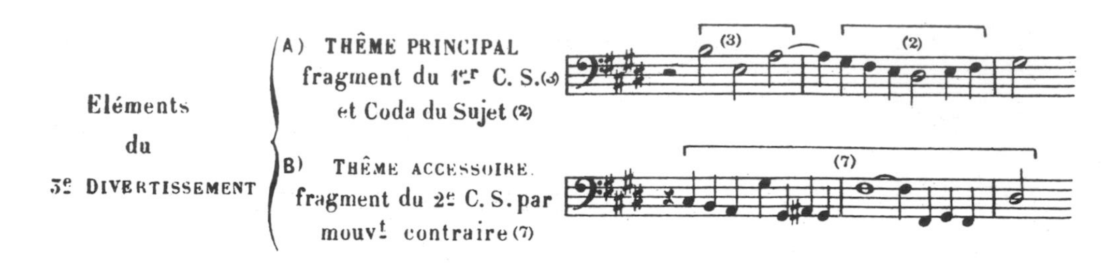
Eléments
du
3e DIVERTISSEMENT
A) THÊME PRINCIPAL
fragment du 1er C. S.(3)
et Coda du Sujet (2)
B) THÊME ACCESSOIRE.
fragment du 2e C. S. par
mouvt contraire (7)
(3)
(2)
(7)

3e DIVERTISSEMENT (canonique)
Plan MELODIQUE
et
HARMONIQUE
du
3e Divertissement
Plan
d'EXÉCUTION
du
3e DIVERTISSEMENT
RÉALISATION
A
B
45
46
47
48

Frag. de A
A
B
49
50
51
52
53
Pédale sur la dominante
54
55
56
57
58

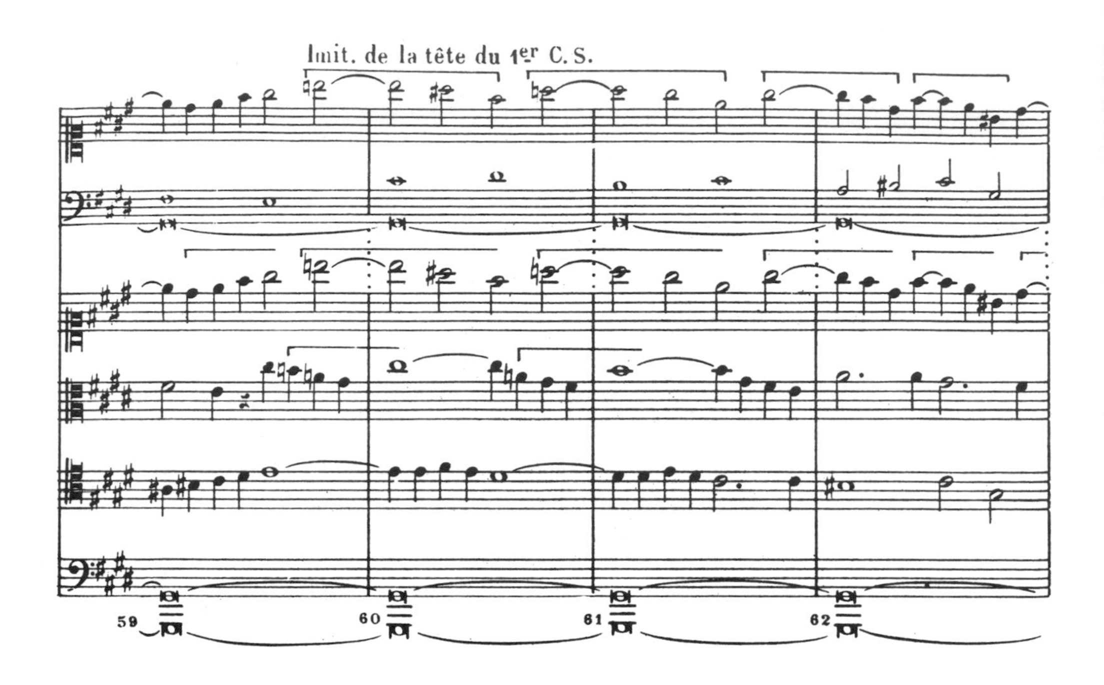
Imit. de la tête du 1er C. S.
59
60
61
62

1er STRETTO
Sujet
Réponse
Sujet
Tête du S. diminué
Réponse
63
64
65
66
67

Rép. par double dim.
Réponse
Sujet
Réponse
Tête du S. diminué
par mt contraire
S. dim. cont.
Sujet
68
69
70
71

2e STRETTO (ton du
en Canon du S. et
S
T. du S. en
double dim.
id.
Sujet par dim.
id.
id.
R. dim. cont.
id.
S
72
73
74
75

5e degré)
de la R. à la 10e supre
R
R
S.cont.en dble dim.
S.diminué (rythme modifié)
76
77
78
79

3e STRETTO (ton du 3e degré)
en Canon du S. à l'8e infre
S
S
S
S
80
81
82
83

4e STRETTO (au ton principal)
en Canon du S. à 2 par mt contraire
et à 3 par mt direct en diminution
S.cont.
S.dimin.
S. cont.
S. par dble dimin.
S.cont.
S.dimin.
S. par mt cont.
84
85
86
87

5e STRETTO
en forme de DIVERTISSEMENT CANONIQUE à 2 (SUJET et RÉPONSE)
Sujet
S
Réponse
R
Sujet
S
Réponse
R
88
89
90
91

S
R
S
R
92
93
94
95

S
S
S
S
96
97
98
99
100

6e STRETTO (canon à 4)
sur Pédale de tonique
S
R
S
rall.
Largo
S
R
S. par
mt cont.
101
102
103
104
105

S
S
106
107
108
109
110
111
112

APPENDIX A

Fugal Subjects

The fugal subjects that follow should be sufficient for this course.

The student should begin by choosing those with large values and simple rhythms in order to avoid unnecessary complications. His rule should be: Keep it simple. It is all too easy to complicate.

10) RADEGLIA
11) GOUNOD
12) A.THOMAS
13) GUILMANT
14) Anonyme
15) REBER
tr
16) MASSENET
17) SAINT-SAËNS
18) A.GEDALGE
19) A.GEDALGE
tr
20) A.GEDALGE
21) MATHESON
22) A.GEDALGE
23) A.GEDALGE

24) BATTIFFERRI
25) J.S.BACH
26) J.S.BACH
27) J.S.BACH
28) KIRNBERGER
29) A.THOMAS
30) MEYERBEER
31) A.GEDALGE
32) J.S.BACH
33) J.S.BACH
34) J.S.BACH
35) GIGOUT
36) GOUNOD

37)
A.GEDALGE
38)
A.GEDALGE
39)
A.GEDALGE
40)
HALÉVY
41)
Anonyme
42)
Anonyme
43)
Anonyme
44)
REBER
45)
A.GEDALGE
46)
Anonyme
47)
AUBER
48)
AUBER
49)
A.THOMAS
50)
G.BIZET

51) A. GEDALGE
52) A GEDALGE
53) HALÉVY
54) A. GEDALGE
55) A. GEDALGE
56) A. GEDALGE
57) SAINT-SAËNS
58) A. GEDALGE
59) A. GEDALGE
60) J. SARTI
61) MASSENET
62) MASSENET
63) MASSENET
64) A. GEDALGE
65) A. GEDALGE

66)
A. GEDALGE
67)
A. GEDALGE
68)
A. GEDALGE
69)
A. GEDALGE
tr
70)
A. GEDALGE
71)
A. GEDALGE
72)
A. GEDALGE
73)
A. GEDALGE
74)
A. GEDALGE
75)
A. GEDALGE
76)
Anonyme
77)
E. GUIRAUD
78)
A. GEDALGE
79)
REBER
80)
REBER

81) Anonyme
82) A. THOMAS
83) REBER
84) ONSLOW
85) Anonyme
86) TH. DUBOIS
87) A. GEDALGE
88) HAENDEL
89) HAENDEL
90) PURCELL
91) J.S. BACH
92) J.S. BACH
tr
93) J.S. BACH
94) J.S. BACH
95) MOZART

96) MOZART
97) ROSSINI
98) CHERUBINI
99) AUBER
100) FENAROLI
tr
101) Anonyme
102) Anonyme
103) AUBER
104) AUBER
105) Anonyme
106) REICHA
107) Anonyme
108) A.THOMAS
109) SAINT-SAËNS
110) Anonyme

111) REBER
112) A.THOMAS
113) EBERLIN
114) CHERUBINI
115) C.M.WIDOR
tr
116) GOUNOD
117) E.GUIRAUD
118) MASSENET
119) A.THOMAS
120) GOUNOD
121) A.GEDALGE
122) A.GEDALGE
123) A.GEDALGE
124) A.GEDALGE
tr
125) A.GEDALGE

138) A. GEDALGE

139) A. GEDALGE

140) A. GEDALGE

141)
A. GEDALGE
142)
A. GEDALGE
143)
A. GEDALGE
144)
A. GEDALGE
tr
145)
A. GEDALGE
146)
A. GEDALGE
147)
A. GEDALGE
tr
148)
PALADILHE
149)
GOUNOD
150)
GOUNOD
151)
A. THOMAS
152)
MASSENET
153)
MASSENET
154)
A. GEDALGE
155)
J. S. BACH

156) ONSLOW
157) GEVAERT
158) AUBER
159) REBER
160) MASSENET
161) MASSENET
162) MASSENET
163) TH. DUBOIS
164) TH. DUBOIS
165) A. THOMAS
166) A. THOMAS
167) A. THOMAS
168) A. GEDALGE
169) A. GEDALGE
170) A. GEDALGE
tr

171) A. GEDALGF
172) A. GEDALGE
173) A. GEDALGE
174) A. GEDALGE
175) A. GEDALGE
176) A. GEDALGE
177) A. GEDALGE
178) A. GEDALGE
179) A. GEDALGE
180) MOZART
181) CHERUBINI
182) AUBER
183) AUBER
184) REBER
185) REBER

186) A. THOMAS
187) A. THOMAS
188) A. THOMAS
189) TH. DUBOIS
190) REBER
191) MASSENET
192) FR. BACH
193) A. GEDALGE
194) A. GEDALGE
195) A. GEDALGE
196) A. GEDALGE
197) A. GEDALGE
198) A. GEDALGE
199) A. GEDALGE

200) AUBER
201) AUBER
202) MARPURG
203) CHERUBINI
204) J.S.BACH
205) MASSENET
206) MASSENET
207) DELIBES
208) A.GEDALGE
209) A.GEDALGE
210) A.GEDALGE
211) A.GEDALGE
212) A.GEDALGE
213) A.GEDALGE
214) A.GEDALGE

215) A. GEDALGE
216) SCARLATTI
217) A. THOMAS
218) A. THOMAS
219) A. THOMAS
tr
220) A. THOMAS
221) A. THOMAS
222) A. GEDALGE
223) A. GEDALGE
tr
224) A. GEDALGE
225) A. GEDALGE
226) A. GEDALGE
227) A. GEDALGE
tr
228) A. GEDALGE

229)
AUBER
230)
A. GEDALGE
231)
A. GEDALGE

APPENDIX B

Fugues with Several Subjects

Definition of the New Subject

473. Until now, we have envisaged a fugue as a musical composition whose development consists solely of elements derived from the exposition. However, many fugues by the masters of the art exist in which there are melodic forms foreign to the subject, the countersubject, and the free parts. Such new musical ideas are introduced to increase the interest of the fugue, both by the contrast they offer to the subject, and by the combinations they are able to form with it.

474. To avoid nullifying unity of expression, the new musical idea must be in a style corresponding to that of the subject. It must not, however, resemble the subject. On the contrary, it must contrast with but not contradict it. It should have a melodic and rhythmic character of its own.

Characteristics of the New Subject

475. Such a melodic or rhythmic figure is called a "new subject." It must be written in invertible counterpoint with the principal subject, and, if possible, with its countersubject as well. The new subject may likewise be accompanied by a countersubject which may or may not be invertible with the principal subject and its countersubject. But, under all conditions, the new subject must be so handled as to be secondary to the principal subject of the fugue. Therefore, not only must it be so designed that it does not overshadow the subject, but it must be subordinated to the principal subject and countersubject, limiting itself to forming two-, three-, or four-part invertible counterpoints with them, as the case may be.

476. Hence, the new subject must be regarded as a supplementary countersubject to the original subject, introduced at an appropriate moment in the fugue. It must, however, have one distinguishing musical characteristic: it must give the impression of complete melodic sense. Moreover, it may sometimes be necessary to give it greater length than the subject.

Place of the New Subject

477. Generally speaking, the new subject is introduced after the second episode, either in a neighboring key or in the principal key of the subject. Sometimes, for emphasis, it is preceded by a cadence on the dominant; it then continues in an exposition of its own, analogous to that of the subject.

478. The new subject is accompanied by its own countersubject or by the countersubject of the principal subject, as the case may be. The principal subject, however, should not be reintroduced until at least the fourth entry of the new subject. Thenceforth, the fugue may continue with both principal and new subjects sounded simultaneously, as well as their countersubjects. All further developments are based on one or another of these themes.

Order of Modulations

479. Here is a suggested outline of the order of arranging the modulations of a scholastic fugue in which a new subject has been introduced. The student may make any other arrangements that he finds convenient:

a) Exposition;

b) Episode;

c) Counterexposition;

d) Episode;

e) Subject in relative major or minor according to mode;

f) Episode in the dominant of the principal key;

g) Exposition of the new subject in the principal key;

h) Episode based on the new subject;

i) New subject and principal subject combined at the second degree, or at the sixth degree in the minor mode;

j) Answers of the new subject and the principal subject combined;

k) Episode based on elements of the new subject and the principal subject;

l) New subject and principal subject combined at the subdominant;

m) Episode and pedal point on the dominant made of elements borrowed from both subjects;

n) Stretto.

480. The order of modulations is not fixed. For example, after the exposition, or after the counterexposition if there be one, episodes may lead the principal subject to the subdominant, followed, after a short episode, by the answer at the second degree. This, supposing the fugue to be in the major mode, may lead to a pause on the dominant of the relative minor, where the new subject is introduced.

Arrangement of the Stretto Section

481. The following arrangement is suggested as a guide to the stretto section. The student is free to proceed according to his convenience, basing the combinations on the nature of both subjects:

a) First stretto of the principal subject;

b) Stretto of the new subject;

c) Strettos on both subjects combined and following, in general, the pattern of strettos based on a single subject.

482. Following are some examples by Bach which show the new subject combined with the principal subject:

a) Organ Fugue in F major:

b) Organ Fugue in C minor:

In the following example, also by Bach, the mutation in the reply of the subject given above engenders a corresponding mutation in the reply of the new subject:

c) *Art of the Fugue*:

In the example immediately above, the new subject and its countersubject begin and end before the principal subject; this both brings out their character and differentiates them from the countersubjects of the principal subject.

Composition of the New Subject

483. It is wise to plan the new subject in advance, that is, while working out the countersubject of the principal subject. This will necessitate the use of three-part invertible counterpoint. If the new subject is to be accompanied by a countersubject that is simultaneously invertible with the principal subject and its countersubject, four-part invertible counterpoint will be necessary. This is analogous to finding three different countersubjects invertible with each other as well as with the subject. (N.B. This is all very well if you are Bach or Mozart, but it is a practical impossibility to the beginner.—F.D.)

One of these, which is to be considered as the new subject, may begin several measures before the principal subject; the others must be shorter than the principal subject.

Analysis of a Fugue with Two New Subjects

484. Beginning at the exposition, here is an analysis of the last fugue in Bach's *The Art of the Fugue,* in which *two* new subjects are heard in succession:

Fugue 15:

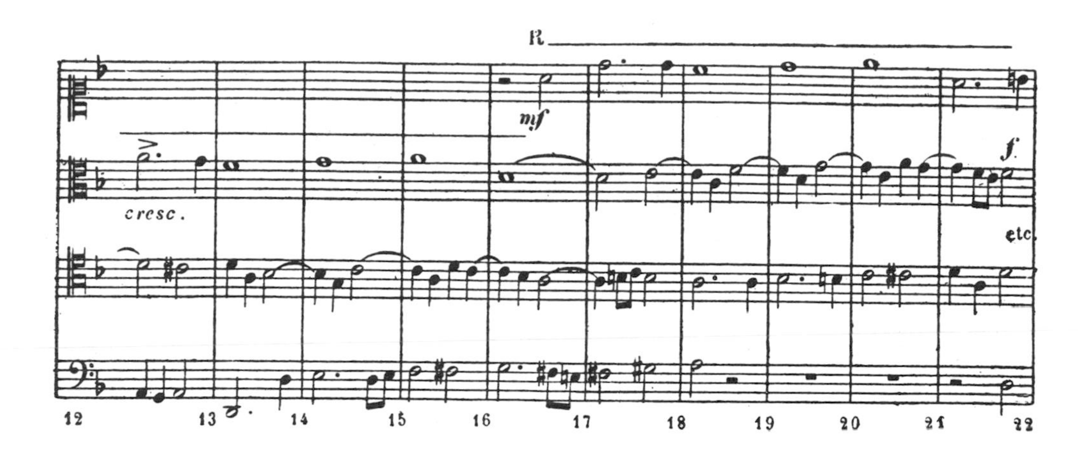

This exposition contains no countersubject in the strict meaning which we have so far attached to that word. However, it should be noted that, beginning at the 13th measure, the two free parts that accompany the subject are almost identically reproduced under the fourth entry of the answer.

485. The entire development which follows the exposition of the principal subject is treated as a series of strettos, alternately direct, inverse, and in contrary movement. The entries are made at various intervals. The themes of the episodes of this part are taken from the phrases which, in the exposition, took the place of the countersubjects.

Inverse and contrary canonical stretto:

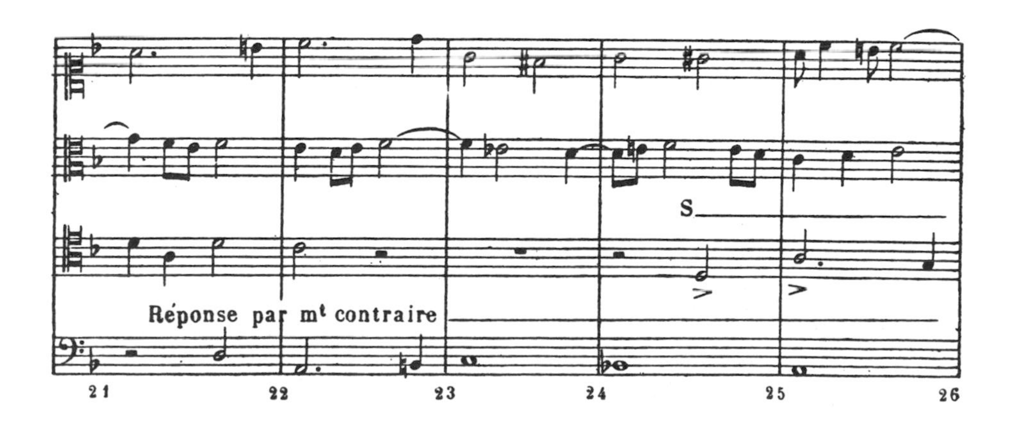

S. par
dim.
cresc.
27
28
29
30
31

mt contraire
p
sf
dim.
p
32
33
34
35
36

Stretto inverse (canonique)
R
S
cresc.
R
37
38
39
40
41
42

Divertis! I
f
cresc.
f
R. au 4e degré
43
44
45
46
47
48

(tiré de la figure de l'Exposition 8e mesure).
dim
cresc.
49
50
51
52
53
54
55

4e degré
dim.
p
p
S. par mt contraire
f
dim.
56
57
58
59
60
61

Stretto canon. S
f
sf
figure annonçant le Divertiss. II
sf
S
62
63
64
65
66
67

Divertissement II
Stretto par mt contraire (canonique)
dim.
p
S. par mt contraire au 3e degré
cresc.
R
68
69
70
71
72
73
74

S. par
f
75
76
77
78
79
80

mt contraire
S
81
82
83
84
85
86

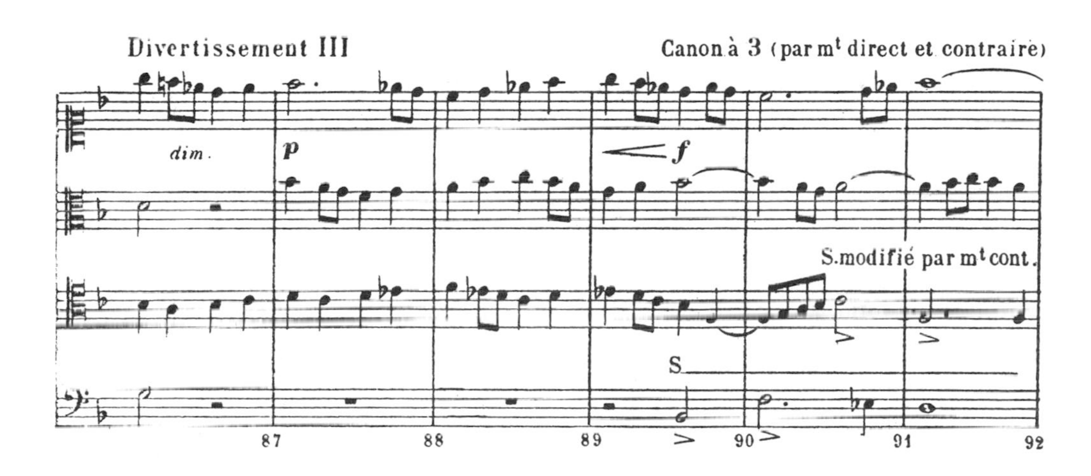
Divertissement III
Canon à 3 (par mt direct et contraire)
dim.
p
f
S.modifié par mt cont.
S
87
88
89
90
91
92

S
dim.
p
S
93
94
95
96
97
98

S
cresc.
99
100
101
102
103
104

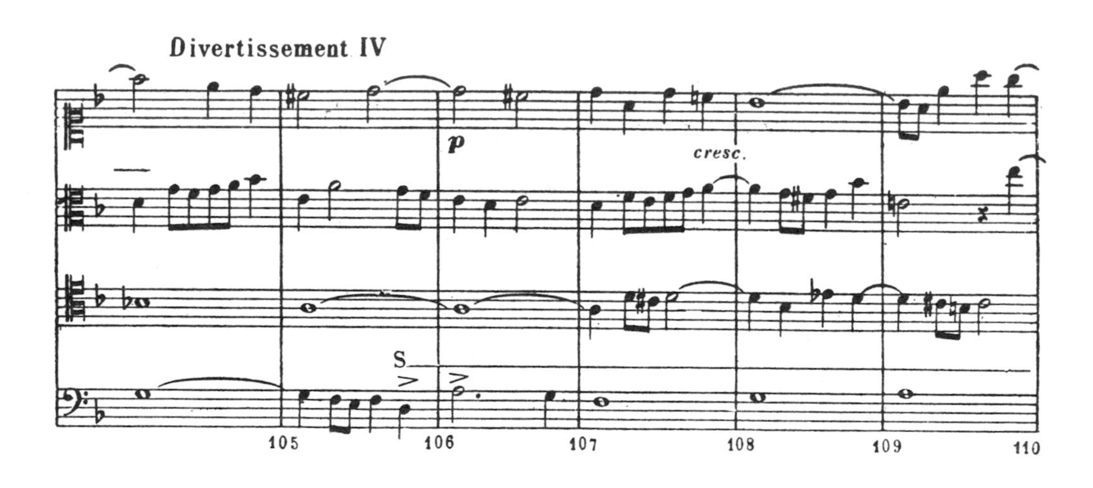
Divertissement IV
p
cresc.
S
105
106
107
108
109
110

111
112
113
114
115

Exposition of a First New Subject

486. The exposition of the first new subject begins at the 114th measure. This exposition is preceded by a short pedal point on the dominant of the principal key, in which the new subject makes its entry. Its melodic character and length differ from that of the principal subject. Its exposition, regular in form, ends at the 140th measure. It is followed by a six-measure partly canonical episode, made of the two phrases heard at the 126th measure. At the 147th measure, the new subject reappears in the principal key, heard this time in the soprano, and combined at the following measure with the principal subject which is sounded in the bass. A very short episode, made of the same elements as before, modulates to the dominant, and the combination of new subject and principal subject reappears at the alto and tenor. A new episode, measures 162 to 167, is followed by a different combination of the two subjects, the principal subject this time not entering until the third measure of the new subject.

After the eighth episode, the new subject reappears in the key of the subdominant, and while it is thus heard in the bass, a canonical stretto of the principal subject and its reply is given beginning at measure 182, joining with an episode that ends at the 193rd measure in a perfect cadence in G minor, the subdominant of the principal subject.

Exposition of the first new subject:

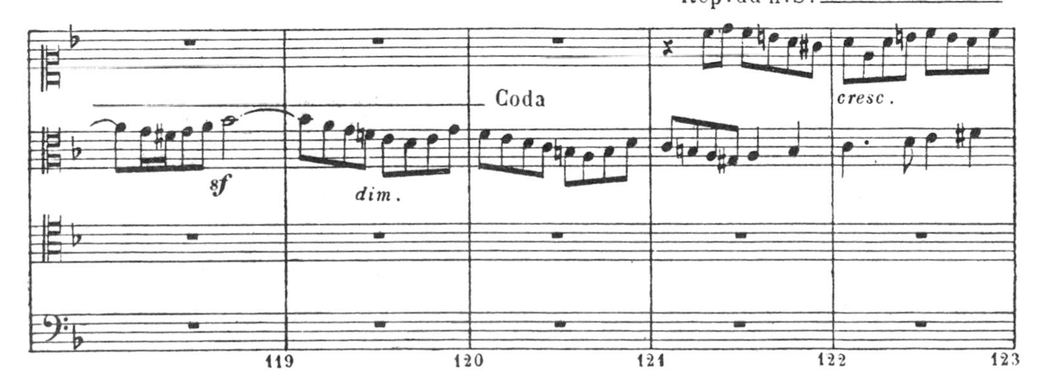

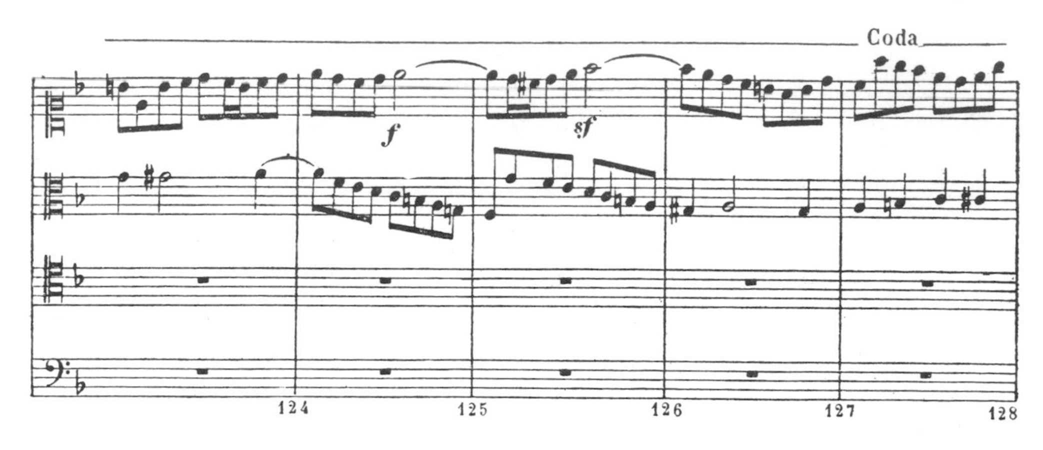
Coda
f
sf
124
125
126
127
128

cresc.
n.S.
f
sf
129
130
131
132
133

cresc.
R
dim.
134
135
136
137
138

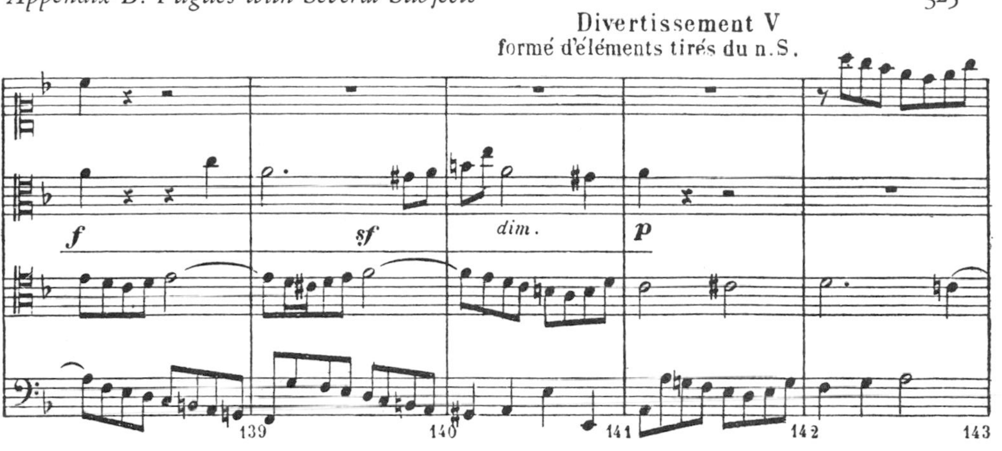
Divertissement V
formé d'éléments tirés du n.S.
f
sf
dim.
p
139
140
141
142
143

n.S.
cresc.
f
144
145
146
147
148

sf
sf
ff
dim.
Sujet principal
f
149
150
151
152
153

Divertissement VI
n.S. à la dte
S. à la dte
154
155
156
157
158

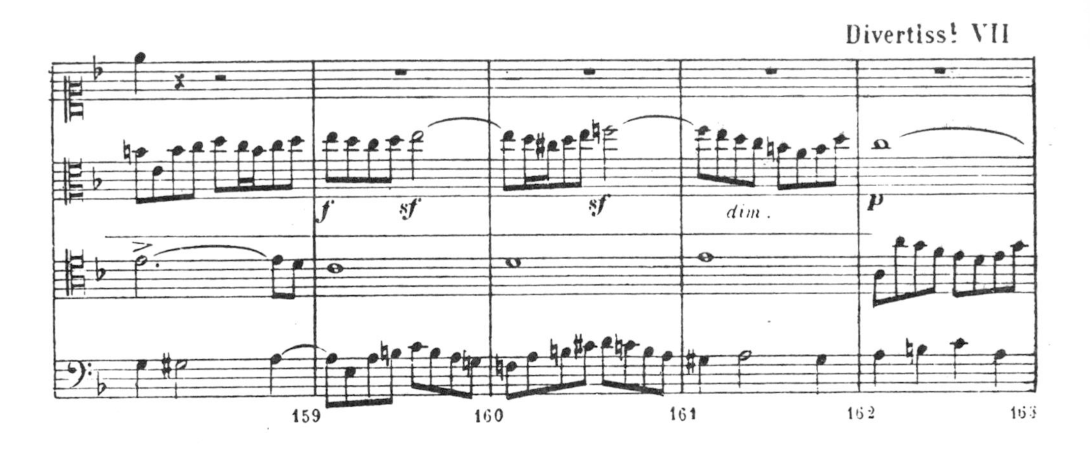
Divertiss! VII
f
sf
sf
dim.
p
159
160
161
162
163

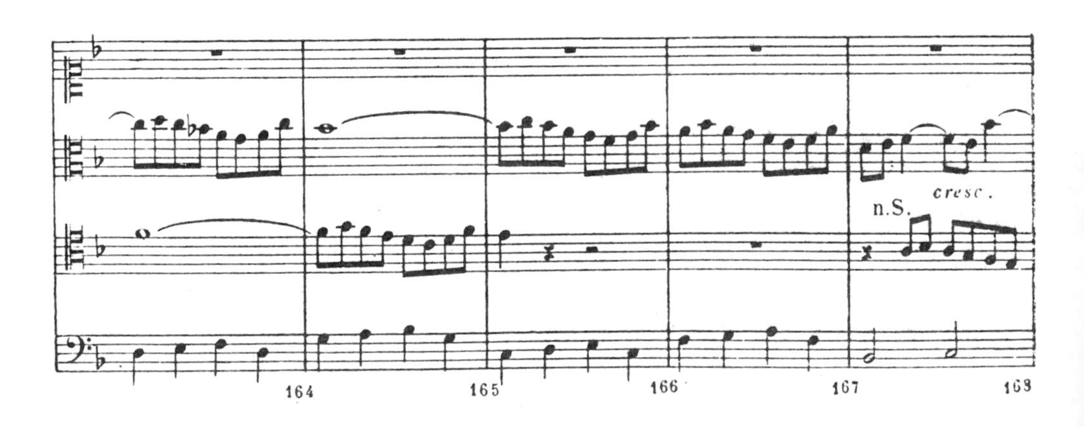
n.S.
cresc.
164
165
166
167
168

S.
169
170
171
172
173

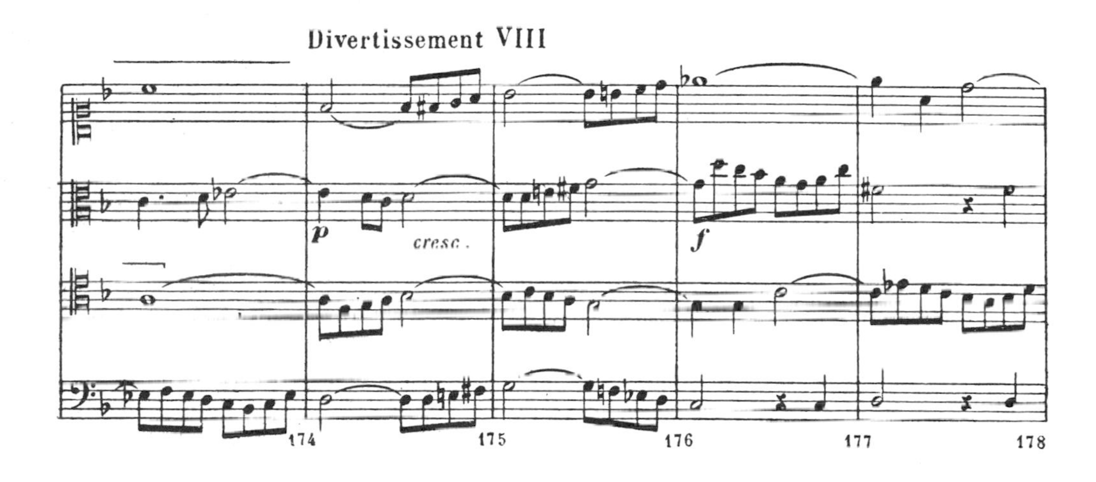
Divertissement VIII
p
cresc.
f
174
175
176
177
178

dim.
p
cresc.
S.
ff
n.S.
179
180
181
182
183

Exposition of the Second New Subject

487. Immediately after the cadence referred to in ¶486, the exposition of the second new subject begins; its four initial notes spell in German the name Bach. This exposition is made in the form of a stretto between the second new subject and its reply, which enters before the second new subject has been heard in its entirety.

488. At the 198th measure, the tenor takes up a figure already heard as a free countersubject in the 8th, 15th, and 20th measures of the exposition of the principal subject, and which has appeared in the episodes of the first part of the fugue. After an episode built on this figure, the second new subject reappears in the tenor, followed, in the measure before the last, by an entry in contrary movement in the alto. A close stretto follows immediately, made up at the distance of half a measure by the second new subject and its reply (measure 220) whose ending is slightly modified. Without interruption, the bass then (measure 222) takes up the second new subject in contrary movement; the alto sounds it again (measure 227) in direct movement at the subdominant, while

various phrases that recall the first new subject appear in the free parts. A short episode built of these same phrases leads to a cadence on the dominant of the principal key.

489. It will be noticed that the answer of the second new subject is not regular, which is of no importance in this instance. Even in a scholastic fugue with several subjects, the answer to a new subject may be made at any desired interval.

Observe that all this part of the fugue is maintained in either the first or fourth degree of the principal key. This is not a rule, though it is well to note that as few modulations as necessary are preferable.

Exposition of the second new subject:

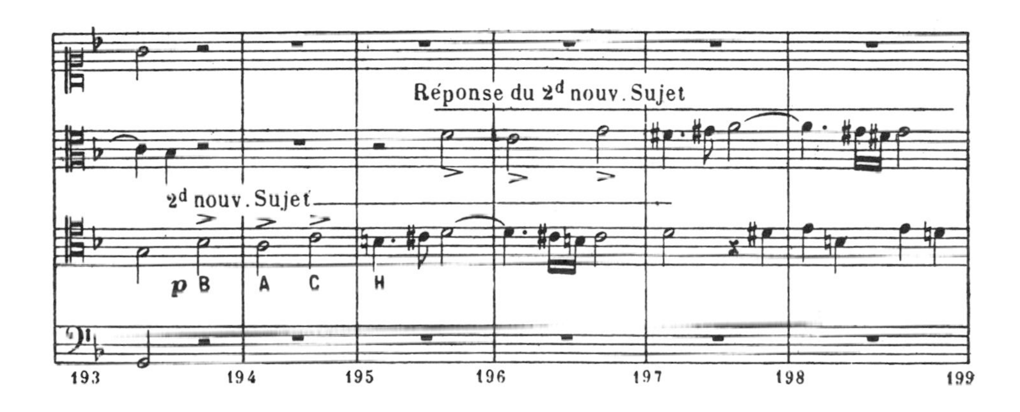

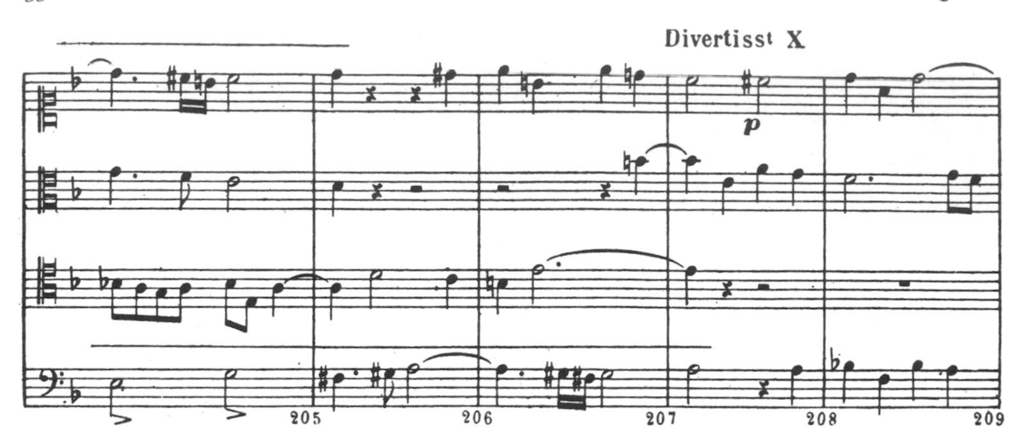
Divertiss^t X
p
205
206
207
208
209

Stretto. du 2^d n.S. par m^t contraire
2^d n.S. par m^t cor.t
f
2^d n. S.
210
211
212
213
214

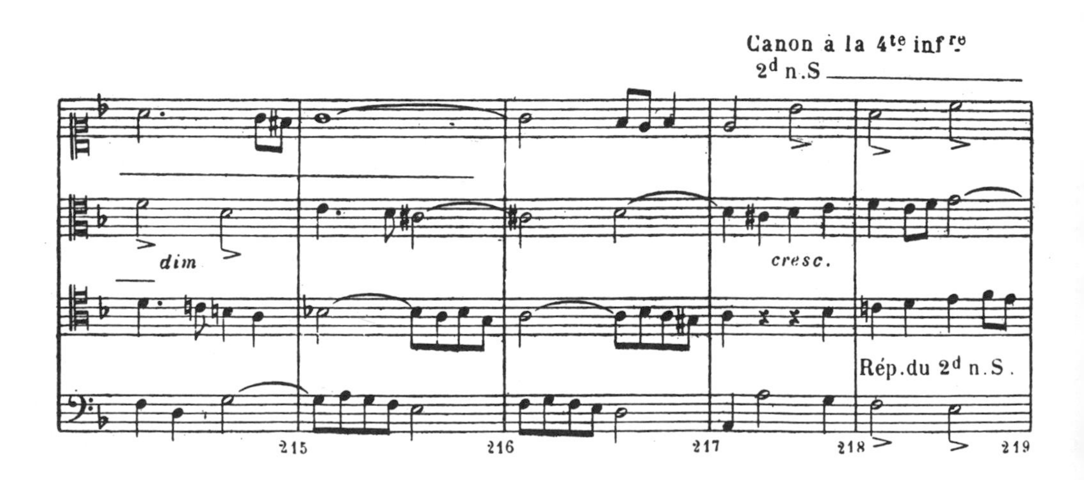
Canon à la 4te inf^re
2^d n.S
dim
cresc.
Rép. du 2^d n.S.
215
216
217
218
219

tr
p
cresc.
2d n.S. par mt cont.
220
221
222
223
224

2d n.S
f
sf
sf
sf
225
226
227
228
229

sf
230
231
232
233

Combinations of the Three Subjects

490. In the last part of the fugue, Bach wrote only six complete measures, the seventh being but a sketch. This last part was intended to include all the combinations that he had in mind for the three subjects. No doubt there is a certain presumption in attempting to finish such a work. Nevertheless, I believe it would be useful for the student to try to complete the fugue, closely following Bach's processes. (N.B. The pupil should be aware that all this should be written in triple and quadruple counterpoint.—F.D.)

Combination of the three subjects:

491. Study of this fugue shows that the new subject permits the introduction of elements quite different from the principal subject and countersubject at a time when the character of the fugue has already been clearly delineated, so that the new ideas do not nullify the unity of the whole. It is for precisely this reason that the new subject should be more strongly characterized than a simple countersubject, and that it make complete musical sense in itself.

492. Obviously no scholastic fugue can reach a development comparable to that attained here. The student should regard it as a model in which almost all

the combinations that can be made in a fugue with several subjects are presented.

493. We may sum up a general outline for a fugue with two or three subjects as follows:

a) Exposition and development of the first subject.

b) Exposition and development of the second subject.

c) Combination of the two subjects, and development of the fugue in conformity with such combinations.

Modifications of the Subject

494. Besides the introduction of a new subject, a fugue may also be diversified by modifying the principal subject and its countersubject.

These modifications may deal with the rhythm of the subject, or, more rarely, with its melodic line, which, however, must never be modified to the extent that it becomes unrecognizable.

In addition to the examples below (¶495 and ¶496), the student will find many for study and guidance in the fugues of Bach, Handel, Mozart, and Mendelssohn.

495. In Fugue XXXIII of the *Well-Tempered Clavier,* the subject:

is sometimes presented in this rhythmically modified form:

and treated in this manner (measures 23 to 26):

496. Bach's *Art of the Fugue* presents several examples of these transforma-

tions of a subject, all of which can be used in a scholastic fugue:

Subject:

Modifications of the Length of the Subject

497. In addition to these rhythmic modifications, the subject may be presented in part, that is, it may be interrupted either to sound the answer or to begin an episode.

Such cutting must be done only at the end of the subject, and must never affect the head of the subject. Moreover, it may only be done with longish subjects.

Modification of the First Note

498. However, the length of the first note of the subject may be modified. When a subject begins like this:

it may occasionally be presented thus:

or, more rarely:

Such modifications must be guided by musical requirements: either because the subject, for harmonic reasons, cannot re-enter with its first note in its original length, or because the re-entry of the subject is made more emphatic by such shortening.

Last Note of the Subject Modified in the Exposition

499. In no case may the changes in ¶498 be made in the exposition, in which the only permitted modification of the subject is that its last note may be retarded at its second entry.

Example (Mendelssohn, Organ Fugue):

The same comment applies to the countersubject.

Modifications in the Answer

500. Likewise, after the first entry of the subject the answer may be modified at its last note, either better to link it to an episode or to a new entry of the subject, replacing a minor by a major interval as in this example by Bach:

But the replacing of a major by a minor interval is never permitted.

501. With this, we end our presentation of the various elements of which a scholastic fugue may be composed.

It should be noted that I have confined myself to the discussion of four-part fugues. I have not thought it fit to formulate special rules for two- and three-part fugues, as the student should have no difficulty in applying rules governing four parts to those with fewer than four parts.

APPENDIX C

Representative Scholastic Fugues

I

Four-Part Fugue
(Contest at the Institute, 1883)

Subject by Massenet

Paul Vidal
(Class of Mr. Massenet)
1st Grand Prix de Rome

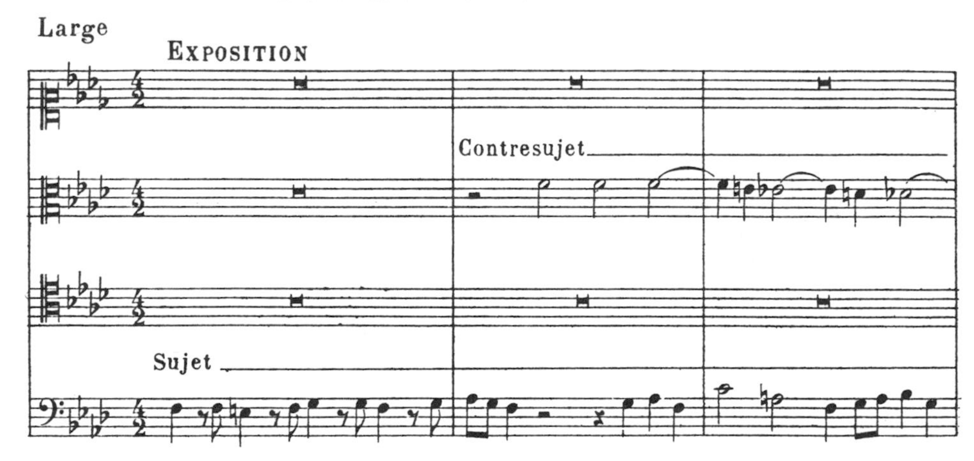

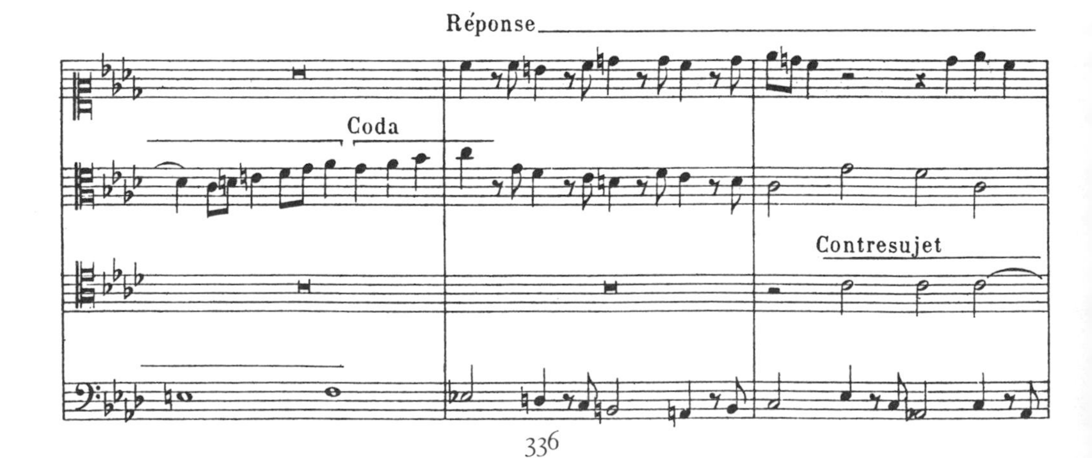

S

Contresujet

Contresujet
Réponse

DIVERTISSEMENT tiré de la Coda
CONTRE-EXPOSITION
Réponse
Contresujet
Contresujet
Réponse

DIVERTISSEMENT tiré du Sujet
TON RELATIF MAJEUR
Sujet
Contresujet

C.S.
R
DIVERTISSEMENT tiré du Sujet et du C.S.
fragt du S.
fragt du C.S.

TON MINEUR DE LA SOUS DOMINANTE
C.S.
Sujet
TON MAJEUR DE LA SUS-DOMINANTE
Sujet
Contresujet
DIVERTISSEMENT
tiré du Contresujet

Pédale de dominante
1er STRETTO
STRETTO
Sujet
Réponse
Sujet

Réponse
C.S.
DIVERTISSEMENT
2e STRETTO
Réponse
Sujet
C.S.
Réponse
Sujet

3e STRETTO par mt contraire
Sujet

Sujet

4e STRETTO par mt contraire
Pédale de tonique

Sujet

dimin.

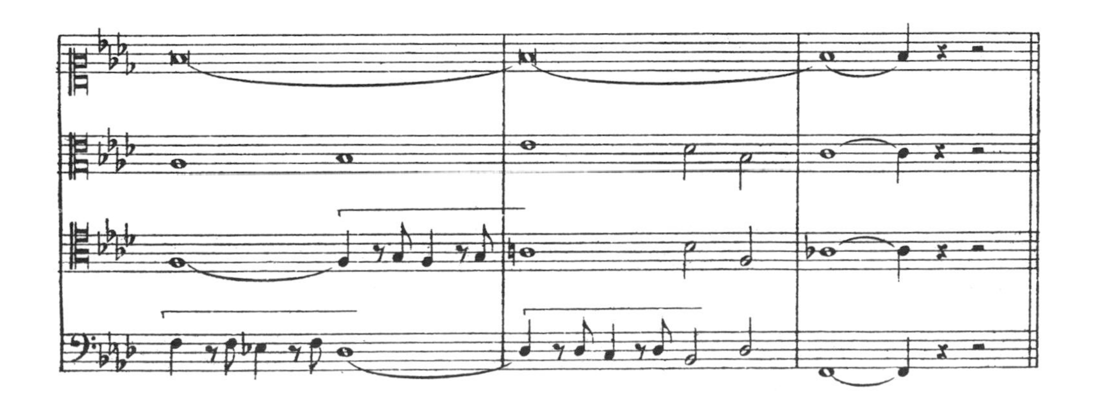

II

Four-Part Fugue

(With Two Countersubjects)

Subject attributed to Halévy — Mlle. R. Depecker

(Class of Mr. Ernest Guiraud)

1st Prize in Fugue, 1892

2e C.S.
1er C.S.
Sujet

mt cont.
1er C.S.
Réponse

2d C.S.

DIVERTt formé avec des frag. des 2 C.S.
frag. du 2d C.S.
B
A
frag. du 1er C.S.

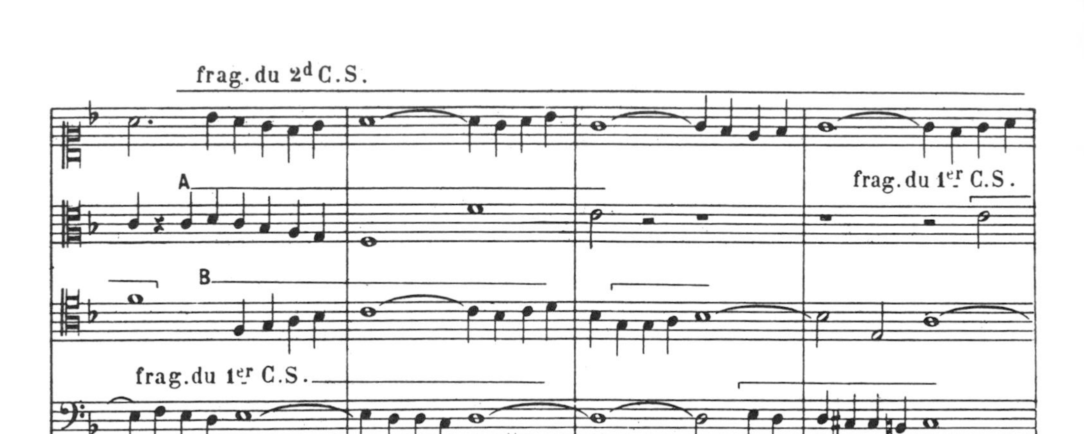
frag. du 2d C.S.
A
frag. du 1er C.S.
B
frag. du 1er C.S.

tête du 2d C.S. par mt cont.
tête du 1er C.S.
frag. du 1er C.S.
tête du 2d C.S. par mt cont.
mt cont.
tête du 2d C.S. par mt cont.
tête du 1er C.S.
tête du 2d C.S. par

tête du 1er C.S.
TON DU 6e DEGRÉ
C
Sujet
tête du 2d C.S.
tête du 2d C.S.
tête du 2d C.S.
mt cont.
tête du 1er C.S.
tête du

C
Coda du 1er C.S.
tête du 2d C.S.
1er C.S.

Réponse au relatif
tête du 2d C.S.
tête du 1er C.S.

DIVERTISSEMENT
Coda du 1er C.S.
Coda du 1er C.S.

Coda du 1er C.S.
tête du 1er C.S.
Coda du 1er C.S.
tête du 1er C.S.

tête du 1er C.S.
Coda du 1er C.S.
C
C

TON DU 5e DEGRÉ
imit.
tête du 2d C.S.
CHORAL (tête de la Réponse)
C
tête du 1er C.S.

mt contraire
tête du 2d C.S.
(Réponse par mt contraire)
frag. du 2d C.S.
1er C.S. combiné avec la

frag. du 2d C.S. par mt cont.
frag. du 1er C.S.
Réponse par mt cont.

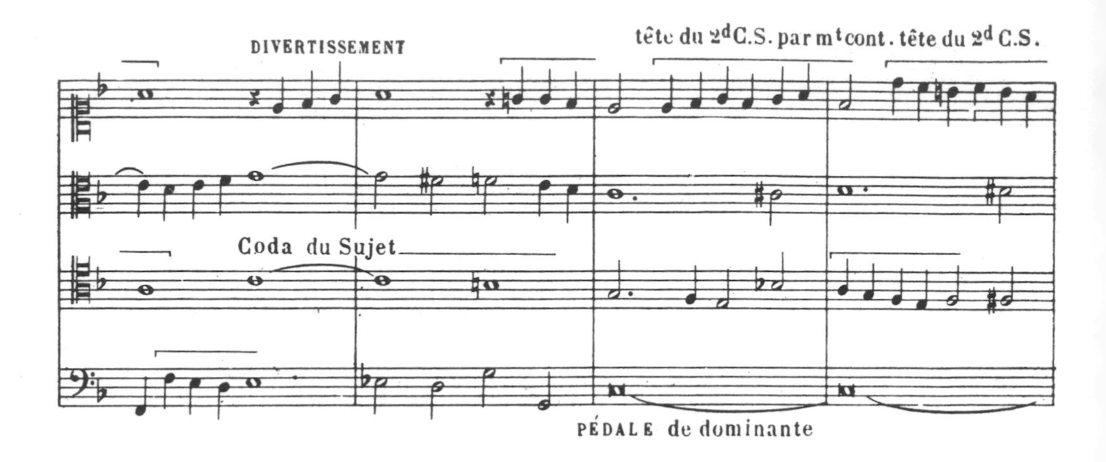
DIVERTISSEMENT
tête du 2d C.S. par mt cont. tête du 2d C.S.
Coda du Sujet
PÉDALE de dominante

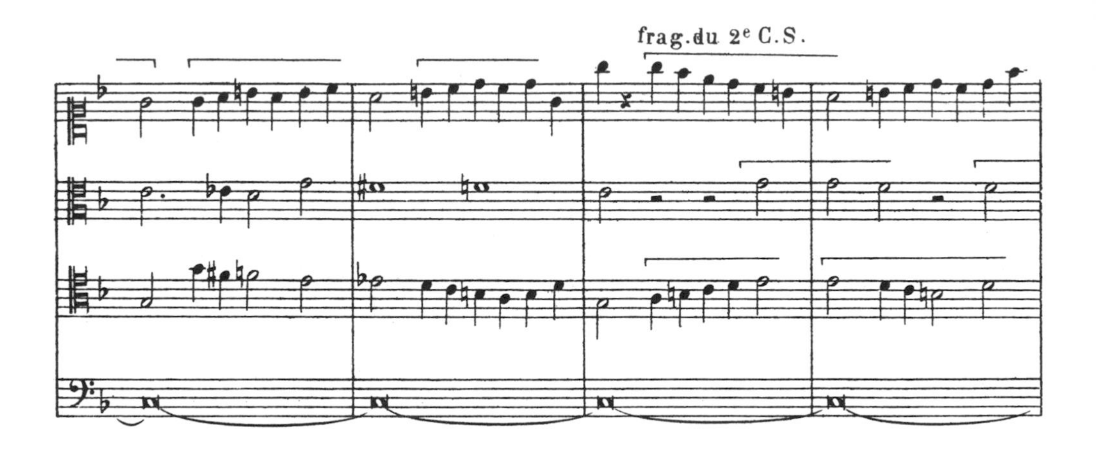
frag. du 2e C.S.

mt contraire
Réponse par diminution

Sujet par diminution

mt contraire

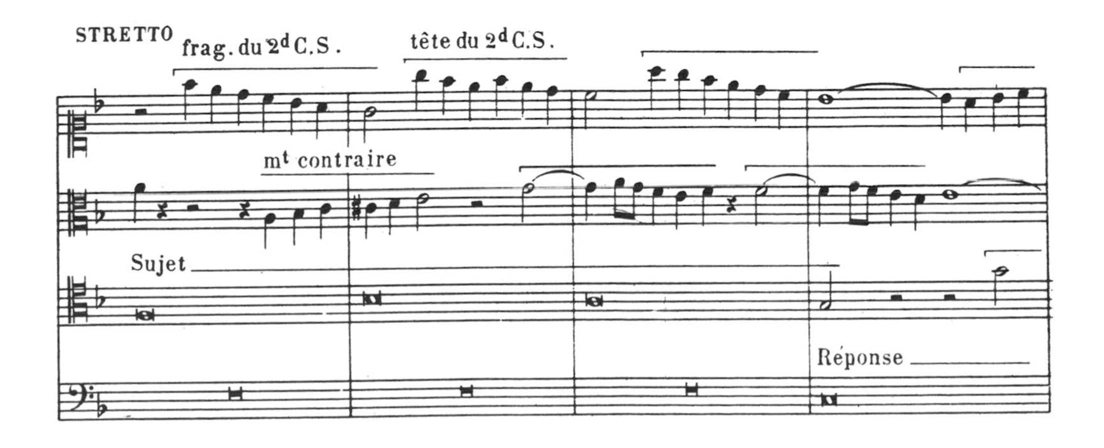
STRETTO
frag. du 2d C.S.
tête du 2d C.S.
mt contraire
Sujet
Réponse

Sujet
D
D

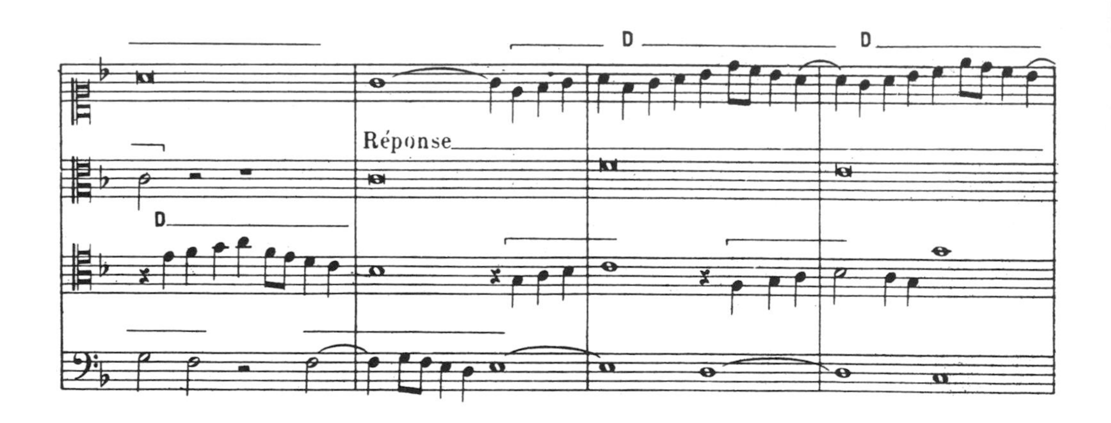
D
D
Réponse
D.

STRETTO LIBRE DES CONTRESUJETS
D
tête du 2d C.S. par diminution
tête du 2d C.S.
mt contraire
frag. du 2d C.S. par dim.
tête du 2d C.S. par dim.

par diminution
frag. du 2d C.S. par dim.
tête du 2d C.S. par dim.

frag. par diminution
tête du 1er C.S.
tête du 2d C.S. par dim
et par mt contraire
tête du 1er C.S

par dim.
tr
tête du 2d C.S. par mt cont.
mt cont.
par dim.

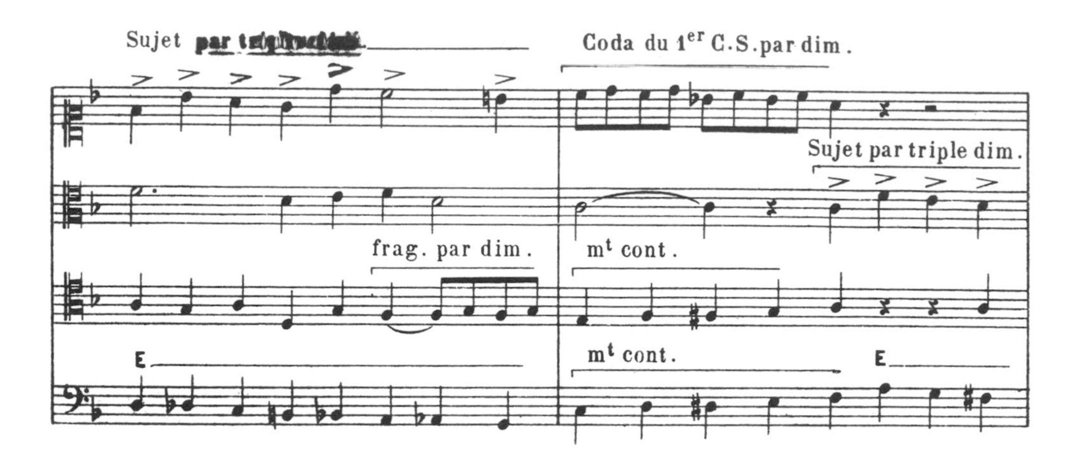
Sujet par
Coda du 1er C.S. par dim.
Sujet par triple dim.
frag. par dim.
mt cont.
E
mt cont.
E

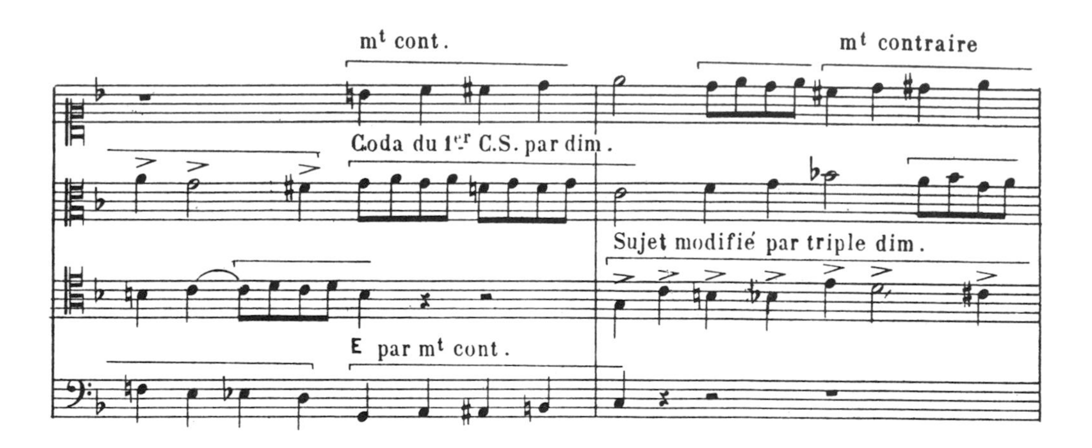
mt cont.
mt contraire
Coda du 1er C.S. par dim.
Sujet modifié par triple dim.
E par mt cont.

mt cont.
mt cont.
E mt cont.
Sujet mod. par triple dim.

frag. du 2d C.S. par dim.
tête du 1er C.S. par dim.
mt cont.
mt cont.

cresc.
tr
cresc.

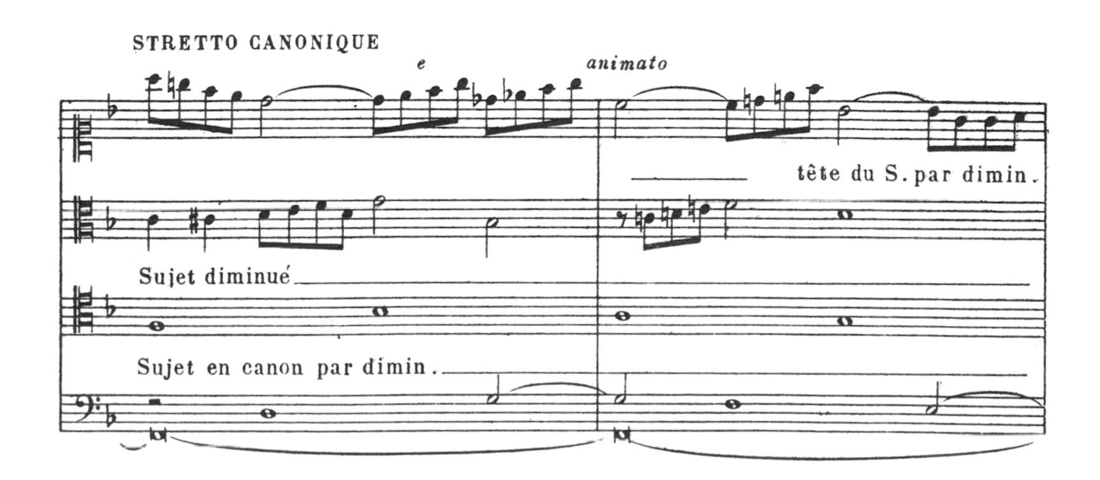
STRETTO CANONIQUE
e
animato
tête du S. par dimin.
Sujet diminué
Sujet en canon par dimin.

ff
ff

toujours ff
f (♮)
allarg.
toujours ff

CHORAL
Sujet
ff
ff
rall.
ff
ff
ff
rall.

1er mouvt
tête du Sujet par dim.
pp
pp
pp
dolce
p
Réponse
rall.
Sujet

III
Four-Part Fugue
(Contest of 1893)

Subject by A. Thomas

F. Van Doren
(Class of Mr. Massenet)

1st Prize in Fugue, 1893

R
C.S.

DIVERTISSEMENT (frag. de la Coda et du C.S.)
A
C
C
C
A
B
C

B
C
A
La 1re partie très expressive
A
A
C
C
C
C

TON RELATIF MINEUR
C. S.
A
S
B
C
C
A

R
C.S.

DIVERTISSEMENT (frag. du S. et du C.S.)
A
B
A
A
B

EXPOSITION D'UN NOUVEAU SUJET
rall.
a tempo
A
rall.
B
Nouveau Sujet
A
a tempo
rall.

Réponse du Nouveau Sujet

TON DE LA SOUS DOMINANTE (Sujet combiné avec le Nouv. S.)
Nouveau S
S

DIVERTISSEMENT (frag. du Nouv. S.)

express.
cresc.
(♯)
cresc.
cresc.
cresc.

dimin.
dimin.
dimin.

rall. molto
rall. molto
rall. molto
rall. molto

1er STRETTO

a tempo
R
S
a tempo

R
S

STRETTO du C. S. canon
C.S.
C.S.

2e STRETTO (inverse) du Sujet
R

S

3e STRETTO du S.(canon)
R
S

DIVERTISSEMENT sur la tête de la R.
cresc.
cresc.
R
cresc.
R
cresc.

R
dimin.
f
dimin.
f
dimin.
f
R

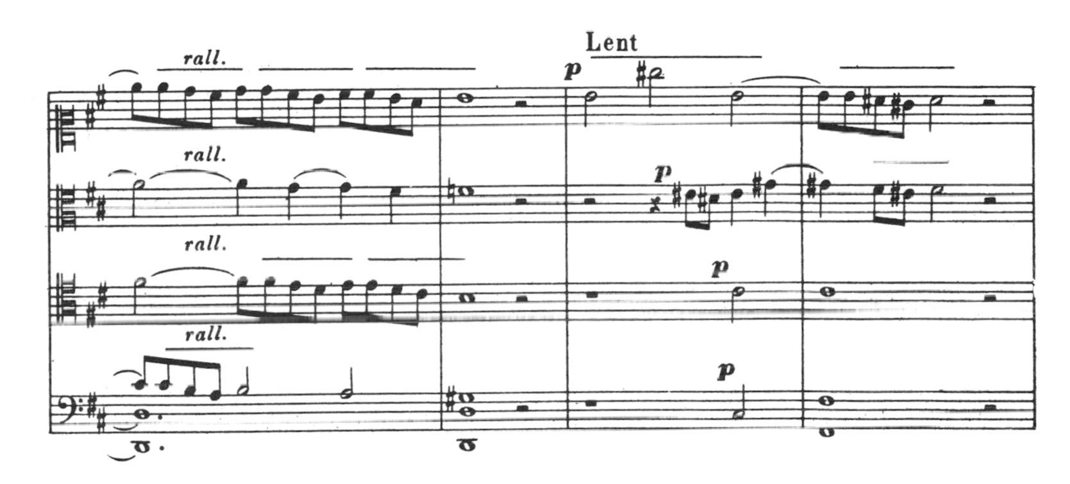
rall.
Lent
p
rall.
p
rall.
p
rall.
p

4e STRETTO du S.
f
S
a tempo
f
f
a tempo
R
S
f
f

R
f
en élargissant
en élargissant
en élargissant

IV
Four-Part Fugue

Subject by A. Gedalge

Charles Koechlin
(Classes of Messrs. Massenet
and Gabriel Fauré)

R
tr
C: S.
partie ad lib.
A
tr

DIVERTISSEMENT sur deux frag. du S. B et C
B
C
B

C
imit. de rythme

frag. de C
TON DU 6e DEGRE
tr
C
S

A
tr
C.S.

R
tr
A

DIVERTISSEMENT sur la partie ad libit. A et sur des fragm. du Sujet
A
tête de A
tr

A
A
A
A

TON DE LA SOUS DOMINANTE
S
tr
C. S.
A

Réponse (au RELATIF MINEUR DE LA SOUS DOMINANTE)
R
tr
A

DIVERTISSEMENT sur la partie ad lib. A
A
A

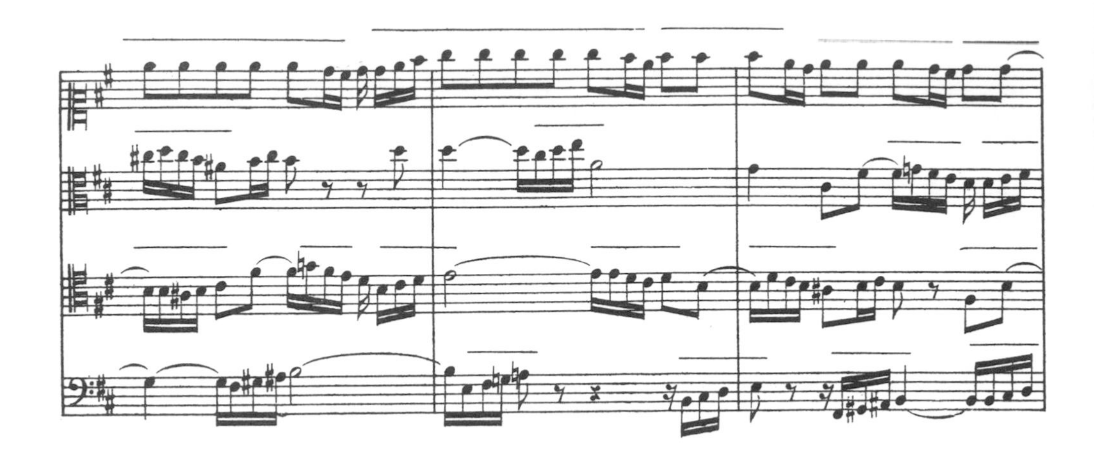

PÉDALE de dominante

1er STRETTO
S

A
R
C.S.

R
A
S
tr

tr
A
C.S.

2e STRETTO
R
tr
S
(#)

S
tr
R

DIVERTISSEMENT sur la tête du Sujet
S. par mouvt contraire

3e STRETTO
Canon du S. et de la R.
R
S
R
S

S
R

tr
tête du S.

V
Four-Part Fugue
(Preliminary Contest, 1896)

Subject by A. Gedalge

Florent Schmitt
(Classes of Messrs. Massenet
and Gabriel Fauré)

1st Grand Prix de Rome, 1900

DIVERTISSE-
R
A
C.S.
B
p
p

-MENT sur la Coda
A
A
B
B
A
A
B

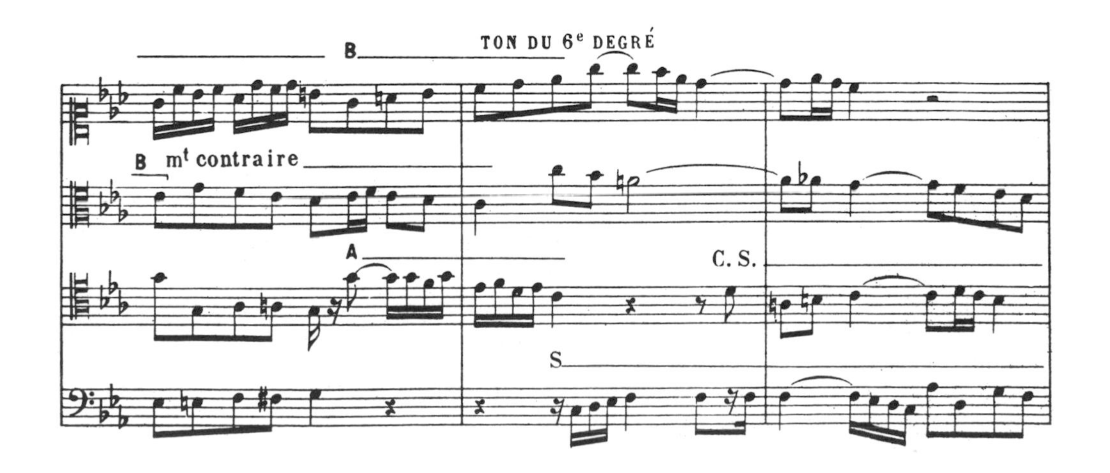
B
TON DU 6e DEGRÉ
B mt contraire
A
C.S.
S

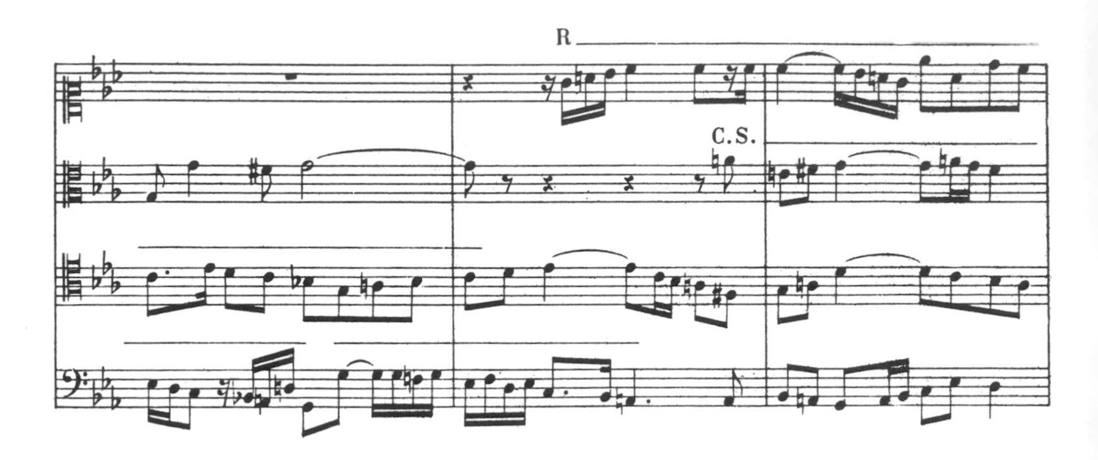
R
C.S.

DIVERTISSEMENT sur un frag. du Sujet
A
A
A

A
TON DU 4e DEGRÉ
A
A
S
A
C.S.

TON DU 2d DEGRÉ
C.S.
S

DIVERTISSEMENT frag. du S. et du C.S.
B
A
B

A
B
B

B
A
A

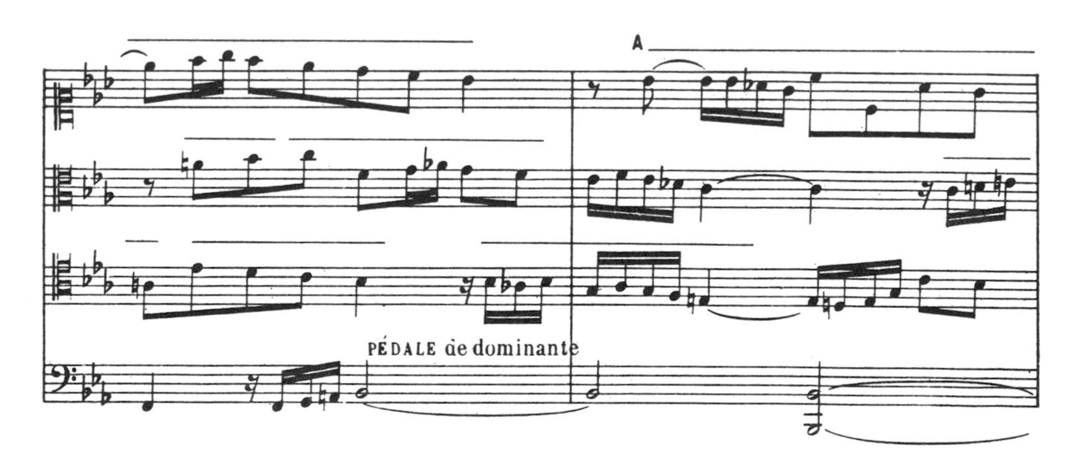
A
PÉDALE de dominante

retenez
retenez
ff
ff

a tempo
1er STRETTO
C.S
S

S
R
C.S.

R
A

2d STRETTO en canon à la 6te
A
A
A

A
A
A
A

3e STRETTO (véritable)
A
S
R
S

R

4e STRETTO (par
R
S
augmentation)
S
S
S
S

dim.
dim.

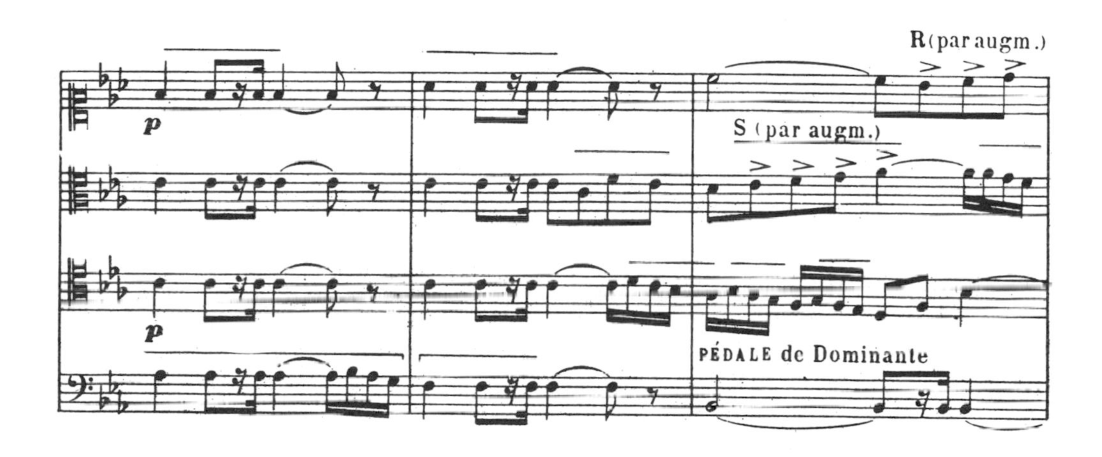
R(par augm.)
p
S (par augm.)
p
PÉDALE de Dominante

dim.
dim.

PÉDALE supérieure
pp
retenez
pp
retenez

VI
Four-Part Fugue

Subject by A. Gedalge

Mlle. J. Boulay
(Class of Mr. Massenet)

1st Prize in Fugue, 1897

DIVERTISSEMENT sur un frag. du Sujet
tr

TON DU 6e DEGRÉ
Sujet
R
C.S.
tr

DIVERTISSEMENT sur un frag. du S. combiné avec un frag. du C.S.
C.S.
tr

TON DU 2d DEGRÉ
C.S.
S

TON DU 4e DEGRÉ
S.
C.S.

DIVERTISSEMENT sur la fin du Sujet

cresc.
cresc.

PÉDALE DE DOMINANTE
f
dim.

1er STRETTO
a tempo
S.
R

R
S.

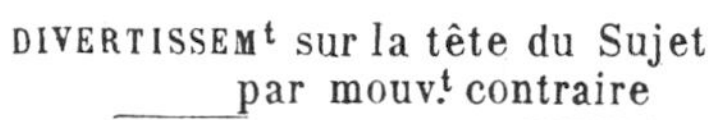
DIVERTISSEMt sur la tête du Sujet
par mouvt contraire

2d STRETTO au 6e degré
R
S

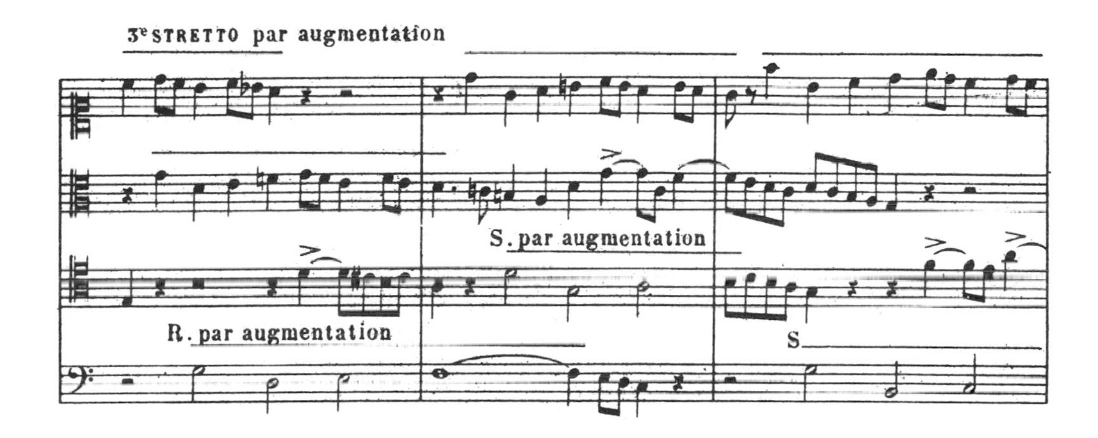
3e STRETTO par augmentation
S. par augmentation
R. par augmentation
S

4e STRETTO (canonique inverse)
R
cresc.
S
R
R
S

5e STRETTO au 4e degré
(par mouvement contraire)
S
R

S
DIVERTISSEMENT
R
cresc.

R

R
rit.

6e STRETTO (libre)
S
S
S
S
S
PÉDALE DE TONIQUE

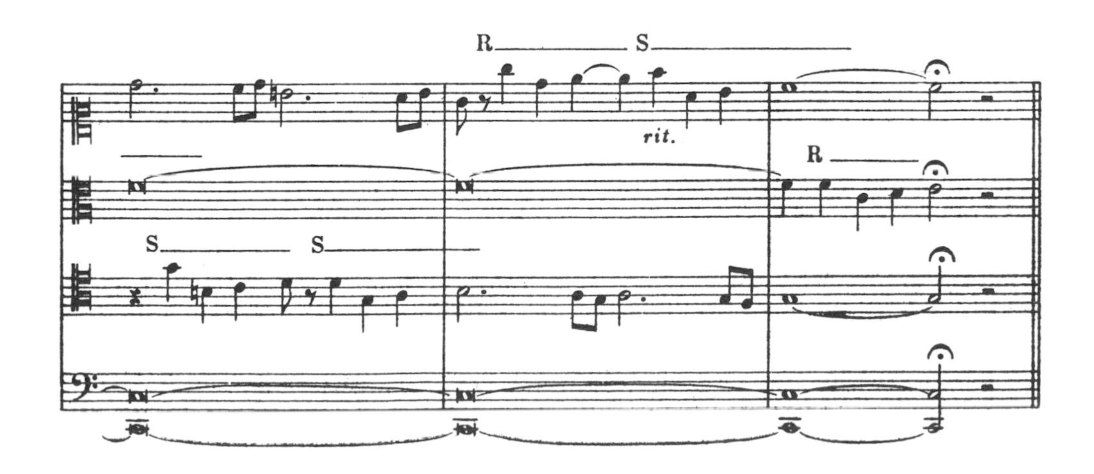
R
S
rit.
R
S
S

VII

Four-Part Fugue
(Preliminary Contest, 1897)

Subject by Theo. Dubois

Edmond Malherbe
(Classes of Messrs. Massenet
and Gabriel Fauré)

1st Grand Prix de Rome, 1899

DIVERTISSEMENT sur la Coda et le C. S.

TON DU 3e DEGRÉ
R
C.S.
C.S.
S

DIVERTISSEMENT
pp
pp

cresc. poco a poco jusqu'à la Pédale

TON DU 4e DEGRÉ
S

TON DU 2d DEGRÉ
C.S.
cresc. poco a poco
S
C.S.

DIVERTISSEMENT
cresc.
cresc.

TON DU 6e DEGRÉ
S
DIVERTISSEMENT
f
f
f
f

rall.
ff
dim.
rall.
ff
PÉDALE DE DOMINANTE
dim.

cre
scen

do
rit.
f
f
rit.
f

1er STRETTO
S
p
Nouvelle Figure
R
p
Nouvelle Figure
p
p
p

Nouv. Fig.
p
S
f
N. F.
R

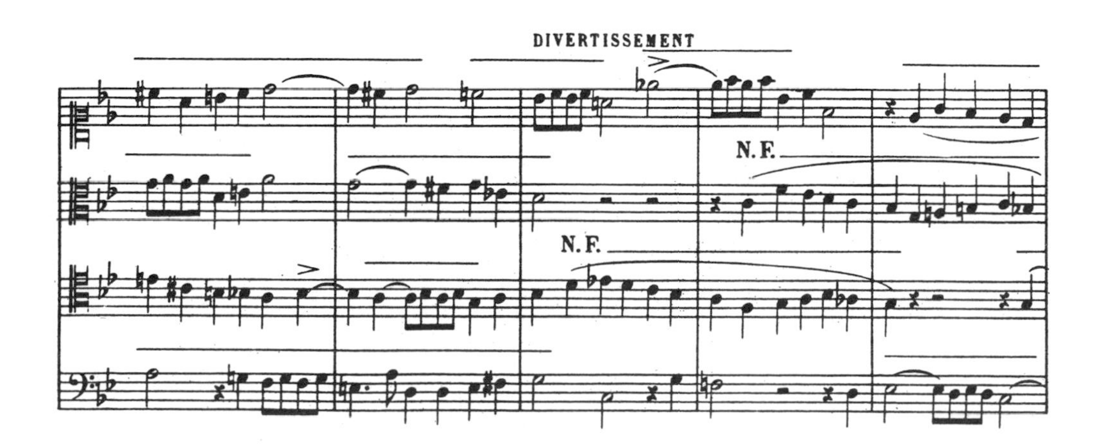
DIVERTISSEMENT
N. F.
N. F.

2d STRETTO
S
R

3e STRETTO
S
f
R
f
S
f

4e STRETTO (canonique)
f
R
f
f
f
f

f rall.
p subito
f rall.
p subito
PÉDALE DE TONIQUE
p

tr
rall.
rall.

VIII
Four-Part Fugue
(With Three Countersubjects)

Subject by Georges Enesco

Georges Enesco
(Class of Mr. Massenet)

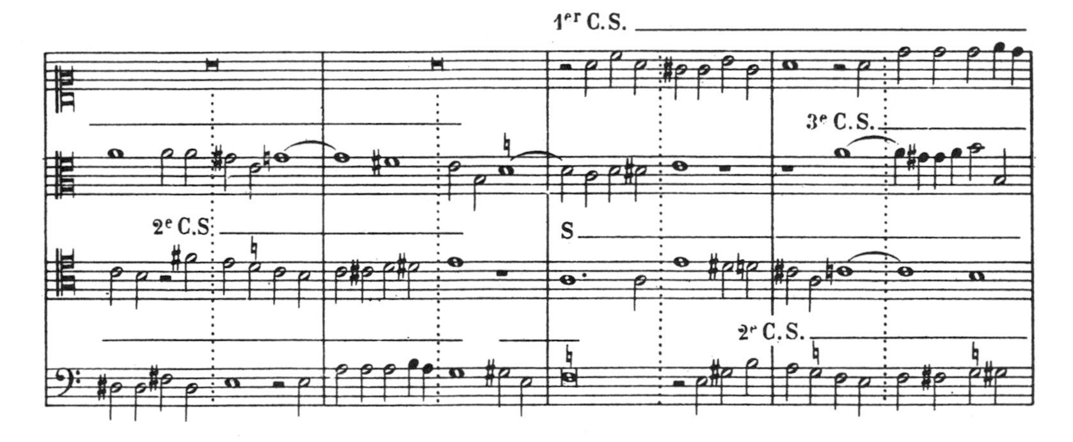

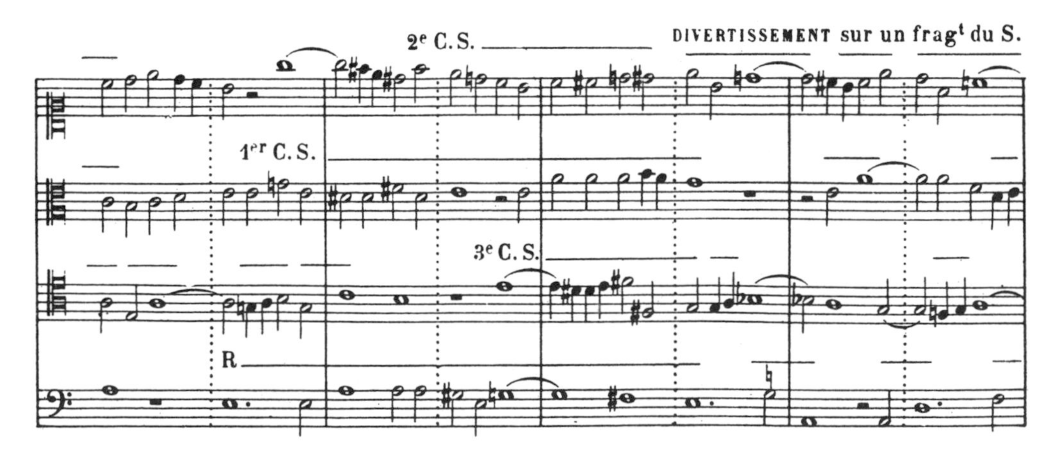

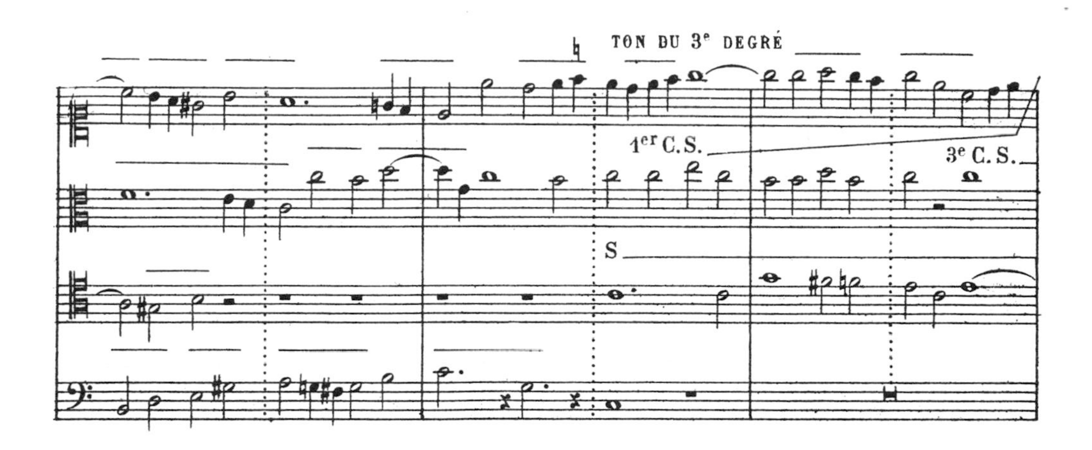
TON DU 3e DEGRÉ
1er C.S.
3e C.S.
S

3e C. S.
R
2e C.S
1er C.S.

DIVERTISSEMENT sur le 3e C.S. et sur un frag. du S.

TON DU 6e DEGRÉ
S
1er C. S.
2e C. S.
R

2e C. S.
DIVERTISSEMENT sur un fragt du 3e C. S.
3e C. S.

TON DU 4e DEGRE
3e C. S.
S
2e C. S.

R
DIVERTISSEMENT
2e C.S.
1er C.S
3e C.S.

sur un fragt du S.
PÉDALE DE DOMINANTE

f
p

1er STRETTO
S
R
2e S.C
S

3e C.S.
2e STRETTO (canon de la Rép. à 4)
R
1er C
S
R
2e C.S.
R
R

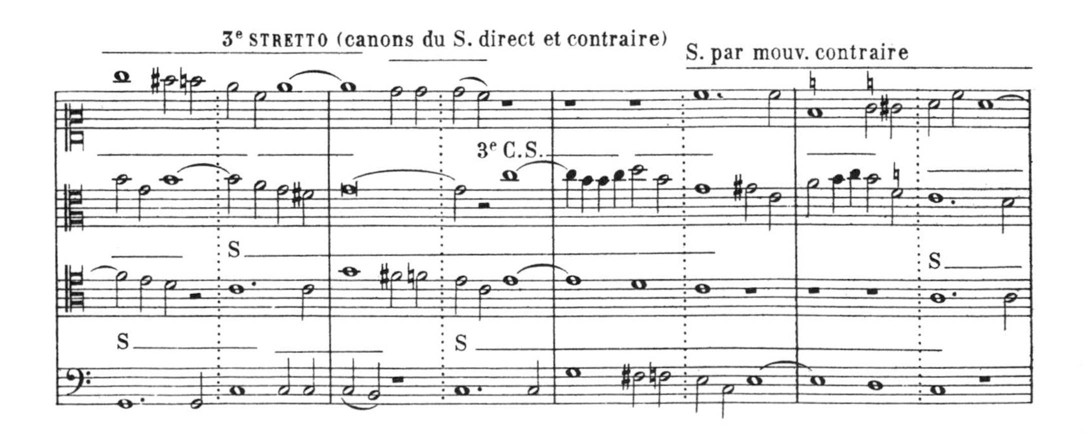
3e STRETTO (canons du S. direct et contraire)
S. par mouv. contraire
3e C.S.
S
S
S
S

4e STRETTO
Sujet par augmentation
S
f
R
S
R. par mt cont.

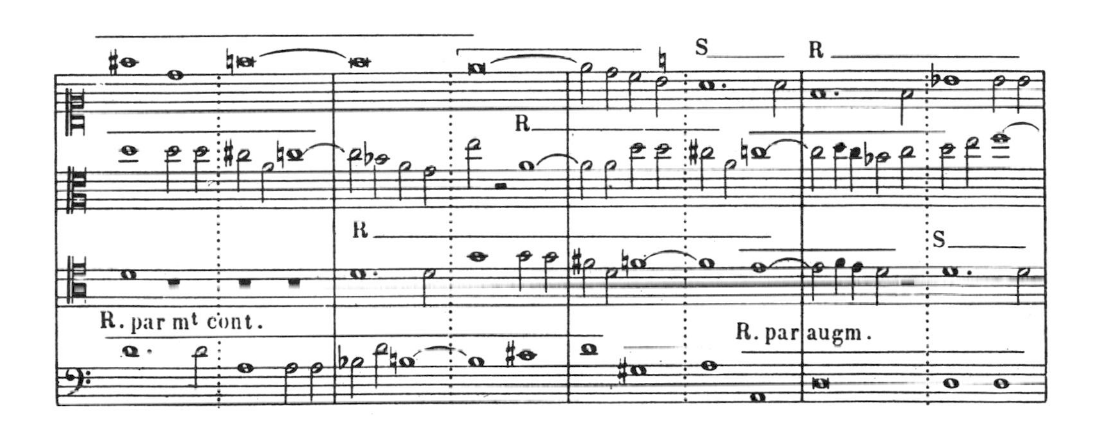
S
R
R
R
S
R. par mt cont.
R. par augm.

5e STRETTO (véritable)
S
R
R
S
S
R

retenu
S
S
S

IX
Four-Part Fugue

Subject by A. Gedalge

M. J. Morpain
(Class of Mr. Gabriel Fauré)

DIVERTISSEMENT sur un frag. du C.S.

TON DU 3e DEGRÉ
S
C.S.

R
C.S.

DIVERTISSEMENT sur la fin du S.

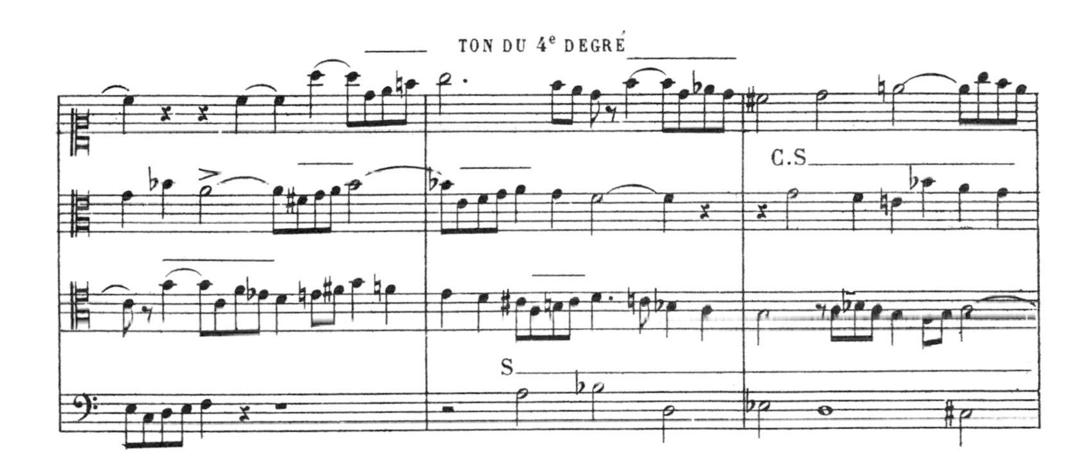
TON DU 4e DEGRÉ
C.S
S

TON DU 6e DEGRÉ
S
C.S

DIVERTISSEMENT sur la tête du C.S.

1er STRETTO
R
S
PÉDALE DE DOMINANTE

S
C.S.
R

2d STRETTO par mt contr. et direct
S.contr.
C.S
S.cont.
S

S
3e STRETTO (canonique)
S
S
R.contr.
S.contr.

4e STRETTO par dimin.
R
S
S.contr.
S.
cont

S
S.contr.
S
S.contr.
S.contr.
S
S
PÉDALE DE DOMINANTE

5e STRETTO
(en canon à contre-temps)
S
S
S.contr.
R

INDEX

(All index numbers refer to paragraphs, not pages.)

Alteration:
characteristic, 33, 44, 74, 77, 78
of the last note of the answer, 500

Alternation:
of subject and answer: 22, 23, 127

Answer:
affected by written or implied alteration of the dominant, 77, 78; examples, 79–84
definition, 22
fundamental harmonies of, 30, 70
general rules for, 28, 29
must consist of keys of first and fifth degrees of the subject, 24
order of modulations in, 25, 26
real, 32
relation of its tonic to tonic of subject, 27
special conventions governing, 30, 31
summary of rules for, 104
tables summarizing answers to
head of subject going from dominant to first degree, 49
head of subject going from tonic to fifth degree, 67, 68
chromatic subject, 47, 48, 92–98
subject beginning on the second, the unaltered fourth, or the sixth degree of the principal key, 103
subject beginning on the dominant, 42, 43, 44
subject beginning on the fifth followed by the altered fourth with immediate return to the fifth degree, 45, 46
subject beginning on the altered fourth degree of the principal key, 102
subject beginning on the seventh degree in major, 100

subject beginning on the altered (raised) seventh degree in minor, 101
subject beginning and ending on tonic or mediant without sounding the fifth degree, 39; sounding it as a passing or neighboring note, 40, 41
subject in which the seventh degree is considered as the third of the key of the dominant, 60, 62, 85
subject ending on the dominant preceded by the unaltered fourth degree of the principal key, 69
subject ending on the dominant or the seventh degree (unaltered in minor), 85; examples, 86, 87, 88
tonal, 32

Augmentation:
double, 254
in contrary, retrograde, or retrograde-contrary movement, 195, 253
in episodes, 251
in the stretto, 326, 327
of the subject, 195, 201

Bass, considered harmonically:
see subject, answer, countersubject, episodes

Cadence:
perfect, 391, 392
perfect, beginning an episode, 408
perfect, during an episode, 407
forbidden in exposition, 410
melodic origin of, 400, 409
use, 399–406

Canons:
in episodes, 234
of subject and answer before the stretto, 465

Chromatics:
allowed in fugal writing, 7
chromatic countersubject, *see countersubject*
chromatic subject, *see subject*

Coda:
as used in episodes, 188, 195, 246 (*b*)
of the subject, definition, 134
extended in two-part fugue, 155
omission, 161

purpose, 134
second coda in exposition, 136

Continuity:
of melodic line, 396; examples analyzed, 396, 397, 398
of style of writing, 390–393, 396

Contrary movement:
in augmentation, 195, 253
in diminution, 195, 253
in episodes, 195, 247, 248
in stretto, 317–320
of the subject, 197
opposed to direct, 247, 376

Counterexposition:
definition, 177
directions for arranging, 178, 179
essential under certain circumstances, 178, 181
vocal arrangements in (in two, three, and four parts), 182, 184

Countersubject:
always investigated with subject, never with answer, 111
beginning of, 106
chromatic, 106 (VI), 121–124
construction of, 116–120, 125
definition of, 105
distinctive characteristics of, 106
essential part of a scholastic fugue, 8
heard after the first entry of the subject, 128, 129
heard at the first entry of the subject, 130
importance of, 115, 413, 414
melodic movements of, 414, 415, 416
mutation of, 107, 108, 109
order of entry of more than one countersubject, 129
place in the exposition, 142–148, 155–160, 162, 171
use of several countersubjects, 106 (III), 113, 114, 150–154, 174–176

Degrees of the scale:
first degree, beginning a subject, 39, 40, 59
considered as fundamental note of the perfect chord on the tonic, 35
ending a subject, 40, 41

second degree, beginning a subject, 103
third degree, beginning a subject, 37, 39, 40
considered as third of the tonic chord, 36
ending a subject, 40, 41
fourth degree, altered, keeps its character as leading note of the dominant key, 45, 102
beginning a subject, 103
unaltered, considered as seventh degree of the key of the dominant, 63, 69, 76
fifth degree, beginning a subject, 37, 42
considered as first degree of the key of the dominant, 37
ending a subject, 85
tonal significance of, 52, 53, 55–58
sixth degree, beginning a subject, 103
seventh degree in major, or unaltered in minor
cannot begin a subject in minor, 101
considered as third of the perfect chord of the dominant, 60, 64, 66, 100
in subjects beginning on the dominant and progressing directly to the seventh degree, 60, 62, 64
tonal and harmonic function of, 60, 64
seventh degree, altered in minor
beginning a subject, considered as leading note of the principal key, 101
considered as third of the perfect chord of the dominant, 64, 66
keeps its character as leading note of the principal key when it follows the tonic and precedes the dominant, 61

Determination of tonality:
of degrees of the subject before the dominant is heard, 62–66

Development:
of a musical idea, 393, 394, 395
of the fugue, 394, 395
see also under episodes

Diminution:
contrary, retrograde, and contrary-retrograde movement, in, 253
double, 254
in episodes, 252
in strettos, 321–325
in strettos, in opposition to original values, 323, 324, 325
of the subject, 195, 201

Entries:
of the answer in the exposition, 133, 138, 140, 141
of the countersubject, after a coda, 134
of the countersubject after the first entry of the subject, 128, 132
of the countersubject on the first entry of the subject, 132
of several countersubjects in succession, 128, 129, 130
made of phrases borrowed from the subject, the countersubject, or free parts of the exposition, 257
number of, in the exposition, 126; in strettos, 278, 356, 357
preceded by a rest, 256, 466
two groups of, in different keys, 466
of the subject in the exposition, 126, 127, 128, 131
of the subject on a dissonance, 403
of the subject after a perfect cadence, 399, 404, 405, 406
summary, 466

Episodes:
augmentation in, examples, 251
augmentation and diminution in contrary movement in, 252
before the stretto section, 432; examples, 446, 447
canonical, examples, 234, 235
canonical, construction of, 236, 237; examples, 238, 239
character of, 194, 214, 420–431
closest imitations reserved for the end of, 259
combining elements of, 215
(*a*) each part imitates itself, setting forth a phrase distinct from the others, 216; examples by Bach, 216
(*b*) all the parts derive from the principal theme which remains intact in one of the parts, 217; examples by Bach, 217, 218, 219, 220, 224
(*c*) two parts imitate each other, alternately stating the principal theme, 225; example by Bach, 225, 226
(*d*) the parts imitate each other two by two, 227; examples by Mozart and Bach, 227
(*e*) the principal theme of the episode is imitated in three parts, 228; examples by Bach, 228, 229, 230
(*f*) the four parts imitate each other, 231; examples by Bach, 231, 233; by Handel, 232
combinations of the above, 241, 242
contrary and direct movement combined in, examples, 247
contrary movement in, 248; example, 248

contrary movement in, linked to stretto in direct movement, 376
definition of, 187, 188
diminution in, 252
double augmentation in, 254
double diminution in, example, 254
established on a harmonic sequence, 189, 190, 191
exposition as a source of themes for, 196–201
free parts developed in, 193, 199
harmonic and melodic plan of, 204–207
harmonic sequences in, 189, 191, 216
interrupted part must make a cadential harmony in, 257
keys to which modulation is made in, 188
length of, 267, 268, 269
melodic design of, 192, 194, 421, 422, 424–429
melodic figures of, extracted from the exposition, 193, 195–199
melodic line of, 202, 203
methods of linkage to first stretto, 374, 375, 376
on a pedal point, 440, 441, 442
parts of, treated melodically, 260
plan of working out, 208, 209, 210
preparation of, 195
principal themes of, 202, 211
retrograde and contrary retrograde movement in, 253
retrograde movement in, examples, 249
several themes in, 211, 212
stretto section, episodes in, 365 (example), 369–373, 376
subject taken as theme of, 250
successive themes in, 242; examples, 243–246
theme of, must be in one key, 213
themes of, derive from the subject, answer, countersubject, coda, or free parts of the exposition, 190, 193

Exposition:
alternation of subject and answer, 126, 133
arrangement of voices in, in two parts, 140; in three parts, 141; in four parts, 141; with countersubject heard after the first entry of the subject, in two parts, 142; example, 155; in three parts, 143; example, 156; in four parts, 144; examples, subject in the soprano, 157–163; subject in the alto, 164, 165, 166; subject in the tenor, 167, 168; subject in the bass, 169, 170, 171; with countersubject heard at the first entry of the subject, in three parts, 145; in

four parts, 146; examples, 172, 173; arrangements to be avoided, 148
coda of the subject and answer, 134, 135, 136
definition, 126
elements of the fugue in, 418
entry of the answer in, 133
entry of the countersubject in, 128, 129, 130
free parts in, 138, 139
number of entries, 127
subject and answer must sound the same beats, 133
subject heard in voice of corresponding range, 131
treated in the principal key, 264
unison avoided in, 137
with two countersubjects, in three parts, 150; in four parts, 151; examples, 174, 175; exceptional arrangements, 152
with three countersubjects, in four parts, 153, 154; example, 176

Free parts:
character of, 139
expressive role of, 417
in exposition, 138
in the stretto, 305

Fugue:
accompanied, 6
answer, *see answer*
as art of developing a musical idea, 470
belonging principally to the key of the subject, 31
countersubjects in, *see countersubject*
definitions, 1, 2, 3, 7
development, *see episodes*
double, 113
essential parts of, 8
etymology of, 2
expressiveness of, 413–418
harmonic filling forbidden in, 139
harmonic sequences in, *see episodes*
harmonies used in, 7
instrumental, 6
invertible counterpoint in, 105, 473–501
length of, 268, 269

melodic movements permitted in, 7
modulations peculiar to the subject of, 34
never silence all parts at once in, 396
parts should present continuous melodic line in, 260
plan and working out of, 472
quadruple, 113
real, 32
style, *see style*
subject, *see subject*
tonal, 32
triple, 113
vocal, 6
writing characterized by use of imitations, 1

Harmony:
harmonic sequences, 187, 189, 191, 216
harmonies used in fugue, 7

Imitations:
see episodes, stretto, fugue

Interruption:
must induce cadential harmony, 257
rules for, 462
subject and answer, *see stretto*

Length:
of episodes, *see episodes*
of the fugue, *see fugue*

Melodic movements:
permitted in parts, 7

Modulations:
at end of subject to key of dominant, 86, 87, 88
from tonic to dominant by characteristic alteration, 33, 74, 80
in episodes, 213
in strettos, 302
order of modulations, 265, 266
to head of subject when progressing to dominant, 34, 37, 44, 59, 77
to neighboring keys, 263
to opposite mode, 270–275

Mutation:
chromatic subject, in, 47, 48, 92–98
definition, 88
effect of, 88–91
may produce oblique movement in answer, 46, 47, 89, 93
must not produce contrary movement in answer, 46, 89

Neighboring keys: 263
see modulations

New subject: 473–501

Order of entries:
see episodes, exposition, stretto

Pedal point:
composition of, 442–446
definition of, 335
degrees most frequently found on, 336
double, 341
entry of, 344
essential part of scholastic fugue, 8
harmonic rules governing, 337
importance of, 437
in episodes, 343
inferior, 340, 345, 346
inner, 340
in strettos, 343
in the stretto section, 377
introduction of, 433–438
musical elements of, 439
on degrees other than tonic or dominant, example, 350(*c*)
on the dominant, 345, 346, 347, 384
on the tonic, 347, 348, 387
ornamented, 349; examples, 350, 351
role of, 338, 339, 433
superior, 340; examples, 348, 351
use in various circumstances, 437, 438

Preliminary drafts:
of the countersubject, 116, 117, 118

of the episodes, 202–208, 420, 472
of the pedal point, 343
of the stretto, 306, 472

Rests:
before entries, 134, 256, 466

Retrograde movement:
in episodes, examples, 195, 249
in the stretto, 332

Stretto:
analysis of, 379, 387
answer, heard in full in, 307, 356
arrangement in four parts, 306
asymmetrical entries in, 309, 310
augmentation and diminution combined in, example, 331(*b*)
augmentation in, 326, 331
canonical, 283, 287–291, 300, 301
classification of, 313
construction of stretto section, 359–388; summary, 377
definitions, 278, 279; of stretto section, 280
diminution in, 321–324
entry at unison to be avoided in, 286
episodes in stretto section, 369–373
equidistant entries in, 289
essential part of fugue, 8
first and last strettos in principal key in four parts, 355, 356
free strettos, 293
harmonic concord of entries in, 292
head of subject and of answer indispensable in, 281
in contrary movement, 317–320
in retrograde movement, 317–320
interrupted entries in, 290
interruption of subject in, 290
inverse, 287
investigation of, 457
linkage of stretto section, 431; examples, 444
melodic arrangement of stretto section, 448
methodology of, 294–320
modulations in, 302(2)

musical quality of, 430
of countersubject, 314, 364
of new subject, 473–501
on the off beat, 302 (4)
order of voices in, 285
outline of, 472
summary of construction of stretto section, 377
supplementary harmonic part in, 297
true stretto, 307

Style:
defined, 411
determined by character of subject and countersubject, 412–415
of a fugue, 1
unity of, 418

Subject:
alternates with answer, 126
analysis from harmonic and tonal standpoints, 71, 72, 73
beginning on tonic, 28, 39, 40, 59
beginning on mediant, 39, 40, 41, 59
beginning on dominant, 37, 42
beginning on seventh degree, 100, 101
beginning on altered fourth degree, 102
beginning on second degree, 103
beginning on unaltered fourth degree, 103
beginning on sixth degree, 103
chromatic, 47, 48, 92–98
considerations in construction of, 10
definition of, 4
ending on tonic, 40, 41
ending on mediant, 40, 41
ending on dominant, 85
ending on dominant preceded by the unaltered fourth degree, 76
ending on unaltered seventh degree in minor, 85
ending theoretically should be only on the tonic, mediant, or dominant, or on the seventh degree unaltered in minor, 99
harmonic and tonal functions of the various degrees encompassed in the head of and ending of the subject, 35–38
head of the subject, 21

length of, 15, 16, 17
melody of, 12, 14
mode, 18
modulation by characteristic alteration, 33, 74, 77
modulation to dominant when beginning on the dominant, 37, 42
modulations peculiar to the head and ending of, 34
no modulation of, 39, 40, 41
return to principal key after beginning modulation, 43, 74
rhythm, 11
should form a complete musical phrase, 12
should lend itself to a close canon with the answer, and other canonical imitations, 13
should sustain a four-part harmony, 14
tonal analysis of, 77–84
tonality of, 19, 20, 43

Supplementary parts:
in strettos, 297
in the pedal point, 347

Unison:
avoid between subject and answer, 137
avoid in stretto, 286

Unity:
melodic, 418–422
of expression, 418, 420
of style, 412; synonymous with expressive unity, 418, 419, 420

University of Oklahoma Press
Norman